QUR'ANIC TERMINOLOGY

A LINGUISTIC AND SEMANTIC ANALYSIS

Balil Abd al-Karim

Translated from the Arabic by
Nancy Roberts

THE INTERNATIONAL INSTITUTE OF ISLAMIC THOUGHT
P.O. BOX 669, HERNDON, VA 20172, USA • www.iiit.org

LONDON OFFICE
P.O. BOX 126, RICHMOND, SURREY TW9 2UD, UK • www.iiituk.com

ISBN 978-1-56564-698-8 *limp*
ISBN 978-1-56564-651-3 *cased*

Layout and Design by Shiraz Khan

Content

Foreword — *v*

Introduction — 1

1 Studying Concepts from an Epistemological Perspective — 3

2 *Maʿrifah, ʿIlm* and *Waḥy* — 13

3 Paths of *Maʿrifah*: Reason and Sensation — 81

4 *Maʿrifah* in the Qur'an — 116

5 *ʿIlm* in the Qur'an — 149

6 Tools for Acquiring Knowledge in the Qur'an — 164

7 *Waḥy* (Revelation) and *Nubuwwah* (Prophethood) — 179

Notes — 184

Foreword

BALIL ABD AL-KARIM'S *Qur'anic Terminology: A Linguistic and Semantic Analysis* is a detailed work aiming to provide a broad glossary of key Qur'anic terms and set forth these terms' meanings, both semantically and linguistically, within their Qur'anic context.

There is no way to understand the Qur'an properly, or elucidate as accurately as possible the meaning of its verses, without studying Qur'anic terminology and concepts. Taken together these not only sum up the universal truths of the religion (the great moral code), but also animate the text and give it incredible life, precision, and flexibility, enriching the communication of the Qur'anic message through their beautiful and comprehensive nature.

The IIIT has undertaken in recent years to produce abridged versions of its key publications, and this translation is taken from the abridged Arabic edition *Al-Mafāḥīm al-Miftāḥiyyah li Naẓariyyah al-Maʿrifah fī al-Qur'ān al-Karīm.*

We live in an age in which time is at a premium in virtually all spheres of life, including those of writing and production. Copious intellectual, cultural and informational output continues unabated as part of efforts to keep pace with changes in the public and private spheres alike, while publishing houses and websites vie to provide people with the latest, and most up-to-date information in the easiest, most effective manner. The knowledge economy that now dominates the world requires a process of 'creative adaptation' of information as one of the building blocks of the world community at large, hence the IIIT's series of abridged works. The aim is to help readers benefit from available information as easily, effectively, and efficiently as possible and to further develop their critical faculties so they become better able to contribute to the development of humanity.

The abridged texts have been written in a clear, easy to read style, and while the essential contents of the original works have been preserved, readers will note that, in the interests of space, the abridged editions contain far fewer endnotes than do the original works. The only notes retained are those needed for clarification or the proper establishment of an idea, since the principle aim of this endeavor is to facilitate rapid absorption of the content being conveyed. Readers who wish to go more deeply into the topics of concern or to find full documentation of quotes may refer to the original works, which contain all necessary citations.

The work is being published to widen discourse, and increase awareness of the question of Islamic artistic expression and its ultimate aims and objectives. No doubt the subject is a specialized one, but it is hoped that for the most part both general and specialist readers alike will benefit from the perspective offered and the overall issues examined.

Where dates are cited according to the Islamic calendar (hijrah) they are labelled AH. Otherwise they follow the Gregorian calendar and labelled CE where necessary. Arabic words are italicized except for those which have entered common usage. Diacritical marks have been added only to those Arabic names not considered modern. English translations taken from Arabic references are those of the translator. Qur'anic verses are quoted either in part or in their entirety.

Since its establishment in 1981, the IIIT has served as a major center to facilitate serious scholarly efforts. Towards this end it has, over the decades, conducted numerous programs of research, seminars and conferences as well as publishing scholarly works specialising in the social sciences and areas of theology which to date number more than four hundred titles in English and Arabic, many of which have been translated into other major languages.

We would like to thank the author, translator, as well as editorial and production team at the IIIT London Office, and all those who were directly or indirectly involved in the completion of this book. May God reward them for all their efforts.

JANUARY, 2017

Introduction

PRAISE BE TO GOD, who revealed the Qur'an from on high as a balance in which to weigh truth and falsehood. He has commanded us to reflect on the Qur'an, bearing in mind that it can only be properly understood by those firmly established in knowledge, and will only be kept in remembrance by those who are endowed with insight.

The epistemological aspect of the Qur'an deals with the act of reflecting and investigating (*al-naẓar*), which jurists and philosophers alike agree to be human beings' foremost duty. This process is essential in order for people to know their Creator, themselves, and the world around them. Knowledge of the Creator and of ourselves leads us to search for satisfying answers to life's pressing questions. The better we understand the sources, types and purposes of knowledge, ways of applying and benefitting from knowledge, and the ways in which knowledge is compiled, transmitted and developed, the better able we will be to test the knowledge we have and to link it to the laws and patterns of the cosmos.

The Qur'anic Revelation sets forth a set of concepts which, taken together, sum up the universal truths of the religion. However, there is no way to understand the Qur'an properly without studying its terminology, which is key to accessing the will of God. Consequently, this study contains a glossary of key terms that sets forth these terms' meanings within their Qur'anic context.

The meaning of a given Qur'anic term will vary depending on the manner and the context in which it is used, and on the issues and questions in relation to which reference is made to it. Just as a concept gives rise to a term, so also does the term and its usage act to shape the concept. As a terminological analysis of the Qur'an, this study examines terms within their respective semantic and linguistic contexts.

Sound communication can only take place when the concepts being discussed are clearly defined and understood, and when terms are used precisely. Unless terms are defined with precision, discussions and debates will revolve not around facts, but around mere words. It is not acceptable to employ terms that are ambiguous or overly general; hence, those who do use such terms should be asked to explain and clarify them in order to make dialogue constructive and genuine. Differences among debaters are often attributable to their use of words, either because various terms are being used to refer to the same entity, or because the same word is being used to refer to more than one entity. But if intended meanings are explained and ambiguities clarified, it becomes possible to distinguish true from false, and what is meant from what is not meant.

BALIL ABD AL-KARIM

1

Studying Concepts from an Epistemological Perspective

CONCEPTS CAN BE viewed from various angles and subjected to a variety of approaches. They can be studied linguistically, psychologically, philosophically, or epistemologically. In the latter case, the structures of concepts are subjected to an analysis which clarifies how relationships among concepts are formed to create integrated epistemological fields.

In this chapter we will be discussing the problem of meaning, that is, the changes that occur in a concept and its signification. In the course of this discussion we will touch upon the epistemological necessity of concepts, concept structure analysis, changes in concepts, networks of key concepts, and the method of categorizing epistemological concepts in the Qur'an. The discussion will take place on three levels of meaning: (1) lexical (*al-dilālah al-muʿjamiyyah*), (2) practical (*al-dilālah al-istiʿmāliyyah*), and (3) interpretative (*al-dilālah al-ta'wīliyyah*).

FIRST: THE EPISTEMOLOGICAL NECESSITY OF CONCEPTS

Any cultural system will be made up of a set of integrated epistemological fields. Such fields include, for example, the realms of religion, metaphysics, mathematics, logic, language and linguistics, society and sociology, and so on. Each of these epistemological fields in turn consists of a set of concepts that are related to each other in specific ways.

1) *The value of concepts*

Each epistemological field is set apart from others by particular features and concepts, while various epistemological fields are linked together to form an integrated epistemological system. The analysis of an epistemological structure is based on three foundations: (1) concepts, (2) the relationships that join concepts into a semantic field, and (3) the relationships that join differing semantic fields into a larger epistemological system. Concepts are a necessary, but not a sufficient, condition for the presence of an epistemological field. It is concepts that highlight the features of a given field; however, the vagueness or distortion of ideas and concepts has caused many writers to conflate or confuse different meanings. Hence, thinkers should make sure to clarify the overall concepts that make up a given field or system.

2) *Concepts in the logical sense*

A concept is a set of specific characteristics and features that distinguish one entity from another. In the context of this discussion, however, we will be adopting the view that the vast majority of concepts are marked by unlimited flexibility. Hence, their meanings broaden at some times and narrow at others, while at the same time preserving their own semantic field. Concepts are to be viewed as a type of universal or abstraction, salient examples of which include: freedom and tyranny, justice and injustice, truth and falsehood, good and evil, beauty and ugliness.

3) *Concept formation*

A concept embodies a meaning or set of meanings which we express by means of either a single word, such as "knowledge," or an expression such as, "divine knowledge." When a particular word is used to communicate a particular meaning, the result is a term which is agreed upon by specialists in a particular field. Such a term may continue to be used exclusively by those who have agreed upon it. However, a problem arises when a particular word comes to be used to communicate several different meanings without the aid of linguistic contexts that make it possible to distinguish which particular meaning of the word is intended. This situation differs from that in which a single word is used to convey two or more different meanings but in which we can deduce which meaning of the word is intended based on the linguistic context.

This difficulty does not arise in relation to concepts with clearly specified meanings. An example of such a situation involves the concept of "democracy," whose lexical definition – 'the rule of the people' – is agreed upon, but whose meaning in actual usage is the subject of debate.

When the order of concepts is disturbed, relationships among members of the Muslim community are affected such that their ties based on doctrine become secondary rather than primary. This sort of reordering might take place due to influences from atheistic and existentialist philosophies which place the individual front and center, and that may even go so far as to make the individual the source of legislation and the measure of what is good and bad, true and false.

SECOND: CONCEPT STRUCTURE ANALYSIS

In order to define a concept, we need to deconstruct its elements and identify their hierarchical arrangement.

1) *Identifying a concept's structure*

A concept's structure consists of numerous elements, some of which are fundamental and others of which are complementary. The fundamental elements enjoy logical priority in the structure, given that they are not derived from anything else. In this respect they resemble the axioms in mathematical and logical systems. Semanticists draw a distinction between basic meanings and additional meanings. The basic meaning performs the most important function of language, which is communication and the transfer of ideas. Therefore, the precise understanding of a concept requires us to analyze its structure and identify its component elements.

2) *The importance of concept structure analysis*

To illustrate the importance of the analytical process for a precise and correct understanding of concepts, let us take as an example the concept of *al-ʿaql*, translated generally as "mind" or "reason." Concepts may be divided into three different types: (1) epistemological concepts such as knowledge (*ʿilm*), understanding (*fahm*), thought (*tafakkur*) and realization or perception (*idrāk*); (2) volitional concepts such as determination (*ʿazm*), choice (*ikhtiyār*), intention (*qaṣd*), and will *(irādah)*; and (3) sensation- or feeling-related concepts, such as anger *(ghaḍab)*, fear *(khawf)*, pleasure *(ladhdhah)* and pain *(alam)*. When we analyze the structure of the concept of *ʿaql* in this manner, we impact the nature of the dialogue that takes place around it, as well as the way in which the dialogue proceeds and the conclusions to which it leads. Scholars have long recognized that there is a link between the structure of language, the structure of mind, and the structure of reality. Analyzing a concept's structure enables us to see further concepts that underlie it, and which evolve over time as their content and range of application expand. It is thus important to observe the meanings acquired by concepts in specific historical phases.

In order to understand a word's precise meaning, you will also need to understand the constellation of words that are semantically related to it. This involves studying the relationships among individual terms within a single semantic field or subfield, since a word's meaning is the outcome of its relationships with other words. Similarly, the aim behind semantic field analysis is to compile all words that belong to a particular semantic field, identify the relationships among them, and clarify their links to the overall concept that ties them together.

THIRD: CONCEPTS AND THE PROBLEM OF MEANING

On what basis can we judge a concept to be clear, vague, or meaningless? We use speech to communicate about things such as doctrine, human affairs, literature, nature, and mathematics, among others. Consequently, the attention Arab scholars down the ages have devoted to the issue of meaning in the linguistic sciences and the philology has been with a view to avoiding what has been termed "semantic maladies" which afflict concepts in various epistemological fields. This concern can be observed particularly in the disciplines of philosophy, linguistics, and the fundamentals of jurisprudence.

1) *The issue of language as approached by linguists*
In his book, *Al-Khaṣāʾiṣ*, Ibn Jinnī stated:

> The Arabs have concerned themselves with the vocabulary of their language, refining it, studying words' particular contexts, and observing

> grammatical structures and rules, whether in poetry, oratory, or the rhymed prose which they have taken such care to perpetuate and preserve. Consequently, the meanings conveyed by their language have a powerful, profound impact on their souls. The words of a language are thus the vessels that convey its meanings and the path along which its ends and purposes are revealed.

Linguists' interest in semantics has manifested itself in their study of lexicology, in compilations of Qur'anic terms that recur with differing facets of meaning (*al-naẓā'ir*), and in the study of metaphors. It should be remembered that the vocalization of the text of the Qur'an was an exercise in semantics. Indeed, the science of grammar and syntax arose in part due to the fact that when reading *Sūrah al-Tawbah*, 9:3, a certain Qur'an reciter had mispronounced the phrase *rasūluhu* ("His Apostle" in the nominative case) as *rasūlihi* ("His Apostle" in the genitive case), which drastically changed the meaning of the verse from "God disavows all who ascribe divinity to aught beside Him, and [so does] His Apostle (*wa rasūluhu*)," to "God disavows all who ascribe divinity to aught beside Him, and [He likewise disavows] His Apostle (*wa rasūlihi*)."

2) *The issue of meaning as approached by rhetoricians*

Rhetoricians have taken a special interest in the semantic aspects of language, such as literal meaning vs. metaphor, sentence structure, and the study of linguistic modes, such as the imperative mode (commands and prohibitions), the interrogative mode (questions), exclamations and others. Al-Jurjānī (d. 474 AH/1078 CE), for example, proposed the notion of *al-naẓm* (meaning order, arrangement, poetic verse), which he developed into a sophisticated literary theory. According to al-Jurjānī:

> The term *al-naẓm* refers to the process of ordering speech in the manner required by the rules of grammar and syntax, and of familiarizing yourself with and adhering to prevailing linguistic norms.

3) *The issue of meaning as approached by philosophers*

The issue of words and meaning has been investigated by a number of

Muslim philosophers, including al-Kindī (259 AH/873 CE), al-Fārābī (339 AH/951 CE), Ibn Sīnā, or Avicenna (428 AH/1037 CE), Ibn Rushd, or Averroes (594 AH/1198 CE), Ibn Ḥazm (456 AH/1064 CE), and al-Ghazālī (504 AH/1111 CE), most of whose treatises on logic and language addressed this topic. Most of these scholars held that words indicate meaning in three different ways, which came to be known as: (1) correspondence (*dilālat al-muṭābaqah*), (2) inclusion (*dilālat al-taḍmīn*), and (3) association (*dilālat al-iltizām*), the last of which refers to the way in which a word or expression points to something beyond what has been named. According to al-Ghazālī:

> Based on the manner in which they are related to meanings, words may be divided into four categories: (1) homonyms (*al-mushtarakah*), (2) generic nouns (*al-mutawāṭi'ah*), (3) synonyms (*al-mutarādifah*) and (4) dissimilar terms (*al-mutazāyilah*). The first type, the homonym, is a single word which is used to refer to several different entities with distinct definitions. The second type, the generic noun, includes a whole group or class and, as such, refers to several different entities that share a feature, or features, in common. The third type, the synonym (*al-mutarādifah*), is a set of different words that refer to the same entity and share the same definition. And the fourth and last type, dissimilar terms (*al-mutazāyilah*), applies to words which have none of these features in common.

4) *The issue of meaning as addressed by scholars of the fundamentals of jurisprudence*

Scholars of the fundamentals of Islamic jurisprudence have concerned themselves with both language and meaning due to the intimate link that exists between the understanding of language and the understanding of the Divine Law revealed in the Arabic tongue.

The science of the fundamentals of jurisprudence aims to deduce legal rulings from specific texts, a process that requires an understanding of the words of the texts from which the rulings are being deduced. Legal scholars divide words into four categories – synonyms (*mutarādifah*), homonyms (*mushtarakah*), unrestricted (*muṭlaqah*) and restricted (*muqayyadah*). Such scholars take a clear interest, of course, in commands and prohibitions given the fact that it is commands and prohibitions which constitute the focal point of all speech addressed to morally responsible agents.

They also concern themselves with context, which determines the meanings of the legal categories into which actions are classified, such as permissibility (*al-ibāḥah*), obligation (*wujūb*), impossibility (*taʿjīz*),[1] and advisement (*irshād*),[2] which are based on the Qur'an's consideration for meaning and structure.

FOURTH: CHANGE IN CONCEPTS

Concepts are embedded in specific environmental and cultural frameworks. Hence, the general, everyday use of terms associated with philosophy, science and literature can cause confusion because, rather than being mere signs pointing to an external reality, the words and expressions we use become bound to a certain mental conceptualization. We should thus be aware of certain words' association with the epistemological content of philosophy and the system of thought to which it gave rise. At the same time, we should take care to distinguish between the phenomenon of conceptual change, and that of conceptual distortion.

1) *Reasons for conceptual change*

Cultural concepts change due to a variety of causes, including the emergence of new needs and psychological and social factors such as bans and taboos. For although the concepts we express through words are abstractions, they are nevertheless shaped by concrete situations.

2) *Conceptual distortion*

The process of semantic change is a natural one. The meaning of a word may pass through various stages of evolution. At each stage, the modification in the concept will then meet with acceptance by speakers of the language concerned, including their academic institutions. However, this process is to be distinguished from semantic distortion, which occurs when the significance a word develops over time is inconsistent with its original meaning.

An example of this phenomenon may be seen in relation to the concept of the mind, or reason (*ʿaql*). At one stage, methods of researching the mind consisted in demonstrating the way in which mind had emerged out of matter. The conclusion that some researchers drew from this was that the mind is nothing but a physical organ. However, this materialistic theory of mind was eventually demolished based on irrefutable scientific evidence.

Materialistic trends in science and philosophy distorted the concept of 'mind' or 'reason' based on their exclusive focus on physical function. The fallacy of materialism lies in confusing the part with the whole, that is, in concluding that because the mind functions via matter, the mind itself consists of matter and nothing more. The Islamic conception of knowledge, by contrast, holds that the human mind is a spiritual entity created by God Almighty in association with the body.

3) *Steps to be followed in the treatments of concepts*

There are specific steps which need to be followed if we are to approach concepts in a proper and precise manner. The first step is to acknowledge the distinguishing features of the language and cultural context in which a concept has been formulated. The second step is to determine whatever lexical and technical meanings are associated with the terms in which the concept is expressed. The third is to identify the semantic process through which the concept has passed by distinguishing between the meanings with which it was linked upon its initial formulation, and the meanings which it has acquired during its historical evolution. And the fourth is to analyze the concept's semantic structure, which involves the identification of its fundamental and complementary elements. This process will help us to distinguish between a concept's natural semantic evolution and its distortion, be it in the form of narrowing, broadening, or whatever else.

FIFTH: THE NETWORK OF KEY CONCEPTS IN THE QUR'AN

Given that for Muslims, the Qur'an is the primary source of knowledge, it will be necessary to enumerate the Qur'anic terms which describe the act of knowing, the means by which knowledge is acquired, and the value of knowledge. We must then translate these terms into concepts. Some Qur'anic terms have clearly defined, relatively self-contained meanings, while others are bound up with additional terms that relate to a given concept. Some terms occur frequently in the Qur'an, and others only rarely. Consequently, we have organized them into thematic groups. Under the category of 'mind', for example, we list all terms having to do with mental processes, such as thought (*tafakkur*), reflection (*tadabbur*), investigation (*naẓar*), hearing (*samʿ*) and sight (*baṣar*), while under the concept of revelation we list terms connected with prophecy (*nubuwwah*), 'the book' (*al-kitāb*), and 'the message' (*al-risālah*).

SIXTH: THE METHOD OF CLASSIFYING EPISTEMOLOGICAL TERMS IN THE QUR'AN

There is a set of Qur'anic terms whose meanings are bound to the concepts of *ʿilm* and *maʿrifah*, and which have been derived through a reading of Qur'anic commentaries.

The meanings of such terms may be classified into three types: (1) lexical, (2) practical, and (3) interpretative.

1) *Lexical meaning (al-dalālah al-muʿjamiyyah)*

The term "lexical meaning" is used to refer to what scholars of the fundamentals of jurisprudence have judged to be a word's original denotation. The original denotation of a term can only be modified based on valid evidence. A term's lexical meaning is based on its relative placement in a semantic field vis-à-vis other related words. Relationships among these different terms needs to be clarified due to the existence of homonyms, synonyms, and antonyms, as well as subtle distinctions among terms. A lexical definition embodies the mental conceptualization that is triggered by the term being defined outside its usual context of social customs and religious beliefs. Apart from a more specific context, however, a word bears numerous possible interpretations. Hence, the linguistic content that precedes and follows a term is the most important factor for determining its meaning and the semantic field to which it belongs.

2) *Practical signification (al-dalālah al-istiʿmāliyyah)*

The term "practical signification" refers to the meaning that a word conveys in actual use or to its metaphorical meanings in a particular context, since individual words are only used to convey their meanings in conjunction with other words. In order to understand particular words in the Qur'an, we need to ascertain what meaning the word in question conveyed during the time when the Qur'an was revealed. There are words which took on precise, heretofore unfamiliar meanings and features based on the way in which they were used in their Qur'anic context or in the overall religious milieu.

3) *Interpretative signification (al-dalālah al-ta'wīliyyah)*

Interpretation (*ta'wīl*) is a means of determining what a speaker intended to say by the words he or she uttered or wrote. However, this aim cannot be attained without adhering to the rules of the language being used. Hence, if one claims that the meaning of something someone has said or written is different from what it appears to be on the surface, one must back up this claim with evidence. Otherwise, we may lose confidence in language and its ability to perform its communicative function. Interpretation involves affirming that a word or set of words conveys a metaphorical rather than a literal meaning. Such an affirmation, in turn, involves understanding the word or words within their surrounding context, and if the affirmation is well-founded, it enables us to arrive at a sounder grasp of the truth being conveyed by the words.

Well-founded interpretation requires that we study the way words were or are actually used in their respective contexts; it requires that we appreciate the link between literal meaning and metaphor, that we be on the lookout for the use of homonyms, and that we be well-versed in scholastic theological thought given the way it has shaped the evolution of certain words' meanings. Al-Shāṭibī stipulated that in order for the interpretation of a word in the Qur'an to be correct, it must be consistent with the word's original lexical meaning, with the meaning it bore in commonly accepted usage at the time the Qur'an was revealed, with its legal definition, and with its metaphorical sense. It must also be consistent with the rules and structure of the language, the semantic context, and what we know about what occasioned the revelation of the verse in question.

2

Maʿrifah, ʿIlm and Waḥy

CONCEPTS ARE clarified through the study of words' lexical meanings. We begin by ascertaining the root and derivations of the word being studied in keeping with the rules of the language we are dealing with. We then examine the ways in which words are used in order to determine their practical significations.

I have gleaned both practical and interpretative approaches from the following works: *Al-Mufradāt* by al-Iṣfahānī, *Al-Taʿrīfāt* by al-Jurjānī, *Al-Kulliyyāt* by al-Kufawī, *Kashshāf Iṣṭilāḥāt al-Funūn* by al-Tahanawī, *Iṣlāḥ al-Wujūh* by al-Dāmighānī, *Nuzhat al-Aʿyun wa al-Naẓā'ir* by Ibn al-Jawzī, and *Wujūh al-Naẓā'ir* by Sulaymān al-Qarʿāwī. Based on a study of the features that distinguish various epistemological concepts from a Qur'anic perspective, I have divided them into three groups based on whether they are related to *ʿilm*, *maʿrifah*, or *waḥy*.

FIRST: CONCEPTS RELATING TO *Maʿrifah*

1) *The concept of maʿrifah*

There are two basic meanings derived from the triliteral root *ʿ-r-f*. The first of these is that of a continuous succession of entities, while the second relates to quietness and tranquility. The verb *ʿarafa*, from which we derive the verbal noun *maʿrifah*, means to know or perceive something as it is, the assumption being that this perception was preceded by ignorance, or that one had forgotten some or all of one's initial perception or realization. Some have defined it as the perception of something through reflection on its effects. Someone who knows something (*al-ʿārif bi al-shay'*) is someone who had a clear perception of it previously, after which he denied it due to some ambiguity or uncertainty. Hence, the term *maʿrifah*, which is associated with sensation, the 'seeing' of the heart, and the distinction between what is known and what is not, is both more specific and more complete than the word *ʿilm*, which is taken from the world of abstract thought. Scholars hold that it is not permissible to attribute *maʿrifah* to God due to its association with a previous lack of knowledge and denial, and due to the fact that it entails an incomplete knowledge that has been arrived at via reflection and contemplation.

The word *maʿrifah*, which appears less often in the Qur'an than the word *ʿilm* and its derivatives, occurs 24 times as a verb with various practical meanings. These meanings may be divided into seven groups: (1) physical recognition (*al-maʿrifah al-ḥissiyyah*). *Sūrah al-Baqarah*, 2:146 reads, "They unto whom We have vouchsafed revelation aforetime know it (*yaʿrifūnahu*) as they know (*yaʿrifūna*) their own children." The word *maʿrifah* signifies the opposite of denial or disavowal. As we read in *Sūrah al-Mu'minūn*, 23:69, "Or is it, perchance, that they have not recognized (*lam yaʿrifū*) their Apostle, and so they disavow him?" (2) Identification (*taʿrīf*), as when one identifies a goal sought. This sense of the word is found in *Sūrah Muḥammad*, 47:6, where we are told that God "will admit them [believers] to the paradise which He has brought them to know (*ʿarrafahā lahum*)." (3) Mutual acquaintance (*taʿāruf*). This sense is illustrated in *Sūrah al-Ḥujurāt*, 49:13, where God declares, "Behold, We have...made you into nations and tribes, so that you might come to know one another (*li taʿārafū*)." (4) Acknowledgment or confession (*iʿtirāf*). In *Sūrah al-Tawbah*, 9:102 we read, "And [there are] others – [people who] have become conscious of their sinning (*iʿtarafū bi dhunūbihim*) after having done righteous deeds side by side with evil ones." (5) An act of goodness (something that people generally acknowledge to be a source of blessing and righteousness) (*maʿrūf*, *ʿurf*). As God declares in *Sūrah Āl ʿImrān*, 3:110, "You are indeed the best community that has ever been brought forth for [the good of] mankind: you enjoin the doing of what is right (*al-maʿrūf*) and forbid the doing of what is wrong," while in *Sūrah al-Aʿrāf*, 7:199, God tells the Prophet to "enjoin the doing of what is right (*al-ʿurf*)." (6) Mount Arafat (*ʿarafāt*): "And when you surge downward in multitudes from Arafat, remember God at the holy place" (*Sūrah al-Baqarah*, 2:198). (7) *Al-aʿrāf*, which refers to an elevated place on the earth. This use is found in *Sūrah al-Aʿrāf*, 7:48, where we read, "The men on the heights (*aṣḥāb al-aʿrāf*) will call to certain men whom they will know from their marks, saying: 'Of what profit to you were your hoards and your arrogant ways?'"

The verb form translated above as mutual acquaintance (*taʿāruf*) is based on what is accessible to the mind and the senses. As for that which is concealed from human perception, it is known to God alone. As we read in *Sūrah Muḥammad*, 47:30, "And God knows (*yaʿlamu*) all that you do." As for the act of acknowledgment (*iʿtirāf*), it derives from knowledge that is certain, but acquired through experience rather than possessed inherently, such as the knowledge of God. The words *maʿrūf* and *ʿurf* both refer to actions and words that are generally agreed to be virtuous and beneficial. Whatever actions or words are not explicitly forbidden by the Divine Law are agreed to be permissible; this principle contributes to the preservation of peoples' cultures, traditions and distinctive identities even when they are ruled by Islamic Law.

A summary of the uses of the term *Maʿrifah* in the Qur'an

The term *maʿrifah* is employed in the Qur'an in the sense of an acquired perception. In numerous places it is accompanied by mention of a visible sign, either in the face, in which case the instrument of perception will be the eye, or in speech, in which case the instrument of perception will be the ear. The Qur'an contains numerous examples of this phenomenon, including God's statement that "upon their faces you will see (*taʿrifu*) the brightness of bliss" (*Sūrah al-Muṭaffifīn*, 83:24).

At times *maʿrifah* reaches the level of complete certainty, as in God's declaration in *Sūrah al-Baqarah*, 2:146 that "They unto whom We have vouchsafed revelation aforetime know it (*yaʿrifūnahu*) as they know (*yaʿrifūna*) their own children: but, behold, some of them knowingly suppress the truth." It might also be noted that most occurrences of the term *maʿrifah* in the Qur'an are coupled with something that stands opposed to it. In *Sūrah al-Naḥl*, for example, it is contrasted with denial: "They [who turn away from it] are fully aware of God's blessings, but none the less they refuse to acknowledge them [as such], since most of them are given to denying the truth" (16:83). In *Sūrah al-Baqarah*, 2:89, *maʿrifah* is contrasted with unbelief: "whenever there came unto them something which they recognized [as the truth], they would deny it (disbelieve in it)." In *Sūrah Yūsuf*, 12:68, we find *maʿrifah* being contrasted with ignorance: "behold, thanks to what We had imparted unto him, he was indeed endowed with the knowledge [that God's will must always prevail]; but most people know it not." In the case of the Prophet, on the other hand, the polytheists' denial of him was a result of lying and knowing denial of the truth he had brought. Moreover, *maʿrifah* as mentioned in the Qur'an is described in different terms depending on whether it is attributed to polytheists or to those who affirm God's oneness. When attributed to the former, it refers simply to acknowledgment – something that is common to the righteous and the unrighteous, the obedient and the disobedient. But when it is attributed to those who worship God in His oneness, it refers to a knowledge that prompts humility before God, love for Him, attachment to Him, and longing for His presence.

Whether supporting evidence is derived from the written Revelation or the Creation, it fosters inward certainty. The written Revelation is being alluded to in the statement, "whenever there came unto them something which they recognized [as the truth], they would deny it" (*Sūrah al-Baqarah*, 2:89). Concerning rational evidence, God declares, "And say: 'All praise is due to God! In time He will make you see [the truth of] His messages, and then you shall know them [for what they are]'" (*Sūrah al-Naml*, 27:93). There are thus two doors to *maʿrifah*: (1) contemplation of the verses of the Qur'an, and (2) reflection on the visible signs in the created order and the divine wisdom, power and mercy reflected therein (cf. *Sūrah Muḥammad*, 47:30).

2) *The concept of nakirah*

The Arabic word *nakirah* is derived from the triliteral root *n-k-r* meaning not to know, to be ignorant of, to disavow or to deny, while the related noun, *munkar*, meaning a wrong or bad deed, is the opposite of *maʿrūf*, meaning a righteous or good deed.

Derivatives of the root *n-k-r* occur 36 times in the Qur'an. God declares in *Sūrah Āl ʿImrān*, 3:110, "You are indeed the best community that has ever been brought forth for [the good of] mankind: you enjoin the doing of what is right (*al-maʿrūf*) and forbid the doing of what is wrong (*al-munkar*)." The word *munkar* refers to whatever a prudent, sound-minded person would find abhorrent, and everything that is forbidden by Islamic Law. The root *n-k-r* is used in contrast to knowledge in the Qur'anic account in which, when Abraham received certain angelic guests, he had misgivings, saying to himself (51:25), "They are strangers (*qawmun munkarūn*)." Similarly in *Sūrah Yūsuf*, 12:58 we are told that although Joseph recognized his brothers (*ʿarafahum*), they did not recognize him (*wa hum lahu munkirūn*). The active participle *munkirūn* in this context conveys the sense of ignoring or disregarding, as if to say that Joseph's brothers related to God's blessings as though they were unaware of their Source. This disregard is a result of ingratitude, which is likewise one of the meanings of the word *kufr*. Another instance of the root *n-k-r*, also in contrast to knowledge, is found in *Sūrah al-Naml*, 27:41, where Solomon commanded the jinn to "alter her [the Queen of Sheba's] throne so that she may not know it as hers (*nakkirū lahā ʿarshahā*)." This use is consistent with the original meaning of the root *n-k-r* as referring to whatever is contrary to trustworthy knowledge.

3) *The concept of kufr*

The triliteral root *k-f-r* means to cover or conceal, and the intensified passive participle *mukaffar* is used to refer to a man covered in armor. The verbal noun *kufr*, often translated as unbelief, is used in contrast to *īmān*, or faith, since the action of *kufr* in relation to God's blessings involves not only denying them, but concealing them as well. The active participle *kāfir*, often translated as unbeliever, originally referred to a dark night (which conceals what would otherwise be visible). Derivatives of the root *k-f-r* occur 503 times in the Qur'an in four different senses: (1) Ingratitude, as in the statement, "Behold, as for those who are bent on denying the truth – it is all one to them whether you warn them or not: they will not believe" (*Sūrah al-Baqarah*, 2:6). (2) Denial. This sense is found in *Sūrah al-Baqarah*, 2:89: "whenever there came unto them something which they recognized [as the truth], they would deny it (*kafarū bihi*)." (3) Disavowal or repudiation. In *Sūrah Ibrāhīm*, 14:22, Satan is quoted as saying to idolaters on the Day of Resurrection, "I have [always] refused to admit (*kafartu*) that there was any truth in your erstwhile belief that I had a share in God's divinity. Verily, for all evildoers there is grievous suffering in store." (4) Turning away. In *Sūrah Ibrāhīm*, 14:13, we read that "they who had turned away from the message (*al-ladhīna kafarū*) spoke [thus] unto their apostles: 'We shall most certainly expel you from our land, unless you return forthwith to our ways!'"

All four of these meanings are related in one way or another to the act of covering or concealment. As we read in *Sūrah al-Baqarah*, 2:88, the unbelievers said of themselves, "Our hearts are the wrappings [which preserve God's Word: we need no more]." In other words, their hearts are closed to whatever truth or knowledge others might attempt to introduce to them.

4) *The concept of idrāk*

The triliteral root *d-r-k* conveys the sense of something's reaching, or catching up with, something else. When one's mind "reaches" or "catches up with" an idea, it has understood it. This root occurs ten times in the Qur'an in four different senses: (1) Restraining, reining in. *Sūrah Yūnus*, 10:90, for example, speaks of Pharaoh's being overwhelmed, and restrained, by the waters of the sea (*...adrakahu al-gharaq*). (2) Overtaking. *Sūrah al-Shuʿarā'*, 26:61 relates that when Pharaoh's army approached, Moses' company cried out, "Behold, we shall certainly be overtaken (*innā la mudrakūn*)!" (3) Coming together (as those at the front of a line and those at its end). Describing the state of those who have rejected God as they approach the hellfire, *Sūrah al-Aʿrāf*, 7:38 tells us that "when they all shall have passed into it, one after another (*ḥattā idhā iddārakū fīhā jamīʿan*), the last of them will speak [thus] of the first of them: 'O our Sustainer! It is they who have led us astray – give, them, therefore, double suffering through fire.'" (4) Seeing. Speaking of God, *Sūrah al-Anʿām*, 6:103 tells us that "No human vision can encompass Him (*lā tudrikuhu al-abṣār*), whereas He encompasses all human vision (*wa huwa yudriku al-abṣār*)."

The meaning of the verb *adraka/yudriku* as used in the Qur'an is consistent with its lexical definition relating to overtaking, catching up with, and the coming together of successive elements. As for its epistemological signification, it consists in the formation of a mental image devoid of judgment, in which case it is referred to as conceptualization. When it is accompanied by judgment, by contrast, it is referred to as affirmation. *Idrāk* is the representation of something's image to the mind of the person engaging in the *idrāk*; in other words, he/she 'witnesses' the entity perceived via said image.

5) *The concept of dirāyah*

The triliteral root *d-r-y* is more or less synonymous with the verb *ʿalima*, to know in a theoretical sense. It occurs thirteen times in the Qur'an as part of the phrase *mā adrāka*, or *mā yudrīka*. One of these occurrences is in *Sūrah al-Aḥzāb*, 33:63: "People will ask you about the Last Hour. Say: 'Knowledge thereof rests with God alone; yet for all you know (*wa mā yudrīka*), the Last Hour may well be near!'" Like the verbs *ʿarafa* and *ʿalima, darā* refers to an act of knowing that follows a state of not knowing. *Dirāyah*, or knowledge, exists in varying degrees; hence, it may be more or less complete. As such, the Arabic term for agnosticism, *lā-dirāyah*, refers to the position taken by someone who holds that the human mind is incapable of grasping the true nature of things.

6) *The concept of ṣidq*

Implying power or strength, the word *ṣidq* refers to the opposite of falsehood, which has no strength or power inherent within it. Other derivatives of this root include the word *ṣidāq*, which refers to a woman's dower, since this is something rightfully hers; *ṣiddīq*, an intensive form referring to someone who is always truthful; *ṣidq*, which refers to the correspondence between a person's words and the reality to which they refer in the belief of the speaker; and *miṣdāq*, which refers to the criterion by which the truth of a statement is determined. Derivatives of the root *ṣ-d-q* occur 127 times in the Qur'an. These include *Sūrah al-Zumar*, 39:32-33: "And who could be more wicked than he who invents lies about God, and gives the lie to the truth (*al-ṣidq*) as soon as it has been placed before him? ... But he who brings the truth (*jā'a bil-ṣidqi*), and he who wholeheartedly accepts it as true (*wa ṣaddaqa bihi*) – it is they, they, who are [truly] conscious of Him!" *Sūrah al-Baqarah*, 2:23 reads, "And if you doubt any part of what We have bestowed from on high, step by step, upon Our servant [Muhammad], then produce a surah of similar merit, and call upon any other than God to bear witness for you – if what you say is true (*in kuntum ṣādiqīn*)!" In *Sūrah al-Zumar*, 39:74, the inhabitants of Paradise exclaim, "All praise is due to God, who has made His promise to us come true (*ṣadaqanā waʿdahu*), and has bestowed upon us this expanse [of bliss) as our portion." We are asked in *Sūrah al-Nisā'*, 4:122, "whose word could be truer (*aṣdaqu*) than God's?" In *Sūrah Maryam*, 19:41, the Prophet Abraham is described as "a man of truth" (*ṣiddīq*). Other derivatives of this root include "friend" (*ṣadīq*), which occurs in *Sūrah al-Nūr*, 24:61, alms (*ṣadaqah*) in *Sūrah al-Baqarah*, 2:196, and bridal dowers (*ṣaduqāt*) in *Sūrah al-Nisā'* 4:4.

7) *The concept of ḥaqq*

The triliteral root *ḥ-q-q* conveys the sense of validity, rightness, justice, duty, worthiness, and truth. Derivatives of this root occur 267 times in the Qur'an. *Sūrah al-Mu'minūn*, 23:71 reads, "But if the truth (*al-ḥaqq*) were in accord with their own likes and dislikes, the heavens and the earth would surely have fallen into ruin," while in a reference to the Qur'an, *Sūrah al-Qaṣaṣ*, 28:48 relates, "And yet, now that the truth (*al-ḥaqq*) has come unto them from Us, they say, 'Why has he not been vouchsafed the like of what Moses was vouchsafed?'" In a reference to Islam, *Sūrah al-Isrā'*, 17:81 reads, "The truth (*al-ḥaqq*) has now come [to light], and falsehood has withered away." In a reference to justice, *Sūrah al-Nūr*, 24:25 declares, "On that day God will pay them in full their just due (*dīnahum al-ḥaqq*)." *Sūrah al-Ṣāffāt*, 37:37 tells us that "he [whom you call a mad poet] has brought the truth (*al-ḥaqq*)," where "the truth" refers to affirmation of the oneness of God. In *Sūrah al-Anʿām*, 6:73, the word *al-ḥaqq* is used to refer to truthfulness ("whenever He says, 'Be,' His word comes true (*qawluhu al-ḥaqq*); and His will be the dominion…"). Set in contrast with falsehood, we read in *Sūrah al-Ḥajj*, 22:62, "Thus it is, because God alone is the Ultimate Truth (*al-ḥaqq*) so that all that men invoke beside Him is sheer falsehood." In *Sūrah al-Baqarah*, 2:282, the word *al-ḥaqq* is used to refer to money: "let him who contracts the debt (*alladhī ʿalayhi*) dictate…" *Sūrah al-Baqarah*, 2:247 uses the superlative *aḥaqqu* to mean "having a better claim to." *Sūrah al-Maʿārij*, 70:24 uses the root *ḥ-q-q* to mean an acknowledged share of someone's possessions (*ḥaqqun maʿlūm*). The word *ḥaqq* is used to mean "need" in *Sūrah Hūd*, 11:79, "we have no use (*ḥaqq*) whatever for thy daughters." In *Sūrah al-Baqarah*, 2:71, the word *ḥaqq* refers to plain truth, while in *Sūrah al-Raʿd*, 13:14 it refers to the affirmation that there is no god but God. *Sūrah al-Tawbah*, 9:111 uses the word *ḥaqq* as an adverbial meaning "in truth." *Sūrah al-Baqarah*, 2:61 speaks of how certain prophets were slain "without right" (*bi ghayri ḥaqq*). All of the aforementioned usages of this root are close to its lexical meaning. For when the Qur'an speaks of God as "the Ultimate Truth (*al-ḥaqq*)" (*Sūrah al-Mu'minūn*, 23:116), it is affirming that God is the One with the right to rule and govern, who always has been and always will be. Similarly, the Qur'an addresses someone whose belief conforms to reality with the words, "that in which you believe is truth self-evident (*innaka ʿalā al-ḥaqq al-mubīn*)" (*Sūrah al-Naml*, 27:79). The word *ḥaqq* is likewise used in contexts that describe a person's words and actions as conforming to what they ought to be. Thus God declares in *Sūrah al-Sajdah*, 32:13, "that word of Mine has come true (*ḥaqq al-qawlu minnī*)," while *Sūrah al-Anfāl*, 8:8 speaks of how God wills to "prove the truth to be true..." (*li yuḥiqqa al-ḥaqqa*), where proving the truth to be true involves a dual aspect of: (1) revealing evidence and signs, and (2) fulfilling the Divine Law.

8) *The concept of yaqīn*

The triliteral root *y-q-n* refers to an end to doubt and uncertainty. Derivatives of this root occur 28 times in the Qur'an in four different senses: (1) Certain truthfulness. *Sūrah al-Naml*, 27:22 quotes the hoopoe bird as saying to Solomon, "I have come to you from Sheba with a tiding sure! (*ji'tuka min saba'in bi naba'in yaqīn*)." This sense is also found in *Sūrah al-Baqarah*, 2:4, where God praises those "who in their innermost are certain of the life to come (*wa bi al-ākhirati hum yūqinūn*)." (2) Death. *Sūrah al-Ḥijr*, 15:99 refers to death with the word *yaqīn*, saying, "worship your Sustainer till death comes to you (*ḥattā ya'tīka al-yaqīn*)." (3) The certainty of an eyewitness. *Sūrah al-Takāthur*, 102:7 warns unbelievers that they will see reality clearly on the Day of Resurrection, when they will surely "behold it with the eye of certainty (*ʿayn al-yaqīn*)." (4) Knowledge. The word *yaqīn* is used adverbially in this sense in *Sūrah al-Nisā'*, 4:157, where we are told that "of a certainty, they did not slay him (*mā qatalūhu yaqīnan*)."

Al-yaqīn is the term with which the Qur'an speaks of verification and the elimination of doubt, a confident realization untainted by illusion, surmise, conjecture, or skepticism. The verb *tayaqqana* cannot be ascribed to God, because *yaqīn* is the knowledge of something that one attains after a state of uncertainty, and after one has accumulated sufficient evidence to make a solid conviction possible. *Yaqīn* is associated with *ʿilm*, but not *maʿrifah* or *dirāyah*. Common collocations containing the term *yaqīn* are *ʿilm al-yaqīn*, *ʿayn al-yaqīn*, and *ḥaqq al-yaqīn*, among which there are certain distinctions.

The person with *yaqīn* has arrived at a clear belief. The hoopoe introduces his report to Solomon with evidence and signs that what he is about to relay is fully truthful and will yield certain knowledge based on the nature of its source and the reliability of its transmission. He begins by saying, "I have encompassed [with my knowledge] something that you have never yet encompassed [with yours]." Only then does he go on to add, "- for I have come to you from Sheba with a tiding sure (*ji'tuka min saba'in bi naba'in yaqīn*)" (*Sūrah al-Naml*, 27:22). The phrase "have encompassed" (*aḥaṭtu*) used by the hoopoe communicates a sense of comprehensiveness, while the noun used for "tiding" (*naba'*) is one generally reserved for a report of weighty significance or a warning of some grave and imminent danger. The hoopoe then describes his tiding with the word *yaqīn*, or "sure." In this way he seeks to demonstrate the veracity of what he is saying and to offer an excuse for his absence.

9) *The concept of kadhib*

The triliteral root *k-dh-b* is associated with untruth, either in the sense of communicating an untruth, usually with the intent to deceive, or of attributing untruth to a statement, a person, one's senses, etc. The Qur'an employs derivatives of this root in 251 places, and in six differing senses. (1) Hypocrisy. The root *k-dh-b* is used in this sense in *Sūrah al-Baqarah*, 2:10, which states that "grievous suffering awaits them [the hypocrites] because of their persistent lying" (*bi mā kānū yakdhibūn*). (2) Slander. *Sūrah al-Nūr*, 24:7 uses this root to refer to the act of bringing a false accusation against one's spouse. (3) Rebuttal. *Sūrah al-Wāqiʿah*, 56:2 uses the noun *kādhibah* to refer to evidence that would disprove the reality of the Resurrection. (4) Denial. Speaking of a vision which the Prophet had, *Sūrah al-Najm*, 53:11 states: "The [servant's] heart did not give the lie to (*mā kadhdhaba*) what he saw." (5) Disbelief. *Sūrah Qāf*, 50:5 speaks of those who "have been wont to give the lie to this truth (*kadhdhabū bi al-ḥaqq*) whenever it was proffered to them." (6) Fabrication of untruths. *Sūrah al-Zumar*, 39:60 speaks of those "who invented lies about God" (*kadhabū ʿalā Allāh*).

The word *kadhib* refers to a verbal report or behavior that does not correspond to reality. The Qur'an thus describes hypocrisy (*nifāq*) as a type of lying, or *kadhib*, since a hypocrite's words and actions do not reflect the reality within his or her conscience. In other words, hypocrisy is to put on an appearance of faith to conceal unbelief and thereby deceive others. *Sūrah al-Baqarah*, 2:8-10 states that

> there are people who say, "We do believe in God and the Last Day," the while they do not [really] believe. They would deceive God and those who have attained to faith – the while they deceive none but themselves, and perceive it not. In their hearts is disease, and so God lets their disease increase; and grievous suffering awaits them because of their persistent lying (*bi mā kānū yakdhibūn*).

Of this group of people we read in *Sūrah al-Mujādalah*, 58:14 that "they swear to a falsehood (*yaḥlifūna ʿalā al-kadhib*) the while they know [it to be false]," and in *Sūrah Āl ʿImrān*, 3:78 that "they tell a lie about God, being well aware [that it is a lie]."

10) *The concept of ifk*

The triliteral root *i-f-k* refers to the act of reversing something or diverting it from its course, and is used in a sense similar to that of *kadhib*. *Al-Mu'tifikāt* is a term that refers to the cities inhabited by the people of Lot and that were overthrown, while the term *ma'fūk* refers to someone who is weak-minded.

Derivatives of the root *i-f-k* occur 30 times in the Qur'an with seven different senses: (1) Lying. *Sūrah al-Aḥqāf*, 46:11 speaks of unbelievers who describe God's message as "an ancient falsehood (*ifkun qadīm*)." (2) False worship. In *Sūrah al-Ṣāffāt*, 37:86, idolaters are asked, "Is it a lie that you want [to worship] as deities besides God (*a'ifkan ālihatan dūn Allāhi turīdūna*)?" (3) Claiming that God has a son. We read in *Sūrah al-Ṣāffāt*, 37:151-152, "Oh, verily, it is out of their own [inclination to] falsehood (*min ifkihim*) that some people assert, 'God has begotten [a son].'" (4) Accusing chaste women of indecent behavior. *Sūrah al-Nūr*, 24:11 refers to "those who would falsely accuse others of unchastity" (*al-ladhīna jā'ū bil-ifk*). (5) Delusion. This sense of the word is found *Sūrah al-Dhāriyāt*, 51:9, which speaks of how "such as would be deluded...are deluded [away from the Truth]" (*yu'faku ʿanhu man ufika*) (Yusuf Ali). (6) Overturning. *Sūrah al-Najm*, 53:53 speaks of "cities that were overthrown" (*al-mu'tafikah*). (7) Sorcery. In relating the account of Moses' encounter with the sorcerers of Pharaoh who caused ropes to appear as though they were serpents, *Sūrah al-Shuʿarā'*, 26:45 tells us that when Moses cast down his staff, "it swallowed up all their deceptions (*mā ya'fakūn*)."

11) *The concept of iftirā'*

The verb *iftarā* is derived from the triliteral root *f-r-y*, one meaning of which is to cut or split something. The verb form *farā* refers to the act of cutting something in a way that distorts or mars it. It can also be used in connection with the fabrication of lies, as in the phrase, *farā al-kidhb*, he invented a lie. When speaking of tanned leather, the verb *afrā* refers to the act of cutting it in order to ruin or destroy it, while the verb form *farā* refers to the act of cutting it in order to repair or improve it.

The verb *iftarā* occurs 60 times in the Qur'an, most frequently in relation to lies or falsehoods. *Sūrah Āl ʿImrān*, 3:94 speaks of those who "invent lies about God" (*man iftarā ʿalā Allāhi al-kadhib*). In some cases it is associated with wrongdoing, as in *Sūrah al-Nisā'*, 4:48, which speaks of someone who worships idols as having "contrived an awesome sin" (*iftarā ithman ʿaẓīman*). *Sūrah Yūnus*, 10:37 declares that the Qur'an "could not possibly have been devised by anyone save God" (*mā kāna hādha al-qur'ānu an yuftarā min dūni Allāh*). It may also be used in connection with some unheard-of action, as in *Sūrah Maryam*, 19:27, which relates that after Mary gave birth to Jesus, her people said to her, "O Mary! Thou hast indeed done an amazing thing (*la qad ji'ti shay'an fariyyan*)!" It is used in *Sūrah al-Qaṣaṣ*, 28:36 in connection with the word for magic (*al-siḥr*), which Muhammad Asad translates as "spellbinding eloquence." We are told that Pharaoh and his entourage described Moses' message from God as "nothing but spellbinding eloquence devised [by man] (*mā hādha illā siḥrun muftaran*)." Similarly, some people of the Prophet's day described the Qur'an as being "nothing but a falsehood invented [by human beings] (*mā hādha illā ifkun muftaran*)" (*Sūrah Saba'*, 34:43). And in *Sūrah al-Mumtaḥanah*, 60:12, the verb is linked to slander. We are told that women wanting to join the Muslim cause must pledge not to "indulge in slander, falsely devising it out of nothingness" (*lā ya'tīna bi buhtānin yaftarīnahu bayna aydīhinna wa arjulihinna*)."

12) *The concept of buhtān*

The word *buhtān* refers to baseless slander, the act of accusing someone wrongly of something he or she did not do. Other senses of the verb *bahita* or *bahuta* include: to be bewildered and confused, to be defeated in an argument, or to fade (said of a color). Derivatives of the root *b-h-t* occur six times in the Qur'an in four different senses: (1) Sexual immorality. The verse quoted above from *Sūrah al-Mumtaḥanah*, 60:12 is translated by Muhammad Sarwar as stating that women must not "bring false charges against anyone (such as ascribing others children to their husbands)" (*lā ya'tīna bi buhtānin yaftarīnahu bayna aydīhinna wa arjulihinna*). (2) Falsehood. In *Sūrah al-Nūr*, 24:16, God tells the Muslim community that they should not believe a vicious rumor but, rather, view it as "an awesome calumny" (*buhtānun ʿazīm*). (3) Dishonest gain. *Sūrah al-Nisā'*, 4:20 tells the man who intends to divorce one wife and take another that he must return the first wife's dower no matter how much it may have been, since otherwise, he will be guilty of a serious wrong (*buhtān*). (4) Bewilderment or confusion. *Sūrah al-Baqarah*, 2:258 describes the denier of truth who disputed with Abraham as being "confounded" (Yusuf Ali) or "dumbfounded" (Asad) (*buhita alladhī kafara*).

13) *The concept of siḥr*

There are three distinct meanings associated with the triliteral root *s-ḥ-r*. When vowelized as *saḥr*, it refers to the pulmonary region of the body immediately next to the esophagus and the trachea. When vowelized as *siḥr*, it refers to the act of deceiving or charming by causing something unreal to appear as real; as such, it relates to magic or sorcery. And when vowelized as *saḥar*, it refers to the early dawn hours.

Derivatives of this root occur 61 times in the Qur'an in five different senses: (1) Knowledge. In *Sūrah al-Zukhruf*, 43:49, the word *sāḥir*, normally translated as "sorcerer," is used in the positive sense of one with knowledge. (2) Delusion. *Sūrah al-Qamar*, 54:2 tells us that if deniers of the truth were confronted with some miraculous sign of the coming judgment, they would deem it to be "an ever-recurring delusion (*siḥrun mustamirr*)." (3) Deception of the eye. We are told in *Sūrah al-Aʿrāf*, 7:116 that when Pharaoh's magicians cast down their staffs, "they cast a spell upon the people's eyes (*saḥarū aʿyun al-nāsi*)." (4) A person who has been charmed or had a spell cast upon him or her. *Sūrah al-Furqān*, 25:8 tells us that some of the Prophet's enemies described him as "a man bewitched (*rajulan masḥūran*)." (5) Being blinded to the truth. *Sūrah al-Mu'minūn*, 23:89 asks those who refused to believe in spite of the evidence, "How, then, can you be so deluded (*fa'annā tusḥarūn*)?"

14) *The concept of qirā'ah*

The triliteral root *q-r-y* or *q-r-'* refers, among other things, to the act of collecting, bringing together. The Qur'an was named thus because it brings together precepts, judgments, stories and the like.

Excluding the terms *al-qur'ān*, *al-qir'*, and *al-qaryah*, forms of the verb *qara'a* appear approximately 17 times in the Qur'an. The term *al-qur'ān* occurs 70 times, while the same term as applied specifically to the speech revealed by God through the Prophet occurs 68 times. It occurs twice in the sense of recitation in *Sūrah al-Qiyāmah*, 75:17-18, where God says to the Prophet concerning the Qur'an: "Behold, it is for Us to gather it [in thy heart,] and to cause it to be read [as it ought to be read] (*ʿalaynā jamʿahu wa qur'ānahu*). Thus, when We recite it, follow its wording (*fa idhā qara'nāhu, fattabiʿ qur'ānahu*)." In *Sūrah al-Aʿlā*, 87:6, an intensive form of the verb is used in the sense of "teach". God tells the Prophet, "We shall teach you (*sanuqri'uka*), and you will not forget." The knowledge gleaned through recitation or reading depends on whether the reading is superficial or deep. Having read and recited the revelation to Moses, the Children of Israel were aware of the validity of what God had revealed to His Prophet Muhammad. Hence, we read in *Sūrah Yūnus*, 10:94 that God said to him, "if you are in doubt about [the truth of] what We have [now] bestowed upon you from on high, ask those who read the divine writ [revealed] before your time."

The verbal noun *qirā'ah* refers to the act of combining letters and words in recitation of something either written or memorized. The word is used in this sense in *Sūrah al-Naḥl*, 16:98, which instructs the Muslims, when reading or reciting the Qur'an, to "seek refuge with God from Satan, the accursed." Similarly, individuals brought before God on Judgment Day are instructed to "read" the book that contains their deeds on earth (*Sūrah al-Isrā'*, 17:14). And in *Sūrah al-ʿAlaq*, 96:1, the Prophet was commanded to "read" in the name of his Sustainer.

15) *The concept of dirāsah*

The triliteral root *d-r-s* denotes hiddenness; the word *dars* means, among other things, a hidden path. The verb *darasa* can refer to the act of threshing, as of wheat, which in olden times was done by tramping the plants with the feet in order to separate them from the grain. The verb *darasa* can also refer to the act of studying, since the person who engages in the act of *dirāsah* is 'treading over' or tracing what was previously read, as one treads on or traces a path. Hence, another meaning of the noun *dars* is a lesson. The verb *darasa* occurs six times in the Qur'an in the present and past tenses, and as a verbal noun. In a challenge to those who disbelieve in the Islamic message, God asks, "Have you, perchance, a [special] divine writ which you study (*tadrusūn*)?" (*Sūrah al-Qalam*, 68:37). In *Sūrah al-Anʿām*, 6:156, the verbal noun is used in the sense of studying and passing on what one studies, while *Sūrah al-Anʿām*, 6:105-106 uses the verb *darasa* in the sense of thorough study and application. God says to the Prophet, "And to the end that they might say, 'You have taken [all this] well to heart (*darasta*) ... follow what has been revealed to you by your Sustainer." The name of the Qur'anic prophet Idrīs is said to be a derivative of the verb *darasa* based on his intensive study of the Divine Revelation.

16) *The concept of taḥṣīl*

The triliteral root *ḥ-ṣ-l* denotes gathering, acquiring and preservation. From this root we get the word *ḥawṣalah*, which refers to the craw of a bird where it stores food it has gathered. It is said that the verb *ḥaṣṣala* originally referred to the act of extracting gold or silver from rock or soil, while the noun *ḥāṣil* refers to the final, enduring outcome of a process. When connected to speech, the verb *ḥaṣṣala* refers to the act of gleaning meaning from what one has heard. The verb *ḥaṣṣala* occurs once in the Qur'an in the passive voice. We read in *Sūrah al-ʿĀdiyāt*, 100:10 about the Day of Resurrection, when "all that is [hidden] in men's hearts is bared (*ḥuṣṣila mā fī al-ṣudūr*)," that is brought out for all to see. In modern-day usage, the verb *ḥaṣṣala* refers not simply to the acquisition of material wealth, but to the acquisition and retention of academic knowledge; hence, it is sometimes used alone to refer to academic performance.

17) *The concept of iḥṣā'*

There are three distinct semantic ranges associated with the root *ḥ-ṣ-y*. The first of these has to do with prevention, and the second with enumeration, comprehension and confinement. As for the third, it takes the form of the noun *ḥaṣā*, which refers to gravel or pebbles.

Derivatives of the root *ḥ-ṣ-y* occur eleven times in the Qur'an in two different senses: (1) Enumeration and computation. This sense is illustrated in *Sūrah Ibrāhīm*, 14:34, where we read, "should you try to count God's blessings, you could never compute them (*lā tuḥṣūhā*)," and *Sūrah al-Ṭalāq*, 65:1, which speaks of "reckoning" (computing, keeping track of) a divorced woman's waiting period. (2) Recording and exhaustive accounting. In *Sūrah Yāsīn*, 36:12 God declares that on Resurrection Day He will say, "We shall record whatever [deeds] they [those who have died] have sent ahead" (*wa kulla shay'in aḥṣaynāhu fī imāmin mubīn*)." We are told in *Sūrah al-Kahf*, 18:49 that upon seeing the record of their unconfessed wrongs on Judgment Day, people will cry out, "Woe unto us!...It leaves out nothing, be it small or great, but takes everything into account (*lā yughādiru ṣaghīratan wa lā kabīratan illā aḥṣāhā*)!" The sense of comprehensive accounting is likewise found in *Sūrah al-Jinn*, 72:28, which reminds us that God "takes count, one by one, of everything [that exists]."

18) *The concept of taqdīr*

The triliteral root *q-d-r* has to do with an entity's extent, scope, and essential nature. The noun *qadar* refers to divine foreordainment and God's power over the creation, while the verbal noun *taqdīr* refers to the act of settling or disposing of affairs, or assessing something or someone with reference to something or someone else.

This root occurs 146 times in the Qur'an in various forms, and in four different senses: (1) Appreciation or assessment. In *Sūrah al-Zumar*, 39:67 we are told that idolaters have "no true understanding of God (*mā qadarū Allāha ḥaqqa qadrihi*)." (2) Scanty apportionment. *Sūrah al-Raʿd*, 13:26 tells us that "God grants abundant sustenance, or gives it in scant measure (*wa yaqdiru*), unto whomever He wills." (3) Power. *Sūrah al-Balad*, 90:5 asks concerning the arrogant and self-sufficient: "Does he...think that no one has power over him (*ayaḥsabu an lan yaqdiru ʿalayhi aḥadun*)?" (4) Determination of human beings' formation in the womb, the cycles of nature, and the measure of everything in existence. In *Sūrah al-Mursalāt*, 77:23 God says, "Thus have We determined [the nature of man's creation] (*faqadarnā*): and excellent indeed is Our power to determine [what is to be]! (*fa niʿma al-qādirūn*)." In *Sūrah Yūnus*, 10:5 we read about how God has "has determined for it [the moon] phases (*qaddarahu manāzila*)" to enable people "to compute the years and to measure [time]." Similarly in *Sūrah al-Muzzammil*, 73:20 we are told that it is "God who determines the measure of night and day" (*yuqaddiru al-layla wal-nahār*)." *Sūrah al-Furqān*, 25:2 tells us that God has made everything and determined its nature (*fa qaddarahu taqdīran*), while *Sūrah al-Ṭalāq*, 65:3 reminds us that "unto everything has God appointed its [term and] measure (*jaʿala Allāhu li kulli shay'in qadran*)."

19) *The concept of baḥth*

In its original meaning, the triliteral root *b-ḥ-th* denotes the act of seeking something in the ground. Its meaning has since been extended to the act of searching for anything or anyone, investigating a matter, or exerting effort in connection with an issue or concern. In more recent times the verb *baḥatha* has been associated more narrowly with academic or scientific research, since it is a process that strives to reveal what has been hidden or unknown. *Sūrah al-Tawbah* (also known as *Sūrah Barā'ah*) has sometimes also been referred to as *Sūrah al-Buḥūth* because of its references to the search for hypocrites in the Muslim community and their secrets.

20) *The concept of kashf*

The triliteral root *k-sh-f* refers to the removal of something from something else in such a way as to reveal it. The noun *kashaf* refers to a bald spot on a horse's forelock; the verb *takashshafa* is used of lightning when it appears in the sky, and the noun *kāshifah* refers to something that reveals or removes something else. Derivatives of this root appear 20 times in the Qur'an. In *Sūrah Qāf*, 50:22 God addresses the godless on the Day of Judgment, saying, "You have been unmindful of this [Day of Judgment]; but now We have lifted from you your veil (*kashafnā ʿanka ghiṭā'aka*), and sharp is your sight today!" Used in nominal form, *k-sh-f* is found in *Sūrah al-Najm*, 53:58 which, speaking of the Last Hour, says that "none but God can unveil it" – literally, it has no unveiler but God (*laysa lahā min dūn Allāhi kāshifah*). Similarly, *Sūrah al-Anʿām*, 6:17 tells us that if God allows misfortune in our lives, no one can remove it but He (*fa lā kāshifa lahu illā huwa*). Similarly, we are told in *Sūrah al-Anʿām*, 6:41 that if He so wills, God can remove affliction when we call upon Him (*fa yakshifu mā tadʿūna ilayhi*).

21) *The concept of naqīb*

The triliteral root *n-q-b* refers generally to an opening in something, or to the act of boring a hole. Another sense of the word is to traverse, as in traversing a country in flight from a pursuer. The noun *naqīb* can refer to a woodwind instrument resembling the oboe (a mizmar) which has holes bored in it, while the noun *naqībah* refers to a person's soul or spirit, or to penetrating vision or insight. The same noun can refer to a large-uddered she-camel, while the verb *naqqaba* can be used to refer to the act of digging up news.

The root *n-q-b* occurs three times in the Qur'an. One of these is found in *Sūrah al-Mā'idah*, 5:12, where it is used in the sense of leader (*naqīb*). In *Sūrah Qāf*, 50:36, the verb *naqqaba* is used in the sense of wandering the land in search of refuge (*fa naqqabū fī al-bilādi hal min maḥīṣ*). In *Sūrah al-Kahf*, 18:97, the root *n-q-b* is used in the sense of piercing a hole in something (*naqb*). This root had the original denotation of digging; the meaning then shifted to the broader sense of searching, so that a scholar or anyone who is intelligent and insightful may be referred to as a *naqqāb*, one who digs or searches for knowledge. The fact that the *n-q-b* root is associated with digging and penetration to reach the heart, or innermost aspect of something, the soul, spirit or mind has been referred to as *al-naqībah*.

22) *The concept of baʿtharah*

The original root associated with this root is *b-th-r*, the letter *ʿayn* being a later addition. Its basic meaning has to do with looking and examining. The verb *baʿthara* means to dissipate, scatter, strew about, or throw into disorder. It can also refer to the act of turning upside down, overturning, or extracting. This root occurs only twice in the Qur'an. One of these instances is in *Sūrah al-Infiṭār*, 82:4, which speaks of graves being overturned (*wa idhā al-qubūru buʿthirat*). A similar usage is found in *Sūrah al-ʿĀdiyāt*, 100:9, which speaks of that which is in the graves being "raised and brought out" (*idhā buʿthira mā fī al-qubūr*). The reference in these two verses is to the swift transfer of those lying in their graves to a place of harsh judgment for what is hidden in their hearts. In both verses the verb is in the passive voice, which serves to draw our attention to the action or movement itself. A point to be noted is that the second verse cited speaks not of *those who* are in the graves, but of *that which* is in the graves. The reason for this might be that most of what lies underground is non-living, hence, the neuter reference. Another way of explaining the use of the neuter is to suppose that when they are raised from their graves, the dead are not conscious, but only become so again after they have been brought out. And in fact, the resurrection is referred to in the Qur'an as *al-baʿth*.

23) *The concept of kitābah*

The root consisting of the letters *k-t-b* denotes the act of joining one thing to another. Derivatives of this root occur 319 times in the Qur'an in five different senses: (1) Prescribe. Addressing the Muslim community, God says, "O you who have attained to faith! Fasting is prescribed for you (*kutiba ʿalaykum al-ṣiyāmu*) as it was prescribed for those before you (*kamā kutiba ʿalā alladhīna min qablikum*)" (*Sūrah al-Baqarah*, 2:183). (2) Ordain. In *Sūrah al-Mujādalah*, 58:21 we read: "God has thus ordained (*kataba Allāhu*): 'I shall most certainly prevail, I and My apostles'..." (See also *Sūrah al-Ḥijr*, 15:4 and *Sūrah al-Baqarah*, 2:235). (3) Inscribe. Speaking of the believers, *Sūrah al-Mujādalah*, 58:22 tells us that God "has inscribed" (*kataba*) faith in their hearts. When the Qur'an says that God has "inscribed faith" in believers' hearts, it means that God has caused, or enabled, them to believe in what they should believe in. (4) Promise. In *Sūrah al-Mā'idah*, 5:21, Moses tells his people to enter the holy land which God has promised (*kataba Allāhu*) them. (5) Write. *Sūrah al-Baqarah*, 2:79 speaks of those "who write down..." (*lilladhīna yaktu- būna al-kitāb*)."

In keeping with the meaning mentioned earlier, the process of writing involves joining letters to one another in the form of script. The image of writing, or a book, is used metaphorically to refer to God's speech even though God's speech is not actually written down (cf. *Sūrah al-Baqarah*, 2:2). Similarly, as we see in the verses quoted above, the image of writing or a book is used metaphorically to speak of divine command, divine ordainment, and divine promise. The basis for this metaphor lies in the fact that before something is written down, it is willed, then spoken. The process begins with an act of will and concludes with an act of writing. *Sūrah al-Aʿrāf*, 7:157 states that the Prophet is "mentioned" (*maktūban*) in the scriptures of the Jews and the Christians. We find the word *kitāb* used to refer to the revelation given to Moses and to the Christian scriptures, just as it is used to refer to the Qur'an (*Sūrah al-Aḥqāf*, 46:12; cf. *Sūrah Fuṣṣilat*, 41:3 and *Āl*

ʿImrān, 3:78). The word *kitāb* is also used in ways that go beyond its original sense. In *Sūrah al-Jāthiyah*, 45:28 and *Sūrah al-Kahf*, 18:49, it is used in the sense of an accounts ledger containing a record of people's deeds for which they will be held accountable on Judgment Day.

24) *The concept of zubur*

The root consisting of the letter *z-b-r* is associated with two distinct meanings. One of these is that of securing or reinforcing something. One might use the verb *zabara* to speak of reinforcing a well with stones, for example. A derivative of this sense of the root is the noun *zubrah* (plural, *zubar*), which refers to a piece of iron. The noun (or adjective) *zubayr* refers to a cunning, self-possessed person. The other set of meanings related to the root *z-b-r* has to do with reading and writing. From this we derive the word *zabūr*, which is used to refer to the Psalms of David, the word *mizbar*, or a pen, and *zubur*, or holy scriptures.

This root occurs nine times in the Qur'an in four different senses: (1) Books of divine wisdom. The word *zubur* is used in this sense in *Sūrah Āl ʿImrān*, 3:184 and *Sūrah al-Naḥl*, 16:44. (2) The revelation given to David. God states in *Sūrah al-Nisā'*, 4:163, "We vouchsafed unto David a book of divine wisdom (*zabūr*)." (3) The divine record of people's deeds (*Sūrah al-Qamar*, 54:52). (4) Pieces of iron (*Sūrah al-Kahf*, 18:96). In *Sūrah al-Mu'minūn*, 23:53, the word *zubur* is used to mean "pieces" in a metaphorical sense.

25) *The concept of sifr*

The triliteral root *s-f-r* conveys the sense of unveiling, exposure, openness and clarity. The noun *safar* is used to refer to travel because, when traveling, people leave their homes and are exposed to new places and people. The verbal noun *safr* refers to writing, since it yields (reveals, brings to light) written material that is needed. As for the noun *sifr* (plural, *asfār*), it refers to a large book or to a section of the Jewish scriptures, while the plural noun *safarah* means "writers" or "messengers," in which sense the word is used in *Sūrah ʿAbasa*, 80:15. The word *safarah* as used here may refer to the angels who "travel" back and forth between God and God's messengers as bearers of revelation. It bears noting that the Arabic word for ambassador is *safīr* (plural, *sufarā'*), the ambassador being one who seeks to promote reconciliation among different parties.

Derivatives of this root occur in twelve places in the Qur'an in five different senses: (1) Journey-stages (*asfār*; see *Sūrah Saba'*, 34:19). (2) Books (*asfār*; see *Sūrah al-Jumʿah*, 62:5). (3) Brightness. *Sūrah ʿAbasa*, 80:38 describes the faces of the righteous on the Day of Resurrection as "bright" (*musfirah*). (4) Daybreak. *Sūrah al-Muddaththir*, 74:34 uses the verb *asfara* to refer to the breaking of dawn. (5) Travel. *Sūrah al-Baqarah*, 2:184 uses the noun *safar* to refer to being "on a journey" (*ʿalā safar*).

26) *The concept of ʿahd*

The root consisting of the letters *ʿ-h-d* has numerous shades of meaning. It has to do with knowledge and familiarity, assignment and commitment, pledge and promise. One meaning of the noun *ʿahd* (plural, *ʿuhūd*) is a dwelling to which a tribe returns again and again. The noun *maʿhad* (plural, *maʿāhid*), defined in modern parlance as 'institute' is likewise a familiar, well-known location. From this root we derive words such as *muʿāhadah* (a treaty or agreement), *al-taʿahhud* (contracting), and *ʿuhdah*, a contract of sale or other contractual obligation. All of the meanings mentioned thus involve a commitment of some sort, as they are entities that need to be adhered to. As such, this root is related to the concepts of sacredness, safety, responsibility, and protection.

Derivatives of this root occur in 46 places in the Qur'an, and in three broad senses: (1) Enjoining or commanding. *Sūrah Yāsīn*, 36:60 uses the verb *ʿahida* in the sense of enjoining or commanding. See also *Sūrah al-Baqarah*, 2:125, where God declares, "thus did We command Abraham and Ishmael: 'Purify My Temple…' (*wa ʿahidnā ilā Ibrāhīma wa Ismāʿīla an ṭahhirā baytī…*)." The same sense of the verb *ʿahida* is found in *Sūrah Ṭāhā*, 20:115 with respect to Adam. (2) Covenant. In *Sūrah al-Aʿrāf*, 7:134, we read that the Children of Israel cried out to Moses in the wilderness, saying, "O Moses, pray for us to your Sustainer on the strength of the covenant [of prophethood] which He has made with you" (*bi mā ʿahida ʿindaka*). (3) Promise or pledge. *Sūrah al-Baqarah*, 2:177 praises those "who keep their promises whenever they promise" (*al-mūfūn bi ʿahdihim idhā ʿāhadū*). Similarly, *Sūrah al-Mu'minūn*, 23:8 praises those who are faithful to their pledges (*ʿahdihim*). (Cf. *Sūrah al-Maʿārij*, 70:32, *al-Baqarah*, 2:80, and *Āl ʿImrān*, 3:76. For the verbal form, see also *Sūrah al-Tawbah*, 9:1, *al-Naḥl*, 16:91, and *al-Fatḥ*, 48:10).

27) *The concept of kalām*

The root consisting of the letters *k-l-m* denotes two sets of meanings, one of which has to do with meaningful speech, and the other with wounds. In its former sense, the *k-l-m* root yields derivatives such as *kalām*, 'speech', and *kalimah*, 'word'. In its latter sense, the *k-l-m* root yields the words *kalm*, 'wound' (plural, *kilām* or *kulūm*). The word *kulām* refers to rugged land.

Derivatives of the root *k-l-m* occur 75 times in the Qur'an in two overall senses: divine speech and human speech. (1) Divine speech. *Sūrah al-Nisā'*, 4:164 tells us that God spoke His word to Moses (*kalla-ma Allāhu Mūsā taklīman*), *Sūrah al-Baqarah*, 2:75 speaks of "the word of God" (*kalām Allāh*) coming to those who reject it, and *Sūrah al-Kahf*, 18:109 states that even if twice the seas' measure were ink for God's words (*kalimātu rabbī*), the seas would be exhausted before God's words were exhausted. Referring specifically to the Qur'an, *Sūrah al-Tawbah*, 9:6 instructs Muslim fighters to grant protection to any polytheist who might request it so that he might "hear the word of God" (*ḥattā yasmaʿa kalām Allāh*). We are told in *Sūrah al-Baqarah*, 2:37 that "Adam received words [of guidance] (*kalimātin*) from his Sustainer," and in a reference to the trials Abraham passed through in connection with circumcision and the possible sacrifice of his son, *Sūrah al-Baqarah*, 2:124 states that God "tried Abraham by [His] commandments" (*bi kalimātin*). (2) Human speech. *Sūrah Maryam*, 19:29 quotes the people of Mary's day asking how they can talk to (*nukallimu*) a newborn infant. Speaking of someone approaching death who cries out to God simply because he fears judgment, we are told in *Sūrah al-Mu'minūn*, 23:100 that this is merely "a word he has spoken" (*innahā kalimatun huwa qā'iluhā*) without meaning what he says. *Sūrah al-Kahf*, 18:5 contains a criticism of those who disseminate distorted spiritual teachings, saying, "dreadful is this saying (*kaburat kalimatan*) that comes out of their mouths (*takhruju min afwāhihim*)."

Jesus is also said to be "the word of God" (*Sūrah al-Nisā'*, 4:171), having been brought into being directly by the creative command, "Be." The title "the word of God" (*kalimat Allāh*) may have been given to Jesus due to the statement he is reported by the Qur'an to have made from the cradle, saying, "Behold, I am a servant of God. He has vouchsafed unto me revelation and made me a prophet" (*Sūrah Maryam*, 19:30).

The Qur'an states that recipients of former revelations "distort the meaning of the [revealed] words, taking them out of their context" (*yuḥarrifūna al-kalima ʿan mawāḍiʿihi*) (*Sūrah al-Mā'idah*, 5:13). Some have understood the phrase *yuḥarrifūna al-kalima ʿan mawāḍiʿihi* to mean that the words of divine writ were actually changed. However, once manuscripts of a scripture have been widely disseminated, it becomes extremely difficult to do such a thing. Hence, this phrase is best understood to refer to distorted interpretations of scriptures.

28) *The concept of qawl*

The root consisting of the letters *q-w-l* relates to the act of speaking or verbal articulation. The noun *qawl* (plural, *aqwāl, aqāwīl*) refers to something said, or to the act of saying it, and can be associated with both good and evil; as for the expression, *al-qīl wa al-qāl*, it is associated with evil, as it bears the sense of harmful innuendo or gossip. Similarly, the expression *taqawwala ʿalayhi* means to fabricate lies or spread rumors about someone, while the verbs *qāwala* and *taqāwala* have to do with negotiating and conferring with.

Derivatives of the root *q-w-l* occur 1,722 times in the Qur'an. The word *qawl* is used in a number of senses, the most prevalent of which have to do with combinations of letters made accessible to the hearer through spoken language, whether in the form of single words, or of complete statements. The verb *qāla* can be used to refer to the thoughts one thinks to oneself. Hence, we read in *Sūrah al-Mujādalah*, 58:8, "They say to themselves... (*yaqūlūna fī anfusihim*)." The verb *taqawwala* is used in *Sūrah al-Ḥāqqah*, 69:44 in the sense of attributing one's own sayings to someone else. What one says might, of course, be inconsistent with what one believes and does. Hence, *Sūrah Āl ʿImrān*, 3:167 tells us that the hypocrites uttered "with their mouths something which was not in their hearts," while we read in *Sūrah al-Shuʿarā'*, 26:226 that poets "say what they do not do."

29) *The concept of nuṭq*

The triliteral root *n-ṭ-q* comprises two basic semantic fields, one of which has to do with speech and articulation, and the other with a type of apparel known as a *niṭāq*, which is a kind of sash or belt. The verb *naṭaqa* refers to the act of articulating meaningful sounds.

Derivatives of the root *n-ṭ-q* occur twelve times in the Qur'an in two basic senses: (1) Sounds that issue from one's mouth. In *Sūrah al-Ṣāffāt*, 37:92, for example, Abraham mocks his people's idols, saying to them, "What is amiss with you that you do not speak (*mā lakum lā tanṭiqūn*)?" (2) Written speech. In *Sūrah al-Mu'minūn*, 23:62, God declares that on Judgment Day there will be "a record that speaks the truth (*kitābun yanṭiqu bil-ḥaqq*)."

The adjective *nāṭiq*, which refers to an entity capable of producing meaningful sound, is applied most often to human beings; when applied to other entities, it is used in a qualified or metaphorical sense. In *Sūrah al-Naml*, 27:16, where Solomon states that he has "been taught the speech of the birds" (*ʿullimnā manṭiq al-ṭayr*), the Qur'an refers to the sounds made by the birds as "speech", since this is how these sounds were perceived by Solomon, who understood what birds such the hoopoe communicated to him. This was something unique to Solomon. To Solomon, then, the birds were "speaking", since he understood their language, whereas to someone who did not understand their language, they would have been, for all intents and purposes, "silent." Similarly in *Sūrah al-Jāthiyah*, 45:29, God tells those gathered on Resurrection Day, "This Our record speaks (*hādha kitābunā yanṭiqu*) of you in all truth." Though in written form, the divine record of people's works "speaks" by communicating a message that is deciphered by the eye; similarly, spoken words can be referred to as a "book" that is deciphered by the ear. God's record bears witness against people, causing them to remember the things they have done.

30) *The concept of lisān*

The root consisting of the letter *l-s-n* denotes a body part that is connected to the rest of the body from one end, and which is of a length appropriate to its location and function. The tongue (*lisān*, plural, *alsun* or *alsinah*) is a known example of such an organ. Derivatives of this root occur 24 times in the Qur'an in four different senses: (1) Language. *Sūrah al-Naḥl*, 16:103 uses the word "tongue" to refer to human language. See also *Sūrah al-Rūm*, 30:22. (2) Words. *Sūrah al-Mā'idah*, 5:78 tells us that those of the Children of Israel who had rebelled against God were "cursed by the tongue (words) of David and of Jesus, the son of Mary" (*ʿalā lisāni Dāwūda wa ʿĪsā Ibni Maryam*). (3) The actual tongue. The word *lisān* is used in this sense in *Sūrah al-Qiyāmah*, 75:16, God instructs the Prophet not to move his tongue in haste when he is receiving the Qur'an. (4) The ability to convey truth (*lisāna ṣidqin*) (*Sūrah al-Shuʿarā'*, 26:84; cf. *Maryam*, 19:50; *al-Shuʿarā'*, 26:195). A similar sense of the word *lisān* is also found in *Sūrah Ṭāhā*, 20:27, where Moses prays for God to "loosen the knot from my tongue" (*waḥlul ʿuqdatan min lisānī*), where the word 'tongue' refers not to the physical member of his body, but to his ability to convey God's message. A related shade of meaning is that of eloquence (see *Sūrah al-Qaṣaṣ*, 28:34). The tongue is likened also to a sword "smite you with sharp tongues" (*Sūrah al-Aḥzāb*, 33:19), to the person speaking (*Sūrah al-Naḥl*, 16:116), and to an instrument for distorting truth (*Sūrah Āl ʿImrān*, 3:78).

31) *The concept of bukm*

The triliteral root *b-k-m* refers to the inability to speak, whether partial (for example, a stammer) or complete. Derivatives of this root occur six times in the Qur'an in association with deafness. *Sūrah al Baqarah*, 2:18 and 171, for example, associate it with deafness and blindness. In *Sūrah al-Isrā'*, 17:97, being "blind and dumb and deaf" is described as the punishment in the afterlife for having refused to use one's faculties in obedience to God during one's life on earth.

32) *The concept of ḥadīth*

The triliteral root *ḥ-d-th* denotes coming to pass or coming to be, as well as newness. Speech, being something from which other realities come to be, is referred to with the verbal noun *ḥadīth*, which can also mean a conversation, or an account of something that the Prophet did, said, or approved. As an adjective, the word *ḥadīth* means new or recent, while the verbal noun *muḥādathah* means conversation or the act of conversing.

Derivatives of the root *ḥ-d-th* occur 36 times in the Qur'an in five different senses: (1) To inform. The verb *ḥaddatha* is used in this sense in *Sūrah al-Baqarah*, 2:76: "Do you inform them of what God has disclosed to you? (*atuḥaddithūnahum bi mā fataḥa Allāhu ʿalaykum*)?" (See also *Sūrah al-Taḥrīm*, 66:3). (2) What one says. *Sūrah al-Nisā'*, 4:87 asks, "Whose word could be truer than God's (*man aṣdaqu min Allāhi ḥadīthan*)?" (3) Discourse. In *Sūrah al-Ṭūr*, 52:34, scoffers are challenged to produce "a discourse" (*ḥadīth*) that can compare in eloquence with the Qur'an. (4) Teachings. *Sūrah al-Zumar*, 39:23 tells us that God has revealed "the best of all teachings" (*aḥsan al-ḥadīth*) in the form of the Qur'an. (5) A tale of things past that serves as an example to others. This sense is found in *Sūrah Saba'*, 34:19, where God states that He scattered the once great people of Sheba, causing them to become "[one of those] tales [of things long past] (*jaʿalnāhum aḥādītha*)." (See also *Sūrah Yūsuf*, 12:101 and *al-Najm*, 53:59).

33) *The concept of khabar*

The triliteral root *kh-b-r* has two primary denotations. The first is knowledge of something. From this denotation we derive the noun *khabar*, meaning report or tiding. The term *khabar* is broader than that of *naba'* in that it implies a more intimate knowledge of the true nature of something. From the same root we derive the adjectives *khabīr*, *khābir*, and *khabir*, meaning knowledgeable or experienced. Used with the definite article and applied to God, the adjective *al-khabīr* means the All-Knowing. The words *khibrah, khubr*, and *mikhbarah* all refer to knowledge or experience of something, while the verbs *istakhbar* and *takhabbar* refer to the act of gathering knowledge or information. The second denotation is that of softness, affluence, and prosperity. The term *khabrā'* refers to soft soil, while the noun *khabīr* refers to a plowman, because he softens and prepares the soil for planting.

Derivatives of the root *kh-b-r* occur 52 times in the Qur'an, all of which have to do with knowledge in some way or another. In *Sūrah al-Naml*, 27:7, we read that Moses, having seen a fire in the distance, told his family that he would investigate it and bring back some "tiding" (*khabar*) concerning what he found (cf. *Sūrah al-Qaṣaṣ*, 28:29; for the plural, "tidings," see *Sūrah al-Zalzalah*, 99:4). *Sūrah al-Tawbah*, 9:94 uses the plural *akhbār* in a similar sense, while *Sūrah Muḥammad*, 47:31 uses the plural *akhbār* to refer to the "assertions" of those who did not want to go to war for the cause of Islam. *Sūrah al-Kahf*, 18:68 and 91 use the nominal form *khubr* to refer to knowledge or experience of something.

The word *khabīr* occurs 45 times in the Qur'an as one of the 99 names of God, Whose knowledge encompasses everything that is, has been, and will be, and all aspects of what is, both outward and inward. The word *khabīr* is applied in the Qur'an to no one but God Himself. *Sūrah al-Baqarah*, 2:234 reads, "God is aware of all that you do" (*Allāhu bi mā ta'malūna khabīr*; cf. *Sūrah Fāṭir*, 35:14), while God is described in *Sūrah Hūd*, 11:1 as the One Who is "Wise, All-Aware" (*ḥakīmin khabīr*). God is "unfathomable [in His wisdom], All-Aware" (*laṭīfun khabīr*) (*Sūrah al-Ḥajj*, 22:63); "All-Knowing, All-Aware" (*'alīmun khabīr*) (*Sūrah Luqmān*, 31:34) and "Fully Aware, All-Seeing" (*Sūrah Fāṭir*, 35:31).

34) *The concept of balāgh*

The root consisting of the letters *b-l-gh* conveys the idea of reaching something, whether temporally or spatially, in a tangible sense or an intangible sense. The verbal noun *balāgh* can mean, among other things, a communiqué or statement, while the verbs *ablagha* (verbal noun, *iblāgh*) and *ballagha* (*tablīgh*) mean to convey a message. Derivatives of this root occur 77 times in the Qur'an; of these instances, twenty-five have to do with the conveyance of knowledge. In ten of the Qur'anic uses of this root, it conveys the sense of delivering the divine message. In *Sūrah al-Mā'idah*, 5:67, God instructs the Prophet to communicate everything he has received by way of revelation, and that if he does not he will "not have delivered His message" (*fa mā ballaghta risālatahu*). In *Sūrah al-Anbiyā'*, 21:106, the word *balāgh* is used to refer to God's message to human beings (cf. *Sūrah Ibrāhīm*, 14:52), and *Sūrah Āl ʿImrān*, 3:20 uses the same term to refer to the act of delivering the message. *Sūrah al-Tawbah*, 9:6 instructs Muslim fighters who have been asked for protection from a polytheist to grant his request and "convey him to a place where he can feel secure" (*ablighhu ma'manahu*). The word *balāgh* is most often qualified in the Qur'an by the adjective *mubīn*, meaning "clear", since a clear message places more of an onus on the message's recipient. Using the verb *balagha* in the sense of 'reaching', *Sūrah Yūsuf*, 12:22 speaks of when Joseph "reached full manhood" (*balagha ashuddahu*).

35) *The concept of bushrā*

The triliteral root *b-sh-r* is related to the emergence of something good and pleasant. The root is occasionally associated with bad tidings; when it is, however, this must be specified by the context. Otherwise, it is assumed that the event concerned is a welcome one. The noun *bushrā* refers to good news, and the verb *bashshara* to the announcement of good news. The words *tabāshīr* and *bushrā* may also refer to the first fruits of date palms or some other plant to be harvested.

Derivatives of the root *b-sh-r* occur in 123 places in the Qur'an in five different senses: (1) Good news. The verb *bashshara* (*bashshartumūnī, tubashshirūn, bashsharnāka*) is used in *Sūrah al-Ḥijr*, 15: 54-55. (2) Sexual intercourse. In *Sūrah al-Baqarah*, 2:187, the verb *bāshara* is used to refer to sexual intercourse in the sense of one person's skin being in direct contact with another's. (3) Nourishing rain. *Sūrah al-Rūm*, 30:46 speaks of God sending winds that "bear glad tidings" (*yursila al-riyāḥa mubashshirāt*) by heralding rain's arrival. (4) Someone who brings good news. *Sūrah al-Baqarah*, 2:119 speaks of God's Messenger as a "bearer of glad tidings" (cf. *Sūrah al-Mā'idah*, 5:19). (5) Human beings (the word *bashar* being both singular and plural). The word *bashar* is used in this sense in *Sūrah al-Mā'idah*, 5:18.

Human beings are referred to as *bashar* in Arabic based on the appearance of hair on their skin (*al-basharah*) as opposed to fur, wool and the like. The association between the verbs *bashshara* and *abshara* and pleasant tidings is that when you give someone good news, it causes the features of his or her face (*basharah*) to brighten and relax. As for the use of the verb *bashshara* in association with unpleasant or dreaded news, this is the exception to the rule (see *Sūrah Āl ʿImrān*, 3:21; *Sūrah al-Naḥl*, 16:59, and *Sūrah al-Zukhruf* 43:17).

36) *The concept of nuṣḥ*

The triliteral root *n-ṣ-ḥ* refers to harmony or reconciliation between two entities; hence, the verb *naṣaḥa* has been used to refer to the act of sewing (which involves joining pieces into a harmonious whole), being pure, and watering or giving to drink. In origin, the active participle *nāṣiḥ* once referred to a tailor. The words *nuṣḥ* and *naṣīḥah*, which refer to heartfelt, sincere advice or counsel, denote the opposite of fraud, deceit or deception. Genuine repentance is thus referred to as *al-tawbah al-naṣūḥ*.

Derivatives of the root *n-ṣ-ḥ* occur thirteen times in the Qur'an and in two primary senses: (1) To admonish or advise. This sense is found in *Sūrah al-Aʿrāf*, 7:62, which relates Noah's statement to his people, "I am...giving you good advice" (*anṣaḥu lakum*), while *Sūrah al-Aʿrāf* 7:79 narrates that the Prophet Ṣāliḥ told his people, "I...gave you good advice" (*naṣaḥtu lakum*), the implication being that the advice has been proffered in good will, and with the sincere hope of helping the person to whom it is addressed. (2) Purity and sincerity. *Sūrah al-Taḥrīm*, 66:8 enjoins those who believe to "turn unto God in sincere repentance" (*tūbū ilā Allāhi tawbatan naṣūḥan*).

37) *The concept of qaṣaṣ*

In its origin, the root *q-ṣ-ṣ* refers to the act of following or tracking. From this we derive the word *qiṣāṣ*, which refers to the legal practice of exacting retribution for physical harm done to others by inflicting similar harm on the perpetrator, since it is as if the person being punished is "following in the tracks" of the one whom he had injured at an earlier time. The verb *qaṣṣa* means to relate or narrate, while the word *qiṣṣah*, or story (plural, *qiṣaṣ*) involves 'following' the events being related.

This root occurs 30 times in the Qur'an in five different senses: (1) To mention or name. In *Sūrah al-Nisā'*, 4:164, God tells the Prophet about messengers He has "mentioned" to him before. There are "apostles whom We have mentioned to you before this..." (*rusulan qad qaṣaṣnāhum ʿalayka min qablu*). (2) To relate or tell (a story). *Sūrah al-Qaṣaṣ* 28:25 tells us how Moses came to his future father-in-law "and told him the story [of his life]" (*wa qaṣṣa ʿalayhi al-qaṣaṣ*). See also *Sūrah al-Aʿrāf*, 7:176 and *Sūrah Ṭāhā*, 20:99. (3) To explain. *Sūrah al-Naml*, 27:76 tells us that the Qur'an "explains to the children of Israel most [of that] whereon they hold divergent views" (*inna hādha al-qur'āna yaquṣṣu ʿalā banī isrā'īla akthar alladhi hum fīhi yakhtalifūn*). (4) To follow a trail. *Sūrah al-Kahf*, 18:64 tells us that Moses and his servant "turned back, retracing their footsteps" (*irtaddā ʿalā āthāri-himā qaṣaṣa*). (5) Just retribution (*qiṣāṣ*) in cases where murder has been committed. See *Sūrah al-Baqarah*, 2:178.

38) *The concept of jalw*

The triliteral root *j-l-w* is used to speak of the act or process of becoming clear or visible. It might be used in a statement such as, "I unveiled the bride" (*jalawtu al-ʿarūs*). The feminine adjective *jalwā'* can be used to describe a clear sky (*samā'un jalwā'u*). Followed by the preposition *ʿan*, the verb *jalā/yajlū* can mean to leave or evacuate a place: *jalā al-qawmu ʿan manāzilihim*, "The people evacuated their homes." As a transitive verb, *jalā* can mean to polish, as in "he polished the sword" (*jalā al-sayf*), to relieve someone of a concern (*jalā ʿanhu al-hamm*), or reveal a matter (*jalā al-amr*).

This root occurs five times in the Qur'an in two different senses: (1) Coming to light or making visible. This is sense is found in *Sūrah al-Shams*, 91:3, which tells us to consider "the day as it reveals the world" (*al-nahāri idhā jallāhā*), in *Sūrah al-Aʿrāf*, 7:187, which tells us that none but God will reveal the Last Hour when the time comes (*lā yujal-līhā li waqtihā illā huwa*), and in *Sūrah al-Aʿrāf*, 7:143, which uses the verb *tajallā* to refer to God's revelation of his glory on Mount Sinai. (2) Leaving home. *Sūrah al-Ḥashr*, 59:3 uses the verbal noun *jalā'* to refer to banishment from one's homeland.

39) *The concept of indhār*

The root *n-dh-r* revolves around the notion of fearing or causing to fear. The verb *andhara*, of which *indhār* is the verbal noun, means to inform someone of something that is to be feared – in other words, to warn. Derivatives of the root *n-dh-r* occur 130 times in the Qur'an, and in four different senses: (1) Warning. In *Sūrah Yūnus*, 10:2, God commands to "warn the people" (*andhir al-nās*). The word *andhar* in the sense of warning is also found in *Sūrah al-Aḥqāf*, 46:21, which tells of a prophet sent to the tribe of ʿĀd who "warned his people" (*andhara qawmahu*). (See also *Sūrah Fuṣṣilat*, 41:13). (2) A warning. *Sūrah al-Najm*, 53:56 states, "This is a warning (*hādha nadhīrun*) like those warnings of old (*min al-nudhuri al-ūlā*)." (3) Messengers from God who came as "warners" (*nudhur*, *Sūrah al-Qamar*, 54:23). *Sūrah Fāṭir*, 35:37 tells how those who were unrepentant in their lifetimes plead with God to be released from their chastisement in the afterlife, only to be reminded that "a warner" (*nadhīr*) had come to them, leaving them without excuse. (4) A vow. Those engaged in the pilgrimage to Makkah should "perform their vows" (*yūfū nudhūrahum*) (*Sūrah al-Ḥajj*, 22:29; *Sūrah al-Baqarah*, 2:270).

40) *The concept of taḥdhīr*

The triliteral root *ḥ-dh-r* conveys the sense of vigilance and wariness. The noun *ḥadhar* denotes avoidance of something out of fear. The adjective *ḥadhir* means cautious, vigilant, on one's guard (cf. *ḥādhir*, "at the ready"), while the noun *taḥdhīr* refers to a warning. Derivatives of this root occur 21 times in the Qur'an, and in three different senses: (1) Instilling fear. In *Sūrah Āl ʿImrān*, 3:28 and 30, we read that "God warns you to beware of Him" (*yuḥadhdhirukumu Allāhu nafsahu*). (2) Exercising caution. See *Sūrah al-Mā'idah*, 5:41, "be on your guard" (*iḥdharū*). (3) To dread. Addressing the hypocrites who sought to do the Muslim community harm, *Sūrah al-Tawbah*, 9:64 declares, "God will bring to light the very thing that you are dreading" (*innā Allāha mukhrijun mā taḥdharūn*). Similarly, *Sūrah al-Zumar*, 39:9 uses the verb *ḥadhara* in the sense of reverent awareness when it speaks of someone who, "ever-mindful of the life to come (*yaḥdharu al-ākhirah*)," spends part of the night in prayer, while *Sūrah al-Nisā'*, 4:71 uses the noun *ḥidhr* in the sense of precautions in war time, saying, "Take your precautions" (*khudhū ḥidhrakum*).

41) *The concept of balā'*

The root *b-l-y* (or *b-l-w*) has two primary denotations: (1) to become worn out, or to wear something out (*baliya/yablā*), and (2) to put to the test (*ibtalā/yabtalī* or *balā/yablū*). The testing or affliction (*balā'*) might come in the form of either evil or good; if in the form of evil (*miḥnah*), it tests a person's faith and patient endurance, and if in the form of good (*minḥah*), it tests one's gratitude.

Derivatives of this root occur 37 times in the Qur'an, and in six different senses: (1) Testing or affliction. In *Sūrah al-Baqarah*, 2:155, God tells believers, "Most certainly shall We try you by means of danger, and hunger, and loss of worldly goods" (*wa la nabluwannakum bi shay'in min al-khawfi wal-jūʿi wa naqṣin min al-amwāli*). Similarly, God declares in *Sūrah Muḥammad*, 47:31, "most certainly We shall try you all (*wa lanabluwannakum*)...We shall put to a test [the truth of] all your assertions" (*wa nabluwa akhbārakum*). The sense of testing is found also in *Sūrah al-Aḥzāb*, 33:11, where we are told that the believers were "tried" (*ubtuliya al-mu'minūn*). *Sūrah al-Baqarah*, 2:124 tells us that God "tried Abraham" (*ibtalā ibrāhīma rabbuhu*) through the commands He had given him. In a related sense, the word *yablū* is used in *Sūrah Yūnus*, 10:30, which tells us that on Judgment Day, each soul will "prove [the fruits of] (*tablū kullu nafsin*) the deeds it sent before (*mā aslafat*)." (3) To be made visible. *Sūrah al-Ṭāriq*, 86:9 tells us that on the Day of Resurrection, secrets will be "laid bare" (*tublā al-sarā'iru*).

SECOND: *ʿIlm*-RELATED CONCEPTS

1) *The concept of ʿilm*

The triliteral root *ʿ-l-m* denotes an effect by which something is distinguished from other entities. From it we derive the noun *ʿalāmah*, which refers to a sign or indication, the word *ʿalam*, which refers to a flag or banner, and *ʿilm*, sometimes translated as 'science', and at other times simply as 'knowledge', and which is contrasted with ignorance, or *jahl*. The active participle *ʿālim* (plural, *ʿulamā'*), which means 'knowing,' refers to a scientist or scholar. It is used of God in *Sūrah al-Mu'minūn*, 23:92, where we read that God is the One Who knows both what is hidden and what is accessible to human perception (*ʿālimu al-ghaybi wa al-shahādah*); similarly we have the noun *ʿalīm*, meaning highly knowledgeable and which, when joined to the definite article (*al-ʿalīm*) is one of the Divine Names meaning All-Knowing. The verb *ʿalima* means to know or discover something, while the intensified form *ʿallama* means to teach (verbal noun, *taʿlīm*), and the verbal noun *maʿlam* refers to a landmark or guidepost (something by means of which a road or path is known, or recognized).

Derivatives of the root *ʿ-l-m* occur 856 times in the Qur'an, and in four basic senses: (1) Marking or distinguishing. In *Sūrah Muḥammad*, 47:31, God declares that He will test people in order to "mark out (*naʿlama*) those of you who strive hard [in Our cause] and are patient in adversity" (*al-mujāhidīna minkum wa al-ṣābirīn*). (2) Knowledge. We are assured in *Sūrah al-Naḥl*, 16:19 that "God knows (*Allāhu yaʿlamu*) all that you keep secret as well as all that you bring into the open" (*mā tusirrūna wa mā tuʿlinūn*). Similarly, the noun *ʿilm* is used in *Sūrah Hūd*, 11:14, where we are told that the Qur'an was revealed by God's knowledge (*unzila bi ʿilmi Allāh*). (3) Teaching. This derivative of the root is found in *Sūrah al-Mā'idah*, 5:4 to refer to the training of hunting animals. The active participle, *muʿallim*, or "teacher," does not occur in the Qur'an. However, the passive participle, *muʿallam*, is used in *Sūrah al-Dukhān*, 44:14, which tells us that the Prophet's opponents accused him of having been taught the Qur'an by others. (4) Learning. The verb *taʿallam*, meaning to learn, is used in *Sūrah al-Baqarah*, 2:102 in relation to people who have been learning about sorcery.

2) *The concept of ḥibr*

The triliteral root *ḥ-b-r* is related to happiness, delight, and beauty, and is used to speak of the remaining traces of something positive and good. The noun *ḥibr* is used to refer to ink, the substance used in writing (a process which may be seen as a form of beautification), while the noun *ḥabr* or *ḥibr* (plural, *aḥbār*) refers to the person who does the writing. (Scholars have disagreed over whether the noun should be written as *ḥibr* or as *ḥabr*; according to al-Jawharī, if the word refers to ink, it is more proper to write and pronounce it as *ḥibr*, whereas if it is associated with learning and prose, it should be pronounced *ḥabr*).

More specifically the noun *ḥabr* is used to refer to a Jewish or Christian scholar or cleric, or simply an upright person. *Sūrah al-Mā'idah*, the fifth surah in the Qur'an, is also known as *Sūrah al-Aḥbār*. Other forms of the noun include *ḥabrah*, *ḥubrah*, *ḥibir*, and *ḥibirah*, while the act of improving or beautifying one's written script or poetry is referred to as *taḥbīr*.

The plural form *aḥbār* occurs four times in the Qur'an in reference to scholars (see, for example, *Sūrah al-Mā'idah*, 5:63), and twice in other senses. Scholars are referred to as *aḥbār* due to the traces of their learning which remain in the form of both written works and memories in people's minds and hearts.

3) *The concept of rabbānī*

The *r-b-b* root conveys a number of different meanings: (1) to repair and/or maintain something. From this sense we derive the noun *rabb*, which refers to an owner, proprietor, master, creator, or caretaker. Hence, the verb *rabba* can also mean to raise or bring up (a child). (2) To remain with (someone) or in (a place). If we speak of land as *marabb*, for example, it implies that it continues to receive rain, and for this reason clouds are sometimes referred to as *rabāb*. (3) To include and embrace something. The noun *rabbānī* refers to someone who has knowledge of God Almighty. It has been said that the word *rabbānī* was introduced into Arabic from Syriac or Hebrew with the meaning of deified, divine, or heavenly.

The word *rabbānī* occurs four times in the Qur'an. *Sūrah al-Mā'idah*, 5:44, for example, refers to "...the [early] men of God (*al-rabbāniyyūn*) and the rabbis (*wa al-aḥbār*)." (See also *Sūrah al-Mā'idah*, 5:63). These were scholars to whom God's word was entrusted, who bore witness to its truth, and who were assigned the task of nurturing people spiritually, teaching them, issuing them rulings based on the Jewish law, and acting in the capacity of prophets and compassionate caregivers. As for the term *al-aḥbār*, it referred to highly influential, leading scholars whose teachings were authoritative and who were known for speaking the truth among their peoples. Those described as *rabbāniyyūn*, being of a higher status than the rabbis, or *aḥbār*, were highly knowledgeable, deeply steadfast individuals endowed with insight into how to guide people, manage their affairs and serve their interests. It has been said that they were the scholarly descendents of Aaron who adhered to the path of the prophets. One notes that while the terms *rabbāniyyūn* and *aḥbār* are linked in the two verses just quoted from *Sūrah al-Mā'idah*, the term *rabbāniyyūn* appears alone in *Sūrah Āl ʿImrān*, 3:146.

4) *The concept of kursī*

The triliteral root *k-r-s* refers to the process of being accumulated, gathered or compressed on top of something else. From this root we derive the noun *kurrāsah* (plural, *karārīs*), meaning notebook or copybook, which consists of pages stacked on top of one another. The noun *kursī* (plural, *karāsin*) can refer to knowledge, or to a seat, chair, throne or bed. The verb *inkiras* means to apply or dedicate oneself to something; the noun *kirs* refers to piled up ruins or remnants, as well as to something's cause or origin; while the noun *karkasah* refers to repetition or intonation.

The term *kursī* occurs twice in the Qur'an in two different senses. In one of these instances it connotes knowledge, as when we are told in *Sūrah al-Baqarah*, 2:255 that God's *kursī* – that is, His knowledge or rule – encompasses the heavens and the earth. In the second instance, and in keeping with the lexical definition of *kursī* as something firm which one sits on, the word is used to refer to Solomon's throne (*Sūrah Ṣād*, 38:34).

Lastly, it has been proposed that the word *kursī* refers to the celestial sphere that encompasses the heavenly bodies.

5) *The concept of athārah*

The triliteral root *a-th-r* conveys three primary meanings: (1) the presentation of something, (2) the mention of something, and (3) the remaining effect of something. The word *athārah* (plural, *athārāt*) refers to a remainder or lasting effect. The words *uthrah*, *ma'tharah* and *ma'thurah* refer to an honorable deed, accounts of which are passed down from one generation to another. The word *athar* refers to what remains of something – a trace or effect; the noun *uthr* refers to a scar, that is, the trace that remains from a wound that has healed, and the noun *ithr* refers to clarified butter extract. In a similar vein, the word *athar* can refer to a protrusion on a camel's hoof which leaves tracks that others can follow, while the noun *athīrah* refers to a pack animal whose hoofs leave large tracks.

Derivatives of the root *a-th-r* occur in 31 places in the Qur'an, and in four different senses: (1) Enduring effects or legacy. *Sūrah Ghāfir*, 40:21 refers to bygone peoples whose lasting impact (*āthār*) on earth was greater than others' (cf. *Sūrah al-Rūm*, 30:9). In *Sūrah Yā Sīn*, 36:12, God speaks of how, on Judgment Day, He will have recorded "the traces [of good and evil]" that people have left behind (*āthāra-hum*). (2) Footsteps. *Sūrah al-Ṣāffāt*, 37:70 criticizes polytheists for being so eager to follow in their forefathers' footsteps (*āthārihim*). (3) Preference. *Sūrah al-Ḥashr*, 59:9 praises those who offer others refuge from harm and "give them preference over themselves" (*yu'thirūna ʿalā anfusihim*). (4) Unique favor. *Sūrah Yūsuf*, 12:91 relates how Joseph's brothers, upon discovering the high position he has attained in Egypt, exclaim, "Most certainly has God raised you high above us" (*la qad ātharaka Allāhu ʿalaynā*).

The verb *athara* denotes the action of transmitting something or passing it on, particularly teaching and knowledge. The word *athārah* or *atharah* refers to a place about which accounts have been told or written with the result that its effects remain to subsequent generations, while the phrase *athāratin min ʿilm* (literally, "vestige of knowledge" – *Sūrah al-Aḥqāf*, 46:4) may also be used to refer to a scholar with an enduring, effective legacy.

6) *The concept of qabas*

The root *q-b-s* in its origin was used in relation to fire, and was then employed in relevant metaphors. In connection with knowledge, one might say that someone *iqtabasa ʿilman*, that is, he sought out or acquired knowledge, or that he passed on or shared knowledge with someone else (*aqbasahu ʿilman*). This root occurs three times in the Qur'an. *Sūrah Ṭāhā*, 20:10 relates how, when Moses sees a fire in the wilderness, he tells his family that he may be able to bring them "a brand therefrom" (*minhā biqabasin*; cf. *Sūrah al-Naml*, 27:7) And in *Sūrah al-Ḥadīd*, 57:13, we are told that on the Day of Resurrection, the hypocrites will say to the believers, "Let us borrow from your Light (*unẓurūnā naqtabis min nūrikum*)!" Hence, the original meaning of *qabas* was related to fire; its meaning was then extended metaphorically to refer to guidance and light.

7) *The concept of rusūkh*

The original denotation of the root *r-s-kh* has to do with firmness, rootedness, and penetration of the soil. When applied to a stream or pond, the verb *rasakha* means for its water to dry up due to its having soaked into the ground. The adjective *rāsikh* means stable, firmly rooted or well-grounded. Hence, *al-rusūkh fī al-ʿilm* that is, well-groundedness in knowledge, refers to a grasp of knowledge based on established and credible evidence and/or irrefutable arguments. The word *rāsikh* occurs twice in the Qur'an. *Sūrah Āl ʿImrān*, 3:7 refers to those who are "deeply rooted in knowledge" (*al-rāsikhūn fī al-ʿilm*), while *Sūrah al-Nisā'*, 4:162 uses the term in the same manner. Abū ʿAmr quotes al-Mubarrad as saying that "those who are deeply rooted in knowledge are those who study together." According to al-Mubarrad, only those who have memorized the Qur'an can become deeply rooted in knowledge, while Ibn ʿAbbās interprets the reference to *al-rāsikhūn fī al-ʿilm* in *Sūrah Āl ʿImrān*, 3:7 as meaning "those who are so fully realized in knowledge that nothing could cast doubt upon it."

8) *The concept of sayyid*

The word *sayyid* is derived from the root *s-w-d*, meaning to rule over/govern. This meaning was in turn derived from the fact that a *sayyid* is someone who rules or governs the majority of a people – that is, the common people (*sawād al-nās*). The word *sayyid* (plural, *sādah*) is thus used to mean a leader, a master, a ruler and, more generally, someone who is discerning, understanding, and possessed of wealth and beneficial influence. The term *sayyid* occurs three times in the Qur'an in reference to a ruler who is magnanimous and knowledgeable. (1) In *Sūrah Yūsuf*, 12:25, the word is used to refer to a husband. (2) *Sūrah al-Aḥzāb*, 33:67 uses the plural form, *sādah*, in the sense of "leaders." (3) Noble or outstanding among men. It is in this sense that the word is used in *Sūrah Āl ʿImrān*, 3:39 in reference to the prophet Yaḥyā (John the Baptist).

9) *The concept of ḥujjah*

The root *ḥ-j-j* conveys four basic senses: (1) to intend – specifically, to intend to reach a given goal or destination. From this we derive the noun *maḥajjah*, which can refer to a destination, a place of pilgrimage, a shrine, or a road, as well as the noun *ḥajj*, which refers to the pilgrimage to Makkah. (2) To argue or dispute with (*ḥājaja*). From this verb we derive the noun *ḥujjah*, meaning evidence, proof, or an argument in favor of a given position. (3) The orbital bone, which is referred in Arabic as the *ḥijāj*. (4) Retreat or withdrawal, referred to as *ḥajḥajah*. Related to this is the word *miḥjāj*, meaning argumentative.

Derivatives of the root *ḥ-j-j* occur 20 times in the Qur'an in two different senses. The first of these is that of enmity or opposition. This sense is found in *Sūrah al-Baqarah*, 2:139, which asks the Jews and Christians, "Do you argue with us about God?" (*a tuḥājjūnanā fī Allāh*). Similarly, *Sūrah Āl ʿImrān*, 3:66 says, "You are the ones who would argue (*ḥājajtum*) about that which is known to you (*fīmā lakum bihi ʿilm*)." And the second is that of clear evidence. This usage is found in *Sūrah al-Anʿām*, 6:149, which reminds us that "the final evidence [of all truth] rests with God alone" (*falillāhi al-ḥujjatu al-bālighah*). Similarly, the evidence advanced by those bent on wrongdoing holds no validity in argumentation. As we read in *Sūrah al-Shūrā*, 42:16, "And as for those who would [still] argue about God (*yuḥājjūna fī Allāh*) after He has been acknowledged [by them] (*min baʿdi ma ustujība lahu*) – all their arguments are null and void in their Sustainer's sight" (*ḥujjatuhum dāḥiḍatun ʿinda rabbihim*). Each side's aim is to dissuade the other side of the stance for which it is arguing, and everything cited in support of one's claims is referred to as a *ḥujjah*, even if it is invalid, as we saw in the quote above from *Sūrah al-Shūrā*, 42:16 ("...all their arguments are null and void..." – *ḥujjatuhum dāḥiḍatun*).

There are two different types of *ḥujjah*. One of these, referred to as a persuasive argument (*ḥujjah iqnāʿiyyah*), is helpful for people who lack the ability to deal with complex rational proofs, and might lead them to certainty by providing multiple types of evidence. The second type, referred to as a *ḥujjah burhāniyyah*, is a well-established argument based on irrefutable evidence. An example of this type of argument is found in *Sūrah al-Anbiyā'*, 21:22: "had there been in heaven or on earth any deities other than God, both [those realms] would surely have fallen into ruin!" If there were multiple deities, they would be in competition for control over all that exists, which would plunge the Cosmos into complete disorder. However, if we define 'God' as the Being that possesses ultimate power, then no alternate deity could even exist, still less compete for control and authority with the one God.

10) *The concept of burhān*

The root of this verbal noun is *b-r-h-n*, which means to establish proof for something. The verb *abraha* likewise means to support proof. The term *burhān* occurs in the Qur'an eight times in four different senses: (1) A manifestation of the truth. We read in *Sūrah al-Nisā'*, 4:174: "O mankind! A manifestation of the truth (*burhān*) has now come unto you from your Sustainer." And in *Sūrah Yūsuf*, 12:24, we are told that when Joseph was tempted to succumb to the seductive advances of his master's wife, he "saw an evidence of his Sustainer's truth" (*burhāna rabbihi*) that strengthened him to resist. (2) Evidence. We are told in *Sūrah al-Mu'minūn*, 23:117 that there is no evidence (*burhān*) for the existence of any god but God. (3) A sign of divinely granted authority. *Sūrah al-Qaṣaṣ*, 28:32 states that after giving Moses the ability to perform two types of miracles before Pharaoh, God referred to these as "two signs" (*burhānān*) that Moses had come bearing a divine message.

The noun *burhān* is on the pattern *fuʿlān* based on the triliteral root *b-r-h*, which means to turn white. The word *burhān* refers to the most certain of all evidence, and denotes uncompromising truthfulness. According to scholars of the principles of jurisprudence, *burhān* is what separates truth from falsehood, the sound from the corrupt.

11) *The concept of sulṭān*

This word is derived from the triliteral root *s-l-ṭ*, which has to do with power, force, authority, and mastery. The word *sulṭān* can refer to a powerful argument or proof, or to the power of a monarch or governor. The *sulṭān* of something is its strength or intensity. Used as a verbal noun, *sulṭān* cannot be pluralized. When used to refer to a ruler, however, its plural is *salāṭīn*.

The word *sulṭān* occurs 35 times in the Qur'an and in two different senses: (1) Power and authority. *Sūrah Ibrāhīm*, 14:22 uses the word in this sense when it states that on the Day of Judgment, Satan will confess to his erstwhile followers, "I had no power (*sulṭān*) at all over you" (cf. *Sūrah Saba'*, 34:21). (2) Proof or evidence of an assertion. It is used in this sense in *Sūrah Yūnus*, 10:68, as well as in 28 other places. The word *sulṭān* is used to mean evidence or proof (*ḥujjah*) because of the force that is sometimes exercised on people's minds and hearts by powerful arguments or evidence, particularly if they are knowledgeable, discerning people of faith. As for its use to denote governing power or sovereignty (*mulk*), the word *sulṭān* points to God's authority over the Earth.

12) *The concept of āyah*

The word *āyah* is derived from the root *a-y-y*, which may refer to sight or consideration, or to the intention to address a particular person. The noun *āyah* refers to a sign. According to al-Aṣmaʿī, a man's *āyah* is his person. Hence, in an example cited by al-Khalīl, if we say that the tribe went out with its *āyāt* (plural of *āyah*), we mean that it went out with all its people together (*kharaja al-qawmu bi āyātihim*). The word *āyah* can also be used to refer to a unit of the Qur'anic text (plural, *āy*), a moral lesson, or time.

The word *āyah* occurs 382 times in the Qur'an in the following senses: (1) A sign. "And among His wonders (signs – *āyātihi*) is this: He creates you out of dust" (*Sūrah al-Rūm*, 30:20; cf. *Sūrah al-ʿAnkabūt*, 29:44). Such "wonders" or "signs" give people access to greater or lesser degrees of knowledge of God depending on their individual capacities or their willingness to reflect and learn. In a divergent but related sense, *Sūrah al-Shuʿarā'*, 26:128 refers to pagan altars as "signs" of wanton folly and idolatry. (2) A unit of the Qur'an. The word *āyah* can refer to any phrase in the Qur'an that communicates a divine ruling, whether this phrase takes up an entire surah or only part of one; the word *āyah* can also be used to refer to each of the units set apart by numbers in the Qur'anic text. For this sense, see *Sūrah Āl ʿImran*, 3:7 and *Sūrah al-Jāthiyah*, 45:8. (3) A miracle. *Sūrah al-Qaṣaṣ*, 28:36 refers to the miracles Moses wrought as *āyāt*. (4) A sign of God's grace. Jesus is referred to in *Sūrah Maryam*, 19:21 as an *āyah*. (5) A command or prohibition. For this sense, see *Sūrah al-Baqarah*, 2:187.

13) *The concept of jidāl*

The meaning associated with the root *j-d-l* is that of a growing rivalry or opposition. The noun *ajdal* is a name for a hawk, while the noun *jadal* can refer to the vehemence of opposition. The verb *jadala* refers to the act of tightly weaving or twisting, as well as to the strengthening and growth of grain in the ear. Similarly, the phrase *jaddalahu* (passive, *injadala, tajaddala*) means, "he wrestled him to the ground" (*ṣaraʿahu ʿalā al-jidālah*).

Derivatives of the root *j-d-l* occur in the Qur'an 29 times in the sense of wrangling, quarreling, debating and discussing. *Sūrah al-Raʿd*, 13:13 speaks of those who "stubbornly argue about God" (*yujādilūna fī Allāh*), *Sūrah al-Baqarah*, 2:197 states that those engaged in the pilgrimage to Makkah must abstain from quarrelling (*jidāl*), and *Sūrah al-Kahf*, 18:54 describes human beings as being primarily "given to contention" (*al-insānu akthara shay'in jadalan*). *Sūrah al-Naḥl*, 16:125 instructs the Prophet to "argue" (*jādil*) with those who disagree with him in a kindly manner. Dialogue or discussion for the purpose of persuasion might be likened to the act of knotting or braiding (*al-jadal*) in the sense of weaving or "plaiting" one's arguments together in such a way that they are strong enough to draw one's opponent to one's side.

14) *The concept of sū'āl*

The root *s-'-l* conveys the notion of a question or inquiry. Derivatives of this root occur 128 times in the Qur'an in the following senses: (1) A request for a legal ruling. *Sūrah al Baqarah*, 2:189 tells us that "They will ask you about the new moons (*yas'alūnaka ʿan al-ahillah*)." (See also *Sūrah al-Baqarah*, 2:215, 217, 219 and 220). (2) Asking for assistance – begging. *Sūrah al-Ḍuḥā*, 93:10 refers to the person who asks for material aid with the active participle *sā'il*, 'one who asks'. (3) Supplication. The word *sā'il* is also used to refer to someone who makes supplication to God (see *Sūrah al-Maʿārij*, 70:1). (4) Petition, request or seek. When Noah asks God to save his unbelieving son from the great flood, God tells Noah not to ask of Him things of which he has no knowledge (*lā tas'alni mā laysa laka bihi ʿilmun* – *Sūrah Hūd*, 11:46). A similar sense of the word is used in *Sūrah al-Raḥmān*, 55:29, which describes how everything in existence seeks God out of need. (Cf. *Sūrah al-Dhāriyāt*, 51:19). (5) Call to account. This sense of the word is used in *Sūrah al-Aʿrāf*, 7:6, where God declares, "We shall most certainly call to account all those unto whom a [divine] message was sent (*falanas'alanna al-ladhīna ursila ilayhim*), and We shall most certainly call to account the message-bearers [themselves] (*wa lanas'a-lanna al-mursalīn*)." (6) To dispute among one another (see *Sūrah al-Naba'*, 78:1).

The verbal noun *sū'āl* refers to the act of seeking knowledge or the means of acquiring it. We are urged to seek knowledge in this way (see *Sūrah al-Anbiyā'*, 21:7). Similarly, it can refer to the act of seeking out material wealth or the means of acquiring it (see *Sūrah al-Dhāriyāt*, 51:19, cited above). It would be contradictory for God to seek knowledge when He is the All-Knowing. Hence, when asking is predicated of God, its purpose is to rebuke, to alert the person questioned to something, or to induce him or her to acknowledge, approve, or do something. In *Sūrah al-Mā'idah*, 5:116, for example, we are told that God asked Jesus son of Mary whether he had told people to worship him and his mother as deities beside God. God asked this question not in order to acquire knowledge, of course, but rather, to communicate something to those around them, to rebuke people for false teachings, and to induce them to acknowledge a truer doctrine.

A question resembles a wish. However, whereas a wish (*umniyah*) has to do with the hope of fulfilling something one has identified as a possibility, a question (*sū'āl*) involves a request for an answer. A rhetorical question may be exactly the same as its answer. However, in the case of a question which is asked in order to learn something or to seek guidance, one's teacher will be like a doctor who strives to heal a sick person. In this role, he pays attention to what the illness requires, not to what the patient says. When answering a question such a teacher may refrain from giving the information that has been requested and instead give the information that the inquirer should have requested or which the inquirer actually needs. This approach is referred to by some as "the sage's approach." When this approach is being employed, the answer will be more general than the question. In *Sūrah Ṭāhā*, 20:17-18, for example, God asks Moses what he is holding in his right hand. To this Moses replies, "It is my staff." Then he adds, "I lean on it; and with it I beat down leaves for my sheep; and [many] other uses have I for it." In *Sūrah al-Shuʿarā'*, 26:70-71, we are told that Abraham asked his father and his people what it was that they worshipped. To this they replied, "We worship idols." Then, as if to anger Abraham, they added, "and we remain ever devoted to them." Answering a question with more information than what was requested might also be intended to motivate the questioner to action. This sort of situation is illustrated in *Sūrah al-Aʿrāf*, 7:113-114, where Pharaoh's sorcerers ask him whether they will be rewarded if they prevail over Moses, and he replies, "Yes; and, verily, you shall be among those who are near unto me." In some situations, the answer might be terser than what the questioner hopes it will be, while in others, the person asked may not answer the question at all, particularly if the query has been posed not with a desire to know, but simply out of obstinacy.

15) *The concept of jawāb*

The triliteral root *j-w-b* conveys two primary meanings. The first is that of piercing, penetrating or traversing. One might say, *jubtu al-arḍa* ("I traversed the land"). In this case, the verbal noun will be *jawb*, while the active participle will be *jā'ib* or *jawwāb*. The second meaning is to reply to something that has been said. One might say, *ajābahu* ("He replied to him"). From this root we derive the nouns *jawāb* (answer, reply), *jā'ibah* (plural, *jawā'ib*), meaning unexpected or extraordinary news, the verb *jāwaba* (verbal noun, *mujāwabah*), meaning to respond to or cooperate with and *tajāwaba* (verbal noun, *tajāwub*), meaning to be responsive or interact harmoniously (with). Still other derivatives include the verb *istajwaba* (verbal noun, *istijwāb*) meaning to interrogate, *istajāba* (verbal noun, *istijābah*), meaning to answer (a prayer), or respond to.

Derivatives of the root *j-w-b* occur 43 times in the Qur'an in the following senses: (1) To cut or penetrate. In *Sūrah al-Fajr*, 89:9 we are told that the people of Thamūd "hollowed out rocks in the valley" (*jābū al-ṣakhra bi al-wād*). (2) To answer, comply with, respond to. God says of Himself 2:186, "I respond to (*ujību*) the call of him who calls" (*daʿwata al-dāʿi idhā daʿāni*). See also *Sūrah Yūnus*, 10:89. (3) To obey. *Sūrah al-Aḥqāf*, 46:31 reads, "Respond to God's call" (*ajībū dāʿīa Allāhi*), while *Sūrah Āl ʿImrān*, 3:172 speaks of the believers "who responded to the call of God" (*istajābū lillāhi*). (4) Response to a question (*jawāb*). See *Sūrah al-Aʿrāf*, 7:82.

If a question mentioned in the Qur'an has already been asked of the Prophet, the answer he is given to say is preceded by the command, "Say" (*qul*) without a preceding *fa*, or "then." In *Sūrah al-Isrā'*, 17:85, for example, we are told that people have asked the Prophet about the nature of inspiration (*yas'alūnaka ʿan al-rūḥ*), and he is commanded to answer them with the word *qul...*, "Say..." (cf. *Sūrah al-Aʿrāf*, 7:187). Elsewhere, by contrast, the question cited is one that has not yet been asked; hence, the present tense used in the Qur'an actually refers to the future. In *Sūrah Ṭāhā*, 20:105, for example, we read, "And they will ask you about [what will happen to] the mountains [when this world comes to an end]. Say, then...". In this case, God's command concerning what to say is preceded by *fa*, meaning "then" (*faqul...*). The meaning is thus: If they ask you...then say...

16) *The concept of fatwā*

The root consisting of the letter *f-t-y* denotes two basic meanings. The first is that of youth, newness and freshness, from which we derive the noun *fatā* (plural, *fityah* or *fityān*), meaning a youth or a young camel. The second is that of clarifying a legal ruling. The verb *aftā* is used to describe the action undertaken by a jurist who rules on a legal question or issue.

Derivatives of the root *f-t-y* occur 21 times in the Qur'an, and in two different senses. (1) A young man. We read in *Sūrah al-Anbiyā'*, 21:60 about Abraham, to whom the people of his day referred as "...a youth" (*fatā*) who had spoken scornfully of their gods. (2) Clarification of a legal ruling. In *Sūrah al-Nisā'*, 4:127 the word *aftā* is used in the sense of providing a legal ruling, as we are told that God Himself would provide the people with a ruling (*Allāhu yuftīkum*) concerning the women of their day. It is the second of these two meanings that concerns us in this context.

The verbal form of *f-t-y* occurs eleven times in the Qur'an in the sense of seeking knowledge and understanding of a specific issue or question. It is in this sense that the word is used in *Sūrah Yūsuf*, 12:43 where, after having a mysterious dream, the king asks his noblemen to explain it to him, saying, *aftūnī fī ru'yāya*: "Enlighten me about [the meaning of] my dream." The word *fatwā* is used to refer to the answer given by a legal scholar concerning a problematic legal matter, while the verbal noun *iftā'* refers to the process of providing such an answer.

17) *The concept of bayān*
The root *b-y-n* yields the verb *bāna/yabīnu*, which refers to a process of separating or distancing one thing from another, or of being exposed, becoming clear, or coming to light. Other verbal derivatives are *abāna, bayyana, istabāna,* and *tabayyana*, while the words *bayān* and *tibyān* (see *Sūrah al-Naḥl*, 16:89) are verbal nouns from the same root.

Derivatives of this root occur 258 times in the Qur'an in the following senses: (1) to give something long, thorough consideration. In *Sūrah al-Ḥujurāt*, 49:6 God tells believers, "If any iniquitous person comes to you with a [slanderous) tale (*in jā'akum fāsiqun bi naba'in*), use your discernment (*fa tabayyanū*)." (2) Evidence and arguments. *Sūrah al-Baqarah*, 2:185 uses the plural noun *bayyināt* to refer the "clear signs" revealed in the Qur'an (for the singular, *bayyinah*, see *Sūrah al-Anʿām*, 6:57). (3) To become clear or manifest. In *Sūrah Ibrāhim*, 14:45, God tells those who are resisting His message how "it was made obvious" (*tabayyana*) to them how He had dealt with disobedient peoples before them. (4) To become distinguishable. During the month of Ramadan, Muslims may continue to break their fast until a black thread is distinguishable from a white one (*hattā yatabayyana... al-khayṭu al-abyaḍu mina al-khayṭi al-aswadi*), 2:187. (5) Clear. God's revelation consists in "messages clearly showing the truth" (*āyātin mubayyinātin*) (*Sūrah al-Nūr*, 24:34). (6) The capacity for self-expression. We are told in *Sūrah al-Raḥmān*, 55:4 that God has granted human beings "articulate thought and speech" (*ʿallamahu al-bayān*)."

The quadriliteral form appears either with a hamzah in the beginning (*abāna*), or with a doubled second consonant (*bayyana*), whereas the triliteral form does not occur in the Qur'an in the sense of revealing or clarifying. Rather, we have the quadriliteral (*abāna*, *bayyana*) and quintiliteral (*tabayyana*) forms in past and present. We also have the active participle *mubayyin* in *Sūrah al-Nūr*, 24:34, and in *Sūrah al-Ṭalāq*, 65:11. As for the imperative voice, it occurs only three times in the form of *tabayyanū* (twice in *Sūrah al-Nisā'*, 4:94, and once in *Sūrah al-Ḥujurāt*, 49:6).

Another active participle derived from this root is *mubīn* (from the verb *abāna/yubīnu*), meaning clear or manifest. *Sūrah Yūsuf*, 12:1, for example, describes the Qur'anic revelation as "a revelation clear in itself and clearly showing the truth" (*mubīn*). The verb form *tabayyana* occurs eighteen times in either the past tense (*Sūrah Saba'*, 34:14), the present tense, or the imperative voice.

The verbal noun *bayān*, used in the sense of revealing or clarifying something, is more general in meaning than the word *nuṭq*, which is used exclusively in relation to human beings and not to other creatures. The process of elucidation entailed in *bayān* can involve either speech or action. Speech can be referred to as *bayān* because it reveals a meaning which a person intends to express. In *Sūrah al-Qiyāmah*, 75:19, God declares that He is the One who will clarify the Qur'an, saying, "It will be for Us to make its [the Qur'an's] meaning clear" (*ʿalaynā bayānuhu*). Indeed, whatever specifies the general or clarifies the obscure, be it speech or action, can be referred to as a kind of *bayān*. In *Sūrah Āl ʿImrān*, 3:138, for example, events from the past are described as a *bayān*, or "a clear lesson."

There are five different ways in which the process of *bayān* can take place through speech and action. The first is referred to as *bayān al-taqrīr*, that is, an act which clarifies and confirms the meaning of something that has been said. In *Sūrah al-Ḥijr*, 15:30-31, we are told that when God commanded the angels to bow down before Adam, all of them did so with the exception of Iblīs. By their action, these angels confirmed the binding nature of what God had commanded. This type of *bayān* is also illustrated in *Sūrah al-Anʿām*, 6:38, which refers to a bird that "flies on its two wings." This is a confirmation of the literal import of what has been said due to the possibility that the statement might have been metaphorical, since it is possible to say, for example, that a person "is flying with enthusiasm," or some such thing. In the present context, the reference to the bird's wings confirms that the Qur'an is speaking here about literal, not figurative, flight. The second is referred to as *bayān al-tafsīr*, that is, interpretation or explanation of words whose meaning may be vague due to the use of homonyms, generalities, or ambiguous expressions. The third is referred to as *bayān al-taghyīr*, which is the act of changing the import of a word or expression through stipulation, exception, or specification. The fourth is known as *bayān al-tabdīl*, which is the same as abrogation. And the fifth is referred to as *bayān al-ḍarūrah*, or clarification by necessity. This type of *bayān* is a clarification which takes place despite a silence about the matter at hand due to some necessity in the surrounding context.

Bayān al-ḍarūrah, or clarification by necessity, is in turn divided into four subtypes: (1) That which is discerned not only by what is stated but by what is unstated. This is illustrated in *Sūrah al-Nisā'*, 4:11 which in a discussion of inheritance rights and distributions, tells us that if the deceased "has left no child and his parents are his [only] heirs, then his mother shall have one-third..." Although it is not stated in the text, we can infer through *bayān al-ḍarūrah* that the remaining two-thirds of the bequest go to the father. We infer this not simply based on the silence concerning the father's portion, but based on the necessary import of what has been said about the need for the inheritance to be shared. (2) That which is made clear by virtue of the identity or specialization of the person speaking (or writing) on the subject in question. (3) That which demonstrates the necessity of protecting the buyer from harm. (4) That which is clarified based on the meaning of the linguistic context. Someone might say, for example, "I owe him one hundred and three dirhams (103) (*lahu ʿalayya mi'atun wa thalāthatu darāhim*)," "three robes (*thalāthatu athwābin*)", "horses (*afrāsin*)," or the like. The phrase *thalāthatu darāhim*, "3 dirhams", which is conjoined via the word "and" (*wa*) to the preceding *mi'atun* (one hundred), makes it clear that the number 100 is associated with dirhams, not with robes or horses. If, by contrast, the person had said, "103 robes (*mi'atun wa thalāthatu athwābin*)," then the phrase "three robes" (*thalāthatu athwāb*), being conjoined by the word "and" (*wa*) to the preceding *mi'atun*, or 100, would make clear that the speaker means 103 robes, not dirhams or horses.

18) *The concept of sharḥ*

The triliteral root *sh-r-ḥ* denotes the act of opening, laying bare, expanding, and clarifying. The verb *sharaḥa* can mean to explain or make clear, while the intensified form *sharraḥa* means to slice (cheese, meat, etc.). Derivatives of the root *sh-r-ḥ* occur five times in the Qur'an in the sense of spreading out or expanding. If one uses the verb *sharaḥa* in relation to the chest, it refers to the act of opening the mind and heart to receive something, such as guidance, knowledge of the truth, and obedience to God, and making it a receptacle of wisdom, self-composure, and courage. The word is used in this sense in *Sūrah al-Zumar*, 39:22, which speaks of the one whose heart has been opened to Islam (*man sharaḥa Allāhu ṣadrahu lil-islām*) and who has received enlightenment (*fa huwa ʿalā nūrin min rabbihi*). (See also *Sūrah al-Anʿām*, 6:125, *Sūrah Ṭāhā*, 20:25, and *Sūrah al-Inshirāḥ*, 94:1). The Arabic word *ṣadr*, though it refers anatomically to the chest, is used to refer in such situations to the heart and mind (cf. *Sūrah al-Nās*, 114:5). The chest can also be seen as the 'fortress' (*ḥiṣn*) within which the heart is shielded from attack by evil forces.

Lastly, it should be noted that the verb *sharaḥa* can also be used to refer to the act of opening someone to evil influences. *Sūrah al-Naḥl*, 16:106, for example, refers to someone who has opened his heart to a denial of the truth (*sharaḥa bil-kufri ṣadran*). The verb *sharaḥa* thus refers originally to a physical act, and is used to refer metaphorically to spiritual realities.

19) *The concept of tafsīr*

The triliteral root *f-s-r* denotes the act of clarifying, uncovering, or bringing to light. The quadriliteral verbal form, *fassara* (verbal noun, *tafsīr*), has been said to be synonymous with the verb *awwala* (verbal noun, *ta'wīl*), which means to interpret, to reveal what is intended by speech that is ambiguous or problematic. *Ta'wīl* is the process of determining which understanding of a word or phrase reflects the meaning it was intended to express in its particular context. The word *fasr* (or *tafsīr*) refers to a physician's examination of water and the act of rendering a judgment concerning it, while the verbal noun *tafsarah* is the process of diagnosing a disease. The noun *tafsīr* occurs once in the

Qur'an in *Sūrah al-Furqān*, 25:33, in which God assures the Prophet that He will provide Him through the Qur'an with "the best explanation" (*aḥsana tafsīran*). Similarly, anything by means of which one comes to know what something means is referred to as *tafsarah*. The difference between *taʿrīf* and *tafsīr* is that while *taʿrīf* refers to an explication of a word's meaning, *tafsīr* is the clarification of a word or phrase through the use of terms that are better understood or more familiar. As for the difference between *tafsīr* and *ta'wīl*, *tafsīr* operates on the level of the apparent meanings of terms or words, while *ta'wīl* operates on the level of hidden or symbolic meanings.

20) *The concept of ḥikmah*

The root *ḥ-k-m* denotes the act of curbing or checking. From this root we derive the noun *ḥukm*, or rule, which refers primarily to the curbing of evil through the prevention of injustice. Similarly, the noun *ḥikmah*, generally translated as 'wisdom', refers to the prevention of ignorance. The active participle *ḥākim*, or ruler, refers to someone who carries out legal rulings (*aḥkām*, singular, *ḥukm*). More generally the word *ḥikmah* is associated with justice (*ʿadl*), knowledge (*ʿilm*), magnanimity (*ḥilm*), prophecy (*nubuwwah*), and revealed scriptures. The verb *aḥkama* is more or less synonymous with the verb *atqana*, which means to master, to do skillfully or properly, or to make something so sound and strong that it cannot be corrupted or undermined. Accordingly, speech described with the derivative adjective *muḥkam* is unambiguous speech whose words and meanings are subject to neither doubt nor equivocation.

Derivatives of the root *ḥ-k-m* occur eleven times in the Qur'an and in five different senses: (1) A means of admonition. In *Sūrah al-Baqarah*, 2:231 God urges the recipients of the Qur'an to take seriously "the revelation and the wisdom which He has bestowed on you from on high in order to admonish you thereby" (*mā anzala ʿalaykum min al-kitābi wa al-ḥikmati yaʿiẓukum bihi*). (2) Understanding and knowledge. Speaking of John the Baptist (Yaḥyā), God declares in *Sūrah Maryam*, 19:12: "We granted him wisdom (*ātaynāhu al-ḥukm*) while he was yet a little boy." Similarly, God declares in *Sūrah al-Nisā'*, 4:54 that He has granted "revelation and wisdom (*al-kitāba wa al-ḥikmah*) unto the House of Abraham." (See also *Sūrah al-Baqarah*,

2:269). (3) The act of ruling on legal matters. Thus God commands the Prophet (5:42), "if you judge, judge between them with equity" (*fa in ḥakamta, faḥkum baynahum bi al-qisṭ*)."

The word *ḥakīm*, meaning "wise" or "a wise man," conveys several different senses. One of these is that of a scholar or learned individual, it being said that in order to be described as *ḥakīm*, one must combine knowledge with action. As *Sūrah Fuṣṣilat*, 41:33 asks: "Who could be better of speech than he who calls [his fellow-men] unto God, and does what is just and right, and says, 'Verily, I am of those who have surrendered themselves to God?'" Another is that of someone who masters (*aḥkama*) the work he does. A third sense conveyed by the word *ḥakīm* is that of 'manifest' or 'clear.' Given the fundamental sense of the root *ḥ-k-m* as that of prevention or curbing, it came to be used to speak of regulating the precision of knowledge and action via direct examination of the meanings of things and the kind of keen observation that comes with accumulated experience. The Arabs once called their nobility *ḥukamā'*, or sages, in recognition of their sound opinions, prudence, and integrity. *Al-Ḥakīm* is also one of the 99 names of God, whose notice nothing escapes, and Who controls, regulates and rules the Universe with His almighty power and knowledge (cf. *Sūrah al-Mā'idah*, 5:118, *Sūrah al-Anʿām*, 6:18, etc.). In this sense, the word *ḥakīm* is more or less synonymous with *ḥākim*, meaning ruler or governor, although the term *ḥukm* (rule, governance, judgment) is broader than *ḥikmah* (wisdom, sagacity).

One proposed definition of *ḥikmah* is knowledge of things as they are. In order to be classified as *ḥikmah*, knowledge must also be accompanied by balanced attitudes and actions, that is, with an avoidance of both excess and neglect. This is consistent with the fact that according to the majority of scholars, *ʿilm* is not simply abstract understanding, but a balance of knowledge and action, with one or the other of the two taking priority depending on the nature of the situation.

The foregoing has been an overview of the Qur'anic terms relevant to the concept of *ʿilm* in its various facets. Other terms might have been included; however, given the length of this study, I have chosen simply to mention them without discussing them in detail. These additional terms include: *ḥilm* (intelligence, understanding), *rushd* (prudence, maturity, sensibility), *luṭf* (subtlety), *iḥsān* (virtue, action on others' behalf), and *īnās* (perception, discernment, observation); *khawf* (fear), *khishyah* (apprehension), and *inābah* (return, repentance); *faṣāḥah* (eloquence, skilled verbal expression) and *laḥn* (grammatical incorrectness); *ʿalan* (public disclosure), *istikhrāj* (extraction, deduction) and *ḥaṣḥaṣ* (to become clear, plain, manifest), all of which relate in one way or another to speech and to information presented to a listener or reader.

21) *The concept of hudā*

The root consisting of the letters *h-d-y* denotes two basic meanings. The first is that of guidance along a path, with the active participle, *hādin*, referring to someone who goes ahead of others to show them the way. As such, the nouns *hidāyah* and *hudā*, meaning right guidance, denote the opposite of error. The second basic meaning of this root is that of a bestowal of grace, that is, a gift (*hadiyyah*). The term *al-hādī* is one of the names of God (*Sūrah al-Ḥajj*, 22:54), who grants sight to His servants and shows them the way of knowledge so that they can perceive and acknowledge His lordship and divinity.

The term *hudā* with its various general and specific meanings occurs in 316 places in the Qur'an. *Sūrah al-Baqarah*, 2:5 speaks of those "who follow the guidance (*hudan*) [which comes] from their Sustainer." Similarly in *Sūrah al-Baqarah*, 2:120, God instructs the Prophet, "Say: 'Behold, God's guidance is the only true guidance'" (*inna hudā Allāhi huwa al-hudā*). For a contrast between *hudā* and *ḍalālah*, guidance and error, see *Sūrah al-Baqarah*, 2:16. The verbal form is found in *Sūrah al-Shūrā*, 42:52, where God tells the Prophet, "you will guide [others] onto a straight path" (*wa innaka la tahdī ilā ṣirāṭin mustaqīm*). (See also *Sūrah al-Baqarah*, 2:38, *Sūrah Ṭāhā*, 20:50, *Sūrah al-Aʿlā*, 87:3, *Sūrah al-Jinn*, 72:2, and *Sūrah Yūnus*, 10:35, and *Sūrah al-Qaṣaṣ*, 28:56). In *Sūrah al-Naml*, 27:41, another form of the verb occurs (*tahtadī, yahtadūn*), meaning 'to allow oneself to be guided.'

All of the aforementioned uses of the derivatives of *h-d-y* thus revolve around the notions of guidance and inspiration. As used in the Qur'an, the word *hidāyah* refers to the act of granting understanding and success, steering others away from the path of error and onto the path of faith which leads in turn to goodness and blessedness. When ascribed to human beings, the word describes the acts of supplication and of showing others the right path. Some apply the word *hidāyah* whether one's efforts to guide others are successful or not, while others apply it only if one's efforts succeed, since *hidāyah* is contrasted with *ḍalālah*, or error.

As for the guidance ascribed to God, it may take one of four different forms. The first form is that which is granted to every morally accountable human being in the form of insight and the ability to reason (see *Sūrah Ṭāhā*, 20:50 and *Sūrah al-Balad*, 90:10). The second is the type of guidance given to the prophets through a special divine call, the revelation of the Qur'an, and the like (see *Sūrah al-Anbiyā'*, 21:73 and *Sūrah al-Anʿām*, 6:90). The third type is the success granted specially to those who have allowed themselves to be guided, and which is denied to those who reject faith. And the fourth is guidance to Paradise in the afterlife.

22) *The concept of ittibāʿ*

The root *t-b-ʿ* denotes the act of following or succeeding. Derivatives of this root occur 175 times in the Qur'an, and in the following eight senses: (1) Accompanying. In *Sūrah al-Kahf*, 18:66, Moses asks a figure of great knowledge and wisdom if he can "follow" him in the sense of traveling with him (*hal attabiʿuka*). (2) Emulating. In *Sūrah Yāsīn*, 36:21 we read the admonishment to emulate (*ittabiʿū*) "those who ask no reward of you" (*ittabiʿū man lā yas'alukum ajran*). (3) Adhering to. People are urged in *Sūrah al-Naḥl*, 16:123, to adhere to (*ittabiʿ*) "the creed of Abraham." (See also *Sūrah al-Mā'idah*, 5:48). (4) Following a path. *Sūrah al-Nisā'*, 4:115 speaks of someone who "follows (*yattabiʿ*) a path other than that of the believers (*ghayra sabīli al-mu'minīn*). (See also *Sūrah al-Anʿām*, 6:153). (5) Engaging in. *Sūrah al-Baqarah*, 2:102

speaks disapprovingly of those who engage in (*ittabaʿū*) certain evil practices that were prevalent during the days of Solomon, (*Sūrah al-Nisā'*, 4:157). (6) Adopting, turning toward. In *Sūrah al-Baqarah*, 2:145, God speaks to the Prophet about how the Jews and Christians have not adopted (*tabiʿū*) his direction of prayer. (7) Obedience. *Sūrah al-Nisā'*, 4:83, God tells the believers that were it not for His grace and generosity, most of them would have obeyed (*laittabaʿtum*) Satan. (8) Seeking. We read in *Sūrah Āl ʿImrān*, 3:162 about the one who "strives after God's goodly acceptance" (*man ittabaʿa riḍwān Allāh*). (See also *al-Mā'idah*, 5:16). (9) Chasing. Moses is warned in *Sūrah al-Shuʿarā'*, 26:52 to move quickly with the Children of Israel as they flee Egypt, since they will be pursued (*innakum muttabaʿūn*).

23) *The concept of shūrā*

The root *sh-w-r* denotes two basic meanings: (1) to reveal or express something, and (2) to take something. One might say, for example, *shurtu al-dābbah*, "I took the pack animal," while the noun *mishwār* refers to the path along which an animal is taken. The same verb might also be used in association with honey, as in *shāra al-ʿasal*, or *ashāra al-ʿasal* (he took the honey) where the beehive from which the honey is taken is referred to as a *mishār*. Another verbal derivation is the verb *shāwara*, meaning to consult with someone (see *Sūrah Āl ʿImrān*, 3:159). The meaning is derived from the verb *shāra* in the sense of taking because, when one consults with another person, one seeks to "take" his or her point of view on something. Similarly, the verb *istashāra/yastashīru* means to seek someone's counsel (*shūrā*), while the noun *shūrā* can refer to the act of mutual consultation (see *Sūrah al-Shūrā*, 42:38). The noun *mustashīr* may also refer to a camel that can distinguish a pregnant she-camel from one that is not pregnant. The verb *ashāra/yushīru* can mean to point or gesture with one's hand, as in *Sūrah Maryam*, 19:29.

24) *The concept of fiṭrah*

The triliteral root *f-ṭ-r* denotes several different notions. These include (1) opening and making visible, (2) creation and newness, (3) breaking fast, (4) granting something a particular nature or constitution.

Derivatives of this root occur 20 times in the Qur'an: (1) Creation. This sense is found in *Sūrah Yūsuf*, 12:101, which uses the active participle to refer to God as the "Originator of the heavens and the earth" (*fāṭir al-samāwāti wal-arḍ*). (2) Fault or weakness. This sense is found in *Sūrah al-Mulk*, 67:3, which tells us that we will see no "flaw" (*fuṭūr*) in God's creation. (3) Innate constitution or temperament. *Sūrah al-Rūm*, 30:30 refers to "the natural disposition which God has instilled into people" (*fiṭrat Allāhi allatī faṭar al-nāsa ʿalayhā*). (4) Splitting or cleaving lengthwise. *Sūrah al-Infiṭār*, 82:1 speaks of the Day of Resurrection as the time when the sky will be "cleft asunder" (*idhā al-samā'u infaṭarat*).

25) *The concept of ḥayy*

The root consisting of the letter *ḥ-y-y* has two primary meanings. The first is that of being alive, while the other is that of shame, timidity, or bashfulness. In relation to the former sense of the root we have the derivatives *ḥayāh* (life) and *ḥayawān* (animal, living creature, derived from *ḥayayān*). Rain has sometimes been referred to as *ḥayy* due its association with life on Earth and its renewal and sustenance. A clear path is sometimes referred to as *ṭarīq ḥayy*, while the verb *ḥayiya/yaḥyā* is synonymous with *istabāna/yastabīnu*, meaning to become plain or evident, or to see, perceive, notice.

The words *ḥayy/aḥyā'* occur 35 times in the Qur'an, *iḥyā'* (bringing to life) 50 times, and *istaḥyā* four times. It occurs once in the sense of living one's life (*Sūrah al-Naḥl*, 16:97), 44 times in the sense of greeting (*taḥiyyah*), four times in the sense of keeping someone alive in order to make a prisoner of war (*Sūrah al-Baqarah*, 2:49; *Sūrah al-Aʿrāf*, 7:127 and 141; *Sūrah Ibrāhīm*, 14:6), and twice in the sense of being alive (*ḥayy*) (see *Sūrah Yāsīn*, 36:70 and *Sūrah al-Anʿām*, 6:122).

26) *The concept of ẓann*

The root consisting of the letters ẓ-n-n actually denotes two opposite meanings: certainty and doubt. The verb *ẓanna/yaẓunnu* can be synonymous with the verb *ayqana/yūqinu*, to be certain. *Sūrah al-Baqarah*, 2:249, for example, refers to certain men "who knew with certainty (*alladhīna yaẓunnūn*) that they were destined to meet God (*annahum mulāqū Allāh*)." This use of the verb is frequent in the Qur'an. On the other hand, this same verb can mean to doubt or suspect. From this sense of the root we derive the word *ẓinnah*, meaning suspicion, misgiving, or accusation. As for the verbal noun *ẓann*, it can refer either to knowledge, or to vacillation between two unconfirmed beliefs.

The term *ẓann* occurs 69 times in the Qur'an, and in four different senses: (1) Cautious certainty with a consciousness of God. *Sūrah al-Baqarah*, 2:230 states that a formerly married man and woman may return to each other "provided that both of them think (*ẓannā*) that they will be able to keep within the bounds set by God." (2) Doubt or unconfirmed belief. *Sūrah al-Jāthiyah*, 45:32 quotes skeptics saying about the Last Hour: "we think it is no more than an empty guess (*in naẓunnu illā ẓannan*), and [so] we are by no means convinced! (*wa mā naḥnu bi mustayqinīn*)." (A similar sense is found in *Sūrah al-Inshiqāq*, 84:14). (3) Paranoid or vain thoughts. *Sūrah al-Aḥzāb*, 33:10 addresses those who were near death on the battlefield, saying, "conflicting thoughts about God passed through your minds" (*taẓunnūna billāhi al-ẓunūna*). The words *ẓann* and *shakk* are related in meaning. However, the word *ẓann* implies that one possibility is more strongly weighted than the other. A person may have reason to believe that a certain thing is true, though he also holds out the possibility that the opposite is true. His belief (*ẓann*) that something is a possibility (rather than a certainty) distinguishes it from knowledge (*ʿilm*), while the existence of evidence supporting a given possibility distinguishes it from mere suspicion (*shakk*).

27) *The concept of ḥasab*

The root *ḥ-s-b* relates to four basic denotations: (1) counting or computation (*ḥasaba/yaḥsubu*), (2) considering, regarding, or supposing (*ḥasaba/yaḥsibu* or *ḥasiba/yaḥsibu*), (3) a small pillow referred to as a *ḥusbānah* (plural, *ḥusbān*), and (4) a disease that causes whitening of the skin and damage to the hair, the person afflicted with it being referred to as *aḥsab*.

Derivatives of this root occur 110 times in the Qur'an, and in five different senses: (1) Counting or computing. *Sūrah Yūnus*, 10:5 uses the word *ḥisāb* in relation to the measurement of time. (2) Holding accountable. This sense of the word is found in *Sūrah al-Ṭalāq*, 65:8, which refers to a severe accounting (*ḥisāban shadīdan*) to which God subjected those who despised His commands. (3) Sufficiency. In *Sūrah al-Tawbah*, 9:129, God instructs the Prophet to say to those who refuse to believe, "God sufficeth me. There is no god but He. In Him have I placed my trust." (4) One who takes account of human beings' actions. The word *ḥasīb* is used in this sense in relation to God in *Sūrah al-Nisā'*, 4:6. (5) Thinking, supposing. The verb *ḥasaba* is used in this sense in *Sūrah al-ʿAnkabūt*, 29:2 and *Sūrah Āl ʿImrān*, 3:142.

We are told in *Sūrah Āl ʿImrān*, 3:37 that when Zachariah visited Mary in the sanctuary and found her with food whose source he could not identify, he asked her where she had gotten it, and she replied, "It is from God; behold, God grants sustenance unto whom He wills, beyond all reckoning (*bi ghayri ḥisāb*)." The phrase *bi ghayri ḥisāb*, translated here as "beyond all reckoning," can be understood to mean that what God grants, He grants without its being deserved. It can also be understood to mean that what God gives, He does not take back again. Thirdly, it can mean that God gives more than human beings could ever measure.

28) *The concept of jahl*

The root *j-h-l* denotes two primary meanings. The first is opposed to knowledge, while the second is opposed to stillness. Used in the first sense, we derive the noun *majhal* (plural, *majāhil*) meaning an unknown, unexplored region or territory, and *mijhalah*, which refers to something that leads to ignorance. The verbal noun is *jahl* or *jahālah*; the verb *tajāhala* means to feign ignorance or lack of knowledge, while the active participle, meaning 'ignorant', is *jāhil* or *jahūl* (plural, *juhhāl* or *juhalā'*). A she-camel with no identifying markings is referred to as a *nāqah majhūlah*; the verb *istajhala* means to regard someone as ignorant or uneducated.

Used in the second sense, we derive the noun *mijhal*, which refers to the poker used to stir embers. Similarly, the statement, *istajhalat al-rīḥu al-ghuṣna* means that the wind stirred a branch as it blew over it.

Derivatives of the root *j-h-l* occur 24 in the Qur'an. In all these cases they relate in one way or another to a lack of knowledge. In many cases the lack of knowledge is viewed as willful and blameworthy (cf. *Sūrah al-Baqarah*, 2:67), but in some cases it is not. In *Sūrah al-Baqarah*, 2:273, the word *jāhil* is used simply to mean "unaware," without any criticism implied. *Sūrah al-Nisā'*, 4:17 states that God accepts the repentance of those who do wrong "out of ignorance" (*bi jahālah*). *Sūrah Āl ʿImrān*, 3:154 refers to "pagan ignorance" (*jāhiliyyah*), while *Sūrah al-Zumar*, 39:64 records words addressed by the Prophet to unbelievers as "O you who are unaware [of right and wrong]" (*ayyuhā al-jāhilūn*).

29) *The concept of bāṭil*

The root consisting of the letters *b-ṭ-l* denotes something's departure or the brevity of its stay or duration (the verb being *baṭala/yabṭulu*, verbal noun *buṭul/buṭūl*). It is frequently used in opposition to the concept of truth. The active participle, *bāṭil* (plural, *abāṭīl*), is used to refer to that which is false, null, void, or invalid.

Derivatives of this root occur in approximately 36 places in the Qur'an, and in three different senses: (1) Falsehood. The word *bāṭil* is used in this sense in *Sūrah Fuṣṣilat*, 41:42. See also *Sūrah al-Isrā'*, 17:81, *Sūrah al-Ḥajj*, 22:62, which describes all that people worship other than God as "falsehood" (*al-bāṭil*) and *Sūrah al-Baqarah*, 2:42, where people are commanded not to "overlay the truth with falsehood" (*lā talbisū al-ḥaqqa bil-bāṭil*). (2) Nullification. People are exhorted in *Sūrah al-Baqarah*, 2:264 not to "nullify" their good works (*lā tubṭilū ṣadaqātikum*) by reminding others of how good they have been to them. (3) Injustice. *Sūrah al-Baqarah*, 2:188 urges people not to consume each other's resources "wrongfully" (*bil-bāṭil*).

30) *The concept of hawā*

The triliteral root h-w-y denotes the idea of falling, and of emptiness. From this root we derive the noun *hawā'*, which refers to air due to its apparent emptiness. The verb *hawā/yahwī* means to fall (verbal noun, *hawā*), from which we derive the noun *hāwiyah*, meaning pit or chasm (something into which one falls). With the definite article, this noun also refers to Hell (*al-hāwiyah*, the pit into which the denier of truth falls). Another sense of the noun *hawā* is caprice, craving, and passion, which are viewed as being devoid of all benefit. Similarly, the word *hawā* can refer to romantic love in both its positive and negative aspects.

Derivatives of this root occur in 38 places in the Qur'an, and in the following senses: (1) To fall. *Sūrah al-Najm*, 53:1 refers to God's message as it "comes down" (*idhā hawā*). Using the verb in a more metaphorical sense, *Sūrah Ibrāhīm*, 14:37 contains Abraham's prayer that people's hearts would "incline" (*tahwī*) toward the inhabitants of the valley where he has settled. (See also *Sūrah al-Ḥajj*, 22:31). (2) Craving. *Sūrah al-Nāziʿāt*, 79:40 uses the term *hawā* to refer to "base desires." (3) To perish. *Sūrah Ṭāhā*, 20:81 employs the verb *hawā* in this sense, telling us that he who brings divine condemnation upon himself "has thrown himself into utter ruin" (*fa qad hawā*). (4) Empty space. *Sūrah Ibrāhīm*, 14:43 describes the hearts of evildoers as "an abysmal void" (*af'idatuhum hawā'*), so terrified and confounded are they from what they witness on the Day of Judgment (cf. *Sūrah al-Qaṣaṣ*, 28:10). (5) Hell. This sense of the word is found in *Sūrah al-Qāriʿah*, 101:9, which, in an indirect reference to Hell, speaks of the "abyss" (*hāwiyah*) in which sinners find themselves. (6) Whim, caprices. For this use, see *Sūrah al-Baqarah*, 2:145, where the plural *ahwā'ahum* is translated by Asad as "errant views" (cf. *Sūrah al-Mā'idah*, 5:48).

THIRD: *Waḥy*-RELATED TERMS IN THE QUR'AN

1) *The concept of Waḥy*

The root consisting of the letter *w-ḥ-y* refers to the act of communicating knowledge of some kind in a rapid, subtle manner. The noun *waḥy* refers to a signal, sign or rapidly delivered message. As for the noun *waḥā*, it refers to an inspiration or quiet voice. The verb *tawaḥḥā* means to hurry or act quickly, while the adjective *waḥiyyun* means hurried or hasty. As for the verb *istawḥā*, it means to call someone and send him out and to seek understanding, insight, or understanding from him. Similarly, the verb *waḥḥā* means to hasten someone or something.

Derivatives of the root *w-ḥ-y* occur 79 times in the Qur'an in five different senses: (1) Sign, signal or gesture. *Sūrah Maryam*, 19:11 tells us how Zachariah came out of the temple and gestured to his people (*awḥā ilayhim*) to praise God morning and evening. (2) To suggest thoughts, whisper. *Sūrah al-Anʿām*, 6:112 describes evil forces that "whisper unto one another" in attempts to deceive and mislead. (3) Inspiration. In *Sūrah al-Qaṣaṣ*, 28:7 God declares, "We inspired [thus] the mother of Moses (*awḥāynā ilā ummi mūsā*): Suckle him [for a time], and then, when thou hast cause to fear for him, cast him into the river." (4) God-given instincts. *Sūrah al-Naḥl*, 16:68 tells us how God has "inspired the bees" (*awḥā...ilā al-naḥl*) to build dwellings for themselves in mountains and trees. (5) Divine revelation. The verb *awḥā* is also used to describe God's communication of His revelation to the prophets, as in *Sūrah al-Nisā'*, 4:163, where God states, "We inspired (*awḥaynā ilā*) Abraham, and Ishmael, and Isaac, and Jacob, and their descendants." The noun *waḥy* is also found in *Sūrah al-Shūrā*, 42:51 in the sense of "sudden inspiration." The process of *waḥy* – sudden inspiration, or revelation – occurs by seeing a messenger from God and hearing what he says, such as when Gabriel delivered God's messages to the Prophet. In other cases, however, one may hear a message without seeing a messenger, such as when Moses heard God speak, yet without seeing Him. The Qur'an warns against claiming falsely to have received divine inspiration; hence we read in *Sūrah al-Anʿām*, 6:93, "And who could be more wicked than he who invents a lie about God, or says, 'This has been revealed unto me' (*qāla ūḥiya ilayya*), the while nothing has been revealed to him (*wa lam yūḥa ilayhi shay'un*)?" The verb *awḥā* can also refer to God's inspiration of people to do good works. In speaking of Isaac and his son, God states in *Sūrah al-Anbiyā'*, 21:73, "We inspired them [with a will] to do good works" (*awḥayna ilayhim fiʿl al-khayrāt*). God inspired Jesus' disciples to believe in him (*Sūrah al-Mā'idah*, 5:111). This same verb, however, can be used to refer to evil insinuations (see *Sūrah al-Anʿām*, 6:121). The Arabic word most often used to refer to inspiration given to people other than the prophets is *ilhām*, while the inspiration granted to other creatures – the bees, for example – is *taskhīr*.

2) *Ilhām*

The triliteral root *l-h-m* denotes the act of devouring, consuming, or swallowing up. Hence, the verb *alhama/yulhimu* in the sense of inspiration is a metaphorical expression derived from the image of 'feeding' someone something that is good. It can describe the act of introducing a good thought into someone's mind with a view to carrying it out in action, or the thought of something evil with a view to avoiding it. The only derivative of the root *l-h-m* found in the Qur'an is the verb *alhama* in *Sūrah al-Shams*, 91:7-8, which tells us that God has 'enlightened' the soul concerning both its vices and its virtues. In other words, He has shown the individual what he or she should pursue by way of goodness and obedience to God, and what to avoid by way of evil and disobedience. Every believer has been a recipient of *ilhām* to some degree by the mere fact of having been guided to faith without his or her having sought out evidence or proof. *Ilhām* thus consists in the knowledge that inspires an individual to undertake whatever action is necessary to achieve the good and provide guidance for others in society.

The process of *ilhām* involves the introduction of ideas into the mind and heart such that the individual immediately grasps their meaning and significance. If we say someone is *mulham*, 'inspired', we mean that he or she comes to know things by virtue of his or her astuteness and intelligence without necessarily having witnessed them directly. *Waḥy* is specific to prophets, while *ilhām* is more general. And whereas *waḥy* takes place through the mediation of an angel or direct communication from God, *ilhām* takes place through the introduction of a thought into one's mind or heart in such a way that the individual realizes the truth without having exerted a special effort to investigate the matter at hand or research evidence for and against it. As for *iʿlām*, meaning notification, it is more general than *ilhām*, since it consists simply in announcing or conveying information to someone about something.

3) *Luṭf*

The root *l-ṭ-f* denotes gentleness, daintiness, and delicacy. When preceded by the definite article, the adjectival form *laṭīf* is one of the 99 names of God (cf. *Sūrah al-Anʿām*, 6:103; *Sūrah al-Ḥajj*, 22:63), and translates roughly as "unfathomable" (Muhammad Asad) or "above all comprehension" (Abdullah Yusuf Ali). The divine name *Al-Laṭīf* often appears in conjunction with *Al-Khabīr* which, as we saw earlier, denotes God's knowledge of all things. *Sūrah al-Mulk*, 67:14 reads, *alā yaʿlamu man khalaqa wa huwa Al-Laṭīf Al-Khabīr*? This is rendered by Asad as, "How could it be that He who has created [all] should not know [all]? Yea, He alone is unfathomable [in His wisdom] (*wa huwa Al-Laṭīfu*), Aware (*Al-Khabīr*)!", and by Abdullah Yusuf Ali as, "Should He not know – He that created? and He is the One that understands the finest mysteries (*wa huwa Al-Laṭīfu*) [and] is well-acquainted [with them] (*Al-Khabīr*)."

As applied to God, the word *laṭīf* describes God's goodness to His servants, which is demonstrated by His gracious, gentle provision of the blessings they need. It also points to God's nature as the One who knows that which is concealed, the intricacies of things. When applied to speech, *laṭif* means mysterious, vague and subtle, and when one says *talaṭṭaftu bi fulān*, it means, "I gained access to his secrets through subterfuge."

Derivatives of the root *l-ṭ-f* occur eight times in the Qur'an. In *Sūrah Yūsuf*, 12:100, Joseph states: *rabbī laṭīfun li mā yashā'u*. This is translated by Abdullah Yusuf Ali as, "Verily my Lord understands best the mysteries of all that He plans to do," and by Muhammad Asad as, "Verily, my Sustainer is unfathomable in [the way He brings about] whatever He wills." Both translations bring out the element of mystery and "beyondness" conveyed by the term *laṭīf* when applied to the Divine. The word *laṭīf* describes someone who operates so covertly and discreetly that his actions escape others' notice. This sense of the root *l-ṭ-f* is found in *Sūrah al-Kahf*, 18:19, where we are told that one of the "Companions of the Cave" is sent out to bring food from the nearby town with instructions that he should "behave with great care (*wal-yatalaṭṭaf*) and by no means make anyone aware of you (*wa lā yushʿiranna bikum aḥadan*)." Similarly, the plural *laṭā'if* refers to realities that are too subtle to be perceived by the senses.

4) *Risālah*

The root *r-s-l* denotes emanation and extension. The noun *rasl* refers to a leisurely gait, while the verb *tarassal* means to proceed leisurely, take one's time. The noun *rasl* can also refer to sheep that have been sent out to pasture. The plural of *rasl* is sometimes used as an adverb, as in *jā' al-qawmu arsālan*, "the people came in one group after another." The noun *rasūl* (plural, *rusul*) refers to a messenger or apostle, while winds are sometimes referred to as *mursalāt*, "sent ones." As for the verb *rassala* (verbal noun, *tarsīl*), it is more or less synonymous with the verb *rattala* (*tartīla*), meaning to chant or sing.

Derivatives of the root *r-s-l* occur 513 times in the Qur'an, and in the following senses: (1) To let loose upon. This sense is found in *Sūrah Maryam*, 19:83, where God declares that He has "let loose all [manner of] satanic forces upon those who deny the truth" (*arsalnā al-shayāṭīna ʿalā al-kāfirīn*). (See also *Sūrah al-Qamar*, 54:27). (2) To send a person out. In *Sūrah al-Nisā'*, 4:79 God tells the Prophet, "We have sent you as an apostle unto all mankind" (*arsalnāka lil-nāsi rasūlan*). Similarly, we read in *Sūrah al-Shuʿarā'*, 26:53 that in the time of Moses, Pharaoh "sent heralds unto all cities" (*arsala firʿawnu fī al-madā'ini ḥāshirīn*). Used in the sense of release from bondage, the word *arsala* is found in *Sūrah al-Shuʿarā'*, 26:17, where Moses tells Pharaoh to "Let the children of Israel go with us!" (*arsil maʿanā banī isrā'īl*). (3) One who releases from affliction (*mursil*). See *Sūrah Fāṭir*, 35:2. (7) To provide. This sense is found in *Sūrah Nūḥ*, 71:11, where we are told that God "will send rain to you in abundance" (*yursili al-samā'a ʿalaykum midrāran* – more literally, will release the sky upon you).

The original meaning of the root *r-s-l* is that of gradual emission or sending out, as in reference, for example, to camels sent out little by little. A similar sense is conveyed by the word *rasūl*, a messenger who is sent out. (In *Sūrah al-Tawbah*, 9:128, the word *rasūl* is used to refer to a single person, while in *Sūrah al-Shuʿarā'*, 26:16 it is used to refer to more than one). The plural form *rusul* is used to refer both to God's prophets (*Sūrah Āl ʿImrān*, 3:144) and to His angels (see *Sūrah Hūd*, 11:81).

5) *Naba'*

The root *n-b-ʿ* denotes movement from place to place. The noun *naba'* refers to a report or piece of news that has been brought from one place to another, the active participle *munbi'* refers to a person who brings the report, and a *nabī*, or prophet (plural, *anbiyā'*) is someone who brings a report on God's authority. The verb *tanabba'a* can mean either to claim to be a prophet, or to prophesy or predict something, while the verbal noun is *nubū'ah* or *tanabbu'*. Another sense conveyed by this root is that of being raised, elevated or prominent. When attributed to a sound or voice, the verb *naba'a* denotes softness, and means to make a low sound. Hence, the noun *naba'* refers to a report that is critical in its importance, that is delivered discreetly, or in a low voice, and that is devoid of all untruth. In order for a *khabar* to be described as a *naba'*, it must display these three qualities.

The root *n-b-'*, derivatives of which appear in 160 places in the Qur'an, occurs as a verb in past and present tenses, and as a noun, plural and singular. All of its occurrences are consistent with the root's lexical definition as a true report. These include, for example, *Sūrah al-Taḥrīm*, 66:3 (*nabba'at bihi*, "she divulged it"), *Sūrah Āl ʿImrān*, 3:15 (*a'ūnabbi'ukum*, "Shall I tell you...?"), and *Sūrah Yūsuf*, 12:15 (*la tunabbi'annahum bi amrihim hādhā*, "Of a surety you shall [one day] tell them the truth of this their affair").

6) *Nubuwwah*

The word *nubuwwah* is derived from the root *n-b-'* discussed above. *Nubuwwah*, or prophethood, is a kind of ambassadorship among thoughtful souls for the purpose of enlightening them concerning both their present life and the life to come. A prophet (*nabī*) is someone who conveys a message that brings peace to those with astute, perceptive minds. The prophet occupies a rank below that of an apostle or messenger (*rasūl*). However, the role of prophet is one for which the individual is chosen, not one he acquires by dint of his own efforts, since the knowledge this station brings is divine in nature and is not dependent on human knowledge in any way.

7) *Īmān*

The root *a-m-n* denotes two basic meanings: (1) faithfulness and honesty that bring inward peace, the verb being *amina/ya'manu*, and the verbal noun being *amānah*, meaning integrity; and (2) affirmation of someone else's truthfulness, the verb being *āmana/yu'minu*, and the verbal noun being *īmān*, or faith (see *Sūrah al-Mā'idah*, 5:5). One of the names of God is *Al-Mu'min*, "the Preserver of Faith" (*Sūrah al-Ḥashr*, 59:23) who, by preserving people's faith, protects them from chastisement in the life to come. As for *īmān*, or faith, it refers to confidence in God demonstrated through reverence and submission to God's Law.

Derivatives of the root *a-m-n* occur 875 times in the Qur'an, and in the following senses: (1) Expression of faith in public, and disbelief in private. This use of the root is found in *Sūrah al-Munāfiqūn*, 63:3, which speaks of certain individuals who "[profess that] they have attained to faith (*āmanū*), whereas [inwardly] they deny the Truth (*thumma kafarū*)." (2) Affirming the truth of Islam both in public and in private. *Sūrah al-Bayyinah*, 98:7 praises those "who have attained to faith, and do righteous deeds" (*alladhīna āmanū wa ʿamilū al-ṣāliḥāt*). (Cf. *Sūrah al-Baqarah*, 2:62). (3) Faith in the one God combined with polytheism (*Sūrah Yūsuf*, 12:106). (4) Affirming the truth of what some other human being says (*Sūrah Yūsuf*, 12:17). (5) Believing in falsehoods that can provide no salvation (*Sūrah al-Nisā'*, 4:51).

Īmān whose object is God entails an affirmation of divine truth which stands opposed to *kufr*, or denial of this truth (cf. *Sūrah al-Naḥl*, 16:106). When its object is God, the verb *āmana/yu'minu* is generally followed by the preposition *bi* in parallel with its opposite, *kafara/yakfuru*, which takes the same preposition. By affirming God's existence and oneness, the believer (*mu'min*) renders himself or herself secure (*fī ma'man*) from divine chastisement. When the object of the verb *āmana/yu'minu* in the Qur'an is something or someone other than God, it is generally followed by the preposition *li*, which conveys the sense of not only affirmation, but following and emulation. *Īmān* customarily refers to belief that goes beyond one's knowledge (which is also true of God-consciousness, or *taqwā*). *Īmān* involves confession with the lips, belief in the heart, and action (cf. *Sūrah al-Naḥl*, 16:106 and *Sūrah al-Baqarah*, 2:143). The greater the knowledge that accompanies faith (*īmān*), the more action one will engage in, and the more the action, the greater the certainty. Certainty thus waxes with obedience to the All-Merciful One, and wanes with obedience to evil or destructive impulses. One can only attain to *īmān* by receiving the light of knowledge from the lantern of prophethood, stripping oneself of base desires and caprices, and ceasing to acquiesce in the will of others. Believers' knowledge is derived from the flame of divine revelation, while their will is devoted to God and the life to come. Firmly established in knowledge and right action, such individuals will be among the leaders who guide others based on God's commands, and successors to His Apostle in guiding his community worldwide.

8) *Ghayb*

The root *gh-y-b* denotes the act of vanishing from sight. It is used of the sun when it sets, for example. We say *ghābat al-shams*, that is, "the sun vanished from sight." The verbal noun *ghayb* denotes doubt or uncertainty, as well as low or depressed parts of the earth. Similarly, the noun *ghayābah* refers to the bottom of a well, pit, etc.

Derivatives of this root occur 60 times in the Qur'an in the following senses: (1) "That which is beyond the reach of human perception," including: the Day of Judgment (*Sūrah al-Baqarah*, 2:3) and death (*Sūrah Saba'*, 34:14). God is identified as the One who knows "all that is beyond the reach of a created being's perception (*al-ghayb*) as well as all that can be witnessed by a creature's senses or mind (*wa al-shahādah*) (*Sūrah al-Raʿd*, 13:9 and *Sūrah al-Sajdah*, 32:6)." See also *Sūrah al-Aʿrāf*, 7:188, *Sūrah al-Anʿām*, 6:59, *Sūrah Maryam*, 19:78, and *Sūrah al-Jinn*, 72:26. (2) The "dark depths" of a well (*ghayābati al-jubbi*, *Sūrah Yūsuf* 12:10). (3) Confidentialities, the privacy of one's home life. *Sūrah al-Nisā'*, 4:34 speaks of righteous women who act as guardians of "what Allah would have them guard" (*lil-ghaybi bi mā ḥafiẓa Allāhu*, Abdullah Yusuf Ali)." In other words, they behave in their husbands' absence as they would behave in his presence. (4) Backbiting (which involves saying hurtful things about people in their absence). See *Sūrah al-Ḥujurāt*, 49:13. (11) Knowledge of the unseen (i.e., divine revelation received). We are told in *Sūrah al-Takwīr*, 81:24 that God does not "withhold grudgingly a knowledge of the Unseen" (*wa mā huwa ʿalā al-ghaybi bi ḍanīn*).

Sūrah al-Baqarah, 2:3 states that the God-conscious are those "who believe in [the existence of] that which is beyond the reach of human perception" (*alladhīna yu'minūna bil-ghayb*) and which, therefore, can only be known through divine revelation. This verse has been interpreted by some to mean that they believe whether they are present to you, or absent (in other words, they are not hypocrites). This relates to *Sūrah al-Mā'idah*, 5:94, which speaks of pilgrims to Makkah being tempted by the game animals available to them (hunting being prohibited during the pilgrimage) such "that God might mark out those who fear Him although He is beyond the reach of human perception" (*li yaʿlama Allāhu man yakhāfuhu bil-ghayb*, Asad), or, as rendered by Yusuf Ali, "that He may test who fears Him unseen" (*man yakhāfuhu bil-ghayb*).

9) *Qaḍā'*

The root *q-ḍ-y* relates to the action of mastering or completing something; bringing it to pass, carrying out, executing, and ruling or judging concerning the law. The verbal noun *qaḍā'* can refer variously to a legal ruling or judgment, or the judiciary. From this root we derive the active participle *qāḍī*, meaning judge or magistrate, who issues rulings and implements them. The related noun *qaḍiyyah*, meaning lawsuit, case, cause or legal question, points to a process of settling, resolution, and clarification, while the feminine active participle, *qāḍiyyah*, is used to refer to death (which finalizes and concludes a life).

Derivatives of the root *q-ḍ-y* occur 63 times in the Qur'an in the following senses: (1) To command, instruct, enjoin as a duty. *Sūrah al-Isrā'*, 17:23 tells us that God "has ordained (*qaḍā*) that you shall worship none but Him" (*allā taʿbudū illā iyyāhu*). (2) To decree or make known. This meaning of the verb *qaḍā* is found in *Sūrah al-Isrā'*, 17:4 and *Sūrah al-Ḥijr*, 15:66. (3) To finish or conclude. In *Sūrah al-Nisā'*, 4:103 God tells believers, "when you have finished your prayer (*idhā qaḍaytum al-ṣalāh*), remember God..." (*fadhkurū Allāh*). (4) To bring about, accomplish. This sense of the verb *qaḍā* is found in *Sūrah al-Anfāl*, 8:42. (5) To kill, put an end to. *Sūrah al-Qaṣaṣ*, 28:15 tells us that Moses struck a man with his fist and thus "brought about his end" (*qaḍā ʿalayhi*). (6) To settle, decide. *Sūrah Yūsuf*, 12:41 tells us that a certain matter "has been decided [by God]" (*quḍiya al-amru*). Of Jesus' miraculous conception, *Sūrah Maryam*, 19:21 tells us that "it was a thing decreed [by God]" (*kāna amran maqḍiyyan*), while, speaking of how each soul must come within sight of the hell fire, 19:71 describes this reality as "a decree that must be fulfilled" (*kāna... ḥatman maqḍiyyan*). (7) To fulfill a term of service. *Sūrah al-Qaṣaṣ*, 28:29 tells us of when "Moses had fulfilled his term" of service (*qaḍā mūsā al-ajala*) in Midian. (8) To rule, pass judgment on. Describing the Day of Judgment with the use of the past tense (for rhetorical emphasis), *Sūrah al-Zumar*, 39:69 tells that when people appear before God, "judgment will be passed on them all in justice" (*quḍiya baynahum bi al-ḥaqq*). (See also *Sūrah al-Zumar*, 39:75, and *Sūrah al-Naml*, 27:78). (9) To form or create. The verb *qaḍā* is used in this sense in relation to God's creation of the heavens in *Sūrah Fuṣṣilat*, 41:12.

The divine action indicated by the word *qaḍā'* is more concrete than that referred to as *qadar*. *Qadar* has to do with divine foreknowledge or predetermination, while *qaḍā'* has to do with the fulfillment, in real time, of such divine knowledge or predetermination.

3

Paths of Maʿrifah: Reasoning and Sensation

FIRST: CONCEPTS RELATING TO *Maʿrifah*

1) *The concept of maʿrifah*

THE ROOT *ʿ-q-l* refers to an impediment in something. Al-Khalīl contrasted the *ʿaql* to ignorance. The verb is *ʿaqala/yaʿqilu*, the verbal noun being *ʿaql* (plural, *ʿuqūl*). The active participle *ʿāqil* means reasonable, sensible, prudent and the like, its plurals being *ʿuqalāʾ* and *ʿāqilūn*. An intensified form of *ʿāqil* is *ʿaqūl*, meaning endowed with exceptional understanding and intellect. The passive participle *maʿqūl* means intelligible, reasonable, and understandable, while the noun *ʿāqilah* refers to a clan whose members share the burden of paying the blood money for the tribe if one of its members is guilty of unintentional homicide. The *ʿāqilah* would consist of the cousins of the person who had committed the murder. The term *maʿqil* (plural, *maʿāqil*) refers to a stronghold or fortress, while charity (*ṣadaqah*) has sometimes been referred to with the term *ʿiqāl*, which is a rope used to hobble a camel. Renowned grammarian al-Aṣmaʿī stated that when attributed to the gazelle, the verb *ʿaqala* is used to mean that the gazelle was stranded (as on a mountain). Similarly, if food has caused someone constipation, it may be said that *al-ṭaʿām ʿaqala baṭnahu*, while the phrase *uʿtuqila lisānu fulān* means that so-and-so's tongue was tied.

When used in the sense of mind, intelligence, or reason, the word *ʿaql* has numerous denotations. It can mean, for example, knowledge of the nature of things, be they good or bad, beautiful or ugly, perfect or imperfect. Similarly, it might refer to the ability to recognize which of two goods is better, and which of two evils is worse. The passive participle *maʿqūl*, meaning reasonable or intelligible, refers to what has been retained in one's heart or understanding. Reason or intelligence is referred to as *ʿaql* because it is what restrains you (*yaʿqiluka*) from surrendering to your cravings and appetites, just as a *ʿiqāl* – a cord used to hobble a camel – restrains and limits the camel's movement. Similarly, it restrains (*yaʿqilu*) the tongue, thereby preventing its owner from uttering careless, harmful words out of ignorance and error.

Derivatives of the root *ʿ-q-l* occur 49 times in the Qur'an. There is no occurrence of the noun *ʿaql*. However, the root appears repeatedly in various verbal forms: *ʿaqalūhu* (once), *taʿqilūn* and *yaʿqilūn* (46 times), *naʿqilu* (once), and *yaʿqiluhā* (once). The interrogative phrase *afalā taʿqilūn* appears 13 times. Examples of these occurrences include: *Sūrah al-Mu'minūn*, 23:80 which, after pointing to God's power over life and death and "the alternation of night and day," asks its listeners, "Will you not, then, use your reason (*afalā taʿqilūn*)?" In *Sūrah al-Naḥl*, 16:67 God reminds us of the nourishment He provides through "date-palms and vines." He then adds that in these things "there is a message indeed for people who use their reason" (*inna fī dhālika la āyatan li qawmin yaʿqilūn*; cf. 16:13) Likewise, *Sūrah al-Mā'idah*, 5:58 states that certain people who mock the call to prayer "do not use their reason" (*lā yaʿqilūn*; cf. *Sūrah al-Anfāl*, 8:22). In other words, their intelligence does nothing to deter them from engaging in morally reprehensible behavior. It has also been suggested that this verse is saying that they fail to realize the reward they would enjoy if they obeyed God and His Messenger. The fact that they "do not use their reason" does not mean that they have no intelligence or understanding, however. Rather, it means simply that they are failing to respond to God's call due either to pride or to a lack of conviction. The evidence against them stands, however, since, despite their lack of conviction, they do understand the message they have heard.

Philosophers and ethicists view the mind as a non-material essence that is nevertheless associated with matter in the course of its operation. The expressive entity to which each of us refers as "I", the mind has been described as a light in the heart that recognizes truth and falsehood. In sum, the *ʿaql* may be described variously as: (1) the attribute that distinguishes human beings from other living creatures, (2) the capacity by which we recognize the possibility of what is possible, and the impossibility of what is impossible, (3) knowledge gleaned from experience, and (4) an instinctive force by means of which a person is able to squelch cravings for immediate gratification, but which differs in strength from one person to another.

2) *The concept of ḥajr*

The triliteral root *ḥ-j-r* denotes the act of hindering, detaining, prohibiting, or denying access to something. One might state that a ruler *ḥajar ʿalā al-safīh*, that is, he denied a legally incompetent person access to his wealth and forbade him to dispose of it. The mind is sometimes referred to with the word *ḥijr*, since it acts to restrain a person from behaving in an unseemly manner. Found only once in the Qur'an, this use of the word *ḥijr* occurs in *Sūrah al-Fajr*, 89:5, which refers to those "endowed with reason" (*dhī ḥijr*). Hence, the roots *ʿa-q-l* and *ḥ-j-r* share in common the denotation of restraining and holding back.

3) *The concept of nuhā*

The root *n-h-y* denotes: (1) the reaching of a goal or end, and (2) prohibition or restraint. The noun *nuhyah* (plural, *nuhā*) is used to refer to reason or the mind because it restrains us from engaging in shameful actions. It has been suggested that another reason the mind is referred to with the word *nuhyah* is that reason (*al-ʿaql*) causes one to stop (*yantahī*, derived from *nahā*) at what God has commanded rather than exceeding the limits He has set. The word *nuhyah* can thus be seen to be related to the noun *nihāyah*, meaning end or limit. Similarly, the verb *anhā/yunhī* (verbal noun, *inhā'*) may be used synonymously with *ablagha/yublighu* (verbal noun, *iblāgh*), meaning to transmit or conduct something to a termination point. The adjective *manhāh* is used to describe someone who is sensible and insightful. Alternate forms of this adjective include *nahī* and *nahin* (plural, *nahīn*).

Derivatives of the root *n-h-y* occur twice in the Qur'an. *Sūrah Ṭāhā*, 20:54 declares that Nature holds messages "for those who are endowed with reason" (*li ūlī al-nuhā*). Only those who use their reason benefit from these messages, since only they take them to heart; only they comprehend the rational evidence God has placed in the natural world for the reality of the resurrection of the dead. Such evidence is found in the way plants are brought back to life after the earth "dies" during the winter months, and in the way God brought us into being out of nothing. In short, people's minds (*al-nuhā*) act to restrain them (*tanhāhum*) from unseemly comport, and stop (*tantahī*) at the limits God has set for them.

4) *The concept of qalb*

The root *q-l-b* has two primary denotations: (1) the essence or best part of something, and (2) to reverse, topple, or overturn. From the first denotation we derive the noun *qalb* (plural, *qulūb*), or heart, which is viewed as the purest, highest and most genuine part of something. From the second we derive the verb *qalaba*, meaning to overturn or turn inside out.

The noun *qalb* occurs 132 times in the Qur'an. Used to refer to the mind, we find the term in *Sūrah Qāf*, 50:37, which tells us that the Qur'an is "a reminder for everyone whose heart is wide-awake" (*li man kāna lahu qalb*), or, as Yusuf Ali renders it, "for any that has a heart and understanding." *Sūrah al-Ḥashr*, 59:14 describes the foes against which the Muslim community was fighting with the words, "their hearts are at odds [with one another]" (*qulūbuhum shattā*). So, although the word *qalb* can refer to the physical organ located in the left half of the thoracic cavity, it is used figuratively in the Qur'an to refer to a person's emotions, thoughts and feelings. The word *qalb* is also used to refer to the seat of reason, knowledge, courage, fear and illness, while the word *ṣadr*, meaning chest, has been used to refer to the seat of cravings, desires, caprice, whim, anger, and the like.

The Qur'an describes the heart in many ways. It speaks of the heart as capable of rancor; of soundness or illness (*Sūrah al-Mā'idah*, 5:52; *Sūrah al-Ṣāffāt*, 37:84 and *Sūrah al-Aḥzāb*, 33:32), pride and overbearingness (*Sūrah Ghāfir*, 40:35), repentance (*Sūrah Qāf*, 50:33), sin and righteousness (*Sūrah al-Baqarah*, 2:283, *Sūrah al-Muṭaffifīn*, 83:14), mercy and harshness (*Sūrah Āl ʿImrān*, 3:159; *Sūrah al-Ḥadīd*, 57:27); tranquility (*Sūrah al-Raʿd*, 13:28), terror (*Sūrah Āl ʿImrān*, 3:151), understanding (*Sūrah al-Anʿām*, 6:25; *Sūrah al-Ḥajj*, 22:46), blindness (*Sūrah al-Ḥajj*, 22:46), revulsion (*Sūrah al-Zumar*, 39:45); denial (*Sūrah al-Naḥl*, 16:22), trembling (*Sūrah al-Nāziʿāt*, 79:8), listening (*Sūrah al-Taḥrīm*, 66:4), reverence (*Sūrah al-Anfāl*, 8:2; *Sūrah al-Ḥadīd*, 57:16), waywardness (*Sūrah Āl ʿImrān*, 3:7; *Sūrah al-Tawbah*, 9:117), regret (*Sūrah Āl ʿImrān*, 3:156), hardness (*Sūrah al-Baqarah*, 2:74; *Sūrah al-Mā'idah*, 5:13), hypocrisy (*Sūrah al-Tawbah*, 9:77); skepticism and faith (*Sūrah al-Tawbah*, 9:45; *Sūrah al-Mujādalah*, 58:22), and God-consciousness (*Sūrah al-Ḥajj*, 22:32; *Sūrah al-Ḥujurāt*, 49:3). It speaks of God sealing or closing hearts (*Sūrah al-Baqarah*, 2:7, *Sūrah al-Aʿrāf*, 7:101; *Sūrah Muḥammad*, 47:24), testing hearts (*Sūrah al-Baqarah*, 3:154); unifying hearts (*Sūrah al-Anfāl*, 8:63); and strengthening hearts (*Sūrah al-Qaṣaṣ*, 28:10). From this sampling of references it will be apparent that the heart (*qalb*) is spoken of in the Qur'an as the seat of thought and emotion, knowledge and faith, as well as that of ignorance and suspicion, doubt and hypocrisy.

5) *The concept of lubb*

The root *l-b-b* conveys two primary meanings: (1) that of remaining, abiding, and steadfastness, and (2) purity, goodness, inner essence. The verb *alabba/yulibbu* means to stay or remain (verbal noun, *ilbāb*), while the phrase *labbayka* which pilgrims in Makkah address to God has been interpreted to mean, "I will remain steadfastly obedient to You." As for the second meaning, it yields derivatives such as *lubb*, which means the essence, gist, or best part of something – hence, also, the mind or heart. From it we derive the adjective *labīb*, meaning intelligent and understanding, and the noun *labbah*, which refers to the upper part of the chest.

The *lubb* is reason purged of all impurities and steeped in the highest human ideals. Hence, every *lubb* may be classified as a *ʿaql*, but not every *ʿaql* qualifies as a *lubb*. The function of the *lubb* in the Qur'an is to convey a reminder that leads to inner purity, openness to the lessons God has to teach us, and obedience to God's commands. The plural *albāb* occurs 16 times in the Qur'an in a reference to those with acute God-consciousness and discerning, willing hearts and minds. *Sūrah Āl ʿImrān*, 3:7, for example, speaks of those who believe in God's revelation and who say, "...The whole [of the divine writ] is from our Sustainer." To this the Qur'an adds that no one bears this truth in mind but "those who are endowed with insight" (*ūlū al-albāb*). Those referred to in the Qur'an as *ūlū al-albāb* are mentioned in four places in connection with God-consciousness (see, for example, *Sūrah al-Baqarah*, 2:179). In ten places, *ūlū al-albāb* are mentioned in association with mindfulness or remembrance (see, for example, *Sūrah al-Baqarah*, 2:269; *Sūrah al-Raʿd*, 13:19; *Sūrah al-Mā'idah*, 5:100), and in *Sūrah Yūsuf*, 12:111, their mention is associated with "a lesson" (*ʿibrah*) addressed to them. In *Sūrah Ghāfir*, 40:54, we are told that the revelations God has sent down are meant "as a [means of] guidance and a reminder for those who were endowed with insight" (*hudan wa dhikra li ūlī al-albāb*). After giving details concerning the "law of retribution" (*al-qiṣāṣ*), *Sūrah al-Baqarah*, 2:178-179 addresses those who are "endowed with insight" (*ūlī al-albāb*), assuring them that this law is a source of life for people. Only *ūlī al-albāb* have the discernment to understand that, despite the harshness of the law of retribution, it embodies divine wisdom and mercy because, by virtue of the fear it instills in people's hearts, it deters them from wrongdoing.

6) *The concept of fū'ād*

The root *f-'-d* denotes fever, heat and intensity. Thus we might say, *fa'adtu al-laḥm*, "I roasted the meat." The heart is sometimes referred to by the noun *fū'ād* due to its warmth, the while the noun *mif'ad* refers to a metal skewer on which meat is roasted. The verb *ifta'ada/yafta'idu* means to be afflicted with a fearful heart.

The term *fū'ād*, which is consistently employed in a positive sense, occurs sixteen times in the Qur'an in the sense of 'heart' (*qalb*). There has been some disagreement as to what the word *fū'ād* means specifically in relation to the *qalb*, with some linguists holding that the *qalb* is located inside the *fū'ād* (in other words, that the word *fū'ād* refers to the membrane surrounding the *qalb*), and others holding that the *fū'ād* refers to the center of the *qalb*. Using the plural *af'idah*, the Qur'an declares God to be the One who has endowed human beings with "hearing, and sight, and hearts" (*al-samʿa wa al-abṣāra wa al-af'idah*) (*Sūrah al-Mulk*, 67:23; cf. *Sūrah al-Naḥl*, 16:78).

7) *The concept of ṣadr*

The root *ṣ-d-r* conveys two basic meanings. The first of these is the act of coming away from a water source (*al-ṣudūr ʿan al-māʾ*) after drinking (as opposed to *al-wird*, the act of coming to water to drink). The second is the chest (*ṣadr*, plural, *ṣudūr*). Used figuratively, the noun *ṣadr* refers to the highest or most anterior part of something.

The word *ṣadr* occurs 44 times in the Qur'an in figurative reference to the human chest, or bosom, as the seat of the will, the passions, faith, unbelief, and knowledge. Qur'anic uses of the word *qalb* refer to the locus of reason and knowledge; its uses of the word *ṣadr* likewise refer to the seat of reason and knowledge; however, the *ṣadr* is also portrayed as the locus of emotions and inward states such as desire, passion, rage, fear and terror. *Sūrah Āl ʿImrān*, 3:154 tells the Muslim community that God had allowed certain trials and temptations in order to "test... and purge (*li yumaḥḥisa*) what is in your hearts (*mā fī qulūbikum*)," since, it goes on to say, "for God is aware of what is in the hearts [of men]" (*dhāt al-ṣudūr*). The fact that both terms – *qulūb* and *ṣudūr* – are used here indicates a distinction between them in terms of function. The Qur'an speaks of God's testing and purging people's hearts (*qulūb*) as the loci of intelligence, discernment and recollection based on what has been stored in their bosoms (*ṣudūr*) by way of surrender to God or unbelief. *Sūrah al-ʿAnkabūt*, 29:10 asks rhetorically, "Is not God fully aware of what is in the hearts of all creatures? (*ṣudūr al-ʿālamīn*)?" The *ṣadr* as the locus of faith or unbelief is spoken of in *Sūrah al-Naḥl*, 16:106, according to which a person can open his or her heart (*ṣadr*) to unbelief (*kufr*). Similarly, it is into people's bosoms (*ṣudūr al-nās*) that deceptive, evil promptings are 'whispered' by the Tempter (*Sūrah al-Nās*, 114:4-5). *Sūrah al-ʿAnkabūt*, 29:49 tells us that the Qur'an consists of clear messages (*āyātun bayyināt*) that make their way into the hearts (*ṣudūr*) of those who have been endowed with knowledge (*alladhīn ūtū al-ʿilm*).

8) *The concept of fiqh*

The root *f-q-h* refers to the act of comprehending. The verb is *faqaha/yafqahu* and the verbal noun is *fiqh*. On one level, all knowledge, or *ʿilm*, is a kind of *fiqh*, or understanding. However, the word *fiqh* has come to be associated particularly with knowledge of Islamic Law and the proper distinctions between the permitted and the prohibited, truth and falsehood.

The verbal form of the root *f-q-h* occurs 20 times in the Qur'an in a sense that is narrower than that of *ʿilm*. *Sūrah Hūd*, 11:91 reports the words of the people of the prophet Shuʿayb, who said to him, "O Shu'ayb! We cannot grasp the purport of much of what you say" (*mā nafqahu kathīran mimmā taqūl*) (cf. *Sūrah al-Isrā'*, 17:44; *Sūrah Ṭāhā*, 20:28, *Sūrah al-Nisā'*, 4:78; and *Sūrah al-Tawbah*, 9:87). It has been suggested that the meaning of the phrase *mā nafqahu* here means not that they did not understand the meaning of what Shuʿayb was saying but, rather, that they were not convinced by it. For had they not understood it, they would not have been held accountable for their rejection of him. The basis for accountability is simply that one understand the prophet's message, not that one be persuaded by it. The act of *fiqh* is attributed to the *qalb*; this may be seen in *Sūrah al-Aʿrāf*, 7:179, which condemns people "who have hearts with which they fail (or, rather, refuse) to grasp the truth" (*lahum qulūbun lā yafqahūna bihā*). (See also *Sūrah al-Tawbah*, 9:127 and *Sūrah al-Anʿām*, 6:25).

Lastly, the verb form *tafaqqah* is used to refer to the pursuit of knowledge, particularly of one's religion. *Sūrah al-Tawbah*, 9:122 contains an exhortation to Muslims to familiarize themselves with Islamic legal rulings, to share this knowledge with others, and to warn them of the dangers of failing to comply with them.

9) *The concept of fahm*

The root *f-h-m* denotes the act of understanding and seeing something as it really is. The verb is *fahima/yafhamu* (verbal noun, *fahm*); the derivative form of the verb *tafahamma/yatafahhamu* (verbal noun, *tafahhum*) means to come to understand something gradually or in stages, and the intensive form *fahhama/yufahhimu* means to cause someone else to understand. This intensive verb form, which takes both a direct and an indirect object, is found in *Sūrah al-Anbiyā'*, 21:79: "We made Solomon understand the case [more profoundly] (*fahhamnāhā sulaymān*)." We are told in *Sūrah al-Anbiyā'*, 21:79 that God endowed Solomon with unique understanding of a case on which he and his father David were ruling. The word *fahm* has likewise been understood to mean a precise, nuanced grasp of something. In other words, there are varying levels of understanding or comprehension, and not everything that is understood is known. Rather, one might reach a certain level of understanding via speculation or guesswork.

10) *The concept of iḥāṭah*

The root *ḥ-w-ṭ* denotes the act of guarding about, protecting, preserving, watching over, surrounding, and taking responsibility for. From this root we derive the active participle, *ḥā'iṭ*, which refers to a wall (plural, *ḥīṭān*). In conjunction with the preposition *bi*, the verb form *aḥāṭa/yuḥīṭu* is used 23 times in the Qur'an in the following senses: (1) Knowing or comprehending. *Sūrah al-Jinn*, 72:28 tells us that God "encompasses [with His knowledge] all that they had [to say]" (*aḥāṭa bi mā ladayhim*), while *Sūrah al-Baqarah*, 2:255 affirms that human beings cannot encompass any of God's knowledge apart from His will (*lā yuḥīṭūna bi shay'in min ʿilmihi illā bi mā shā'*) (cf. *Sūrah Yūnus*, 10:39; *Sūrah al-Kahf*, 18:68; and *Sūrah al-Naml*, 27:22). (2) Encompassing. *Sūrah al-Baqarah*, 2:19 tells us that "God encompasses [with His might] all who deny the truth" (*muḥīṭun bil-kāfirīn*) (cf. *Sūrah Fuṣṣilat*, 41:54). (3) Destruction. *Sūrah al-Baqarah*, 2:81 tells us that the unrepentant on Judgment Day will be encompassed (i.e., destroyed) by their sins (*aḥāṭat bihi khaṭī'atuhu*) (cf. *Sūrah al-Kahf*, 18:29, 42; and *Sūrah al-ʿAnkabūt*, 29:54).

11) *The concept of tamḥīṣ*

The root *m-ḥ-ṣ* denotes an act of purifying, testing, examination or refinement. The verb is *maḥaṣa/yamḥaṣu* (verbal noun, *maḥṣ*), or *maḥḥaṣa/yumaḥḥiṣu* (verbal noun, *tamḥīṣ*). The verb *maḥḥaṣa* occurs twice in the Qur'an. *Sūrah Āl ʿImrān*, 3:141 tells us that God tests people with both bad fortune and good in order to "render pure of all dross those who have attained to faith" (*li yumaḥḥiṣa Allāhu al-ladhīna āmanū*). Similarly, God declares to the Muslim community in *Sūrah Āl ʿImrān*, 3:154 that "[all this befell you] so that God might...render your innermost hearts pure of all dross" (*li yumaḥḥiṣa mā fī qulūbikum*). Hence, by testing believers through affliction and suffering, God purifies them of their sins and faults.

12) *The concept of tamyīz*

The root *m-y-z* denotes the separation of one thing from another. From this root we derive the verb *māza/yamīzu* (*mayz*) and *mayyaza/yumayyizu* (*tamyīz*). The verb *mayyaza* means to prefer someone or something over another, to set apart or isolate. The verbal noun *tamyīz* refers to the faculty of discernment – the mind's ability to recognize distinctions and similarities among entities. Muslim jurists define the age of discernment as the age at which one can distinguish between what is beneficial and what is harmful.

The verbal form of this root occurs in four places in the Qur'an, including *Sūrah al-Anfāl*, 8:37, which tells us that when judging human beings after death, God will "separate the bad from the good" (*yamīza Allāhu al-khabītha min al-ṭayyib*), and *Sūrah Yāsīn*, 36:59, where we are told that on the Day of Judgment God will say to those who had rejected Him, "...stand aside today, O you who were lost in sin!" (*imtāzū ayyuhā al-mujrimūn*).

13) *The concept of tafakkur*

The root *f-k-r* denotes the act of meditating, pondering, reflecting on, or examining over and over. From it we derive the verbs *fakkara/yufakkiru* (*tafkīr*), meaning to think or cogitate, and *tafakkara/yatafakkaru* (*tafakkur*), meaning to reflect or ponder on evidence or phenomena toward the formation of an image, understanding or conceptualization. The intensive adjective *fikkīr* describes someone who is thoughtful and meditative. However, due to the process of change that is involved in *tafakkur*, it is not attributable to God in His immutability.

Verbal derivatives of the root *f-k-r* occur eighteen times in the Qur'an, while the Qur'anic concepts of *tadhakkur*, *tadabbur*, *ta'ammul*, *istibṣār*, and *iʿtibār* share some common features with that of *tafakkur*. *Sūrah Āl ʿImrān*, 3:191 commends those who keep God in mind throughout the day and night, and who thus "reflect on the creation of the heavens and the earth" (*wa yatafakkarūn fī khalqi al-samāwāti wa al-arḍ*). Similarly, the Qur'an urges us to give thought to the variety in people's races, languages and cultures, deriving as they do from one Single Source. *Sūrah al-Rūm*, 30:21 declares: "And among His wonders is this: He creates for you mates out of your own kind, so that you might incline towards them, and He engenders love and tenderness between you: in this, behold, there are messages indeed for people who think (*inna fī dhālika la āyātin li qawmin yatafakka-rūn*)!" Hence, the phenomena of reproduction, marriage and loving companionship shared by husbands and wives are presented as topics for reverent reflection.

Other references to the act of reflection are found in *Sūrah al-Rūm*, 30:8, which asks concerning people who have no awareness of things ultimate, "Have they never learned to think for themselves (*alam yatafakkarū*)?" In *Sūrah al-Aʿrāf*, 7:176, the Prophet is urged to tell people stories that convey spiritual lessons "so that they might take thought" (*laʿallahum yatafakkarūn*). *Sūrah al-Ḥashr*, 59:21 tells us, in a similar vein, that God compares the power of the Qur'an with that of a force that breaks even mountains asunder. To this He adds, "And [all] such parables We propound unto men, so that they might [learn to] think" (*laʿallahum yatafakkarūn*)."

14) *The concept of tadabbur*

The root *d-b-r* denotes the end, final part, or rear of something. From it we derive the noun *dubur* (the opposite of *qubul*), which refers to the rear part or back side of something. The intensified verb *dabbara/yud-abbiru* (*tadbīr*) means to manage, organize, dispose of, or bring about. It can also refer to the act of freeing a slave after his/her death (literally, "from behind", *min dubur*). As for the verb *tadabbara/yatadabbaru* (*tadabbur*), it denotes the act of thinking about or investigating something's final outcomes or ultimate consequences.

Derivatives of the root *d-b-r* occur 46 times in the Qur'an in the following senses: (1) Back. In *Sūrah al-Anfāl*, 8:15, God commands the Muslim fighters to stand their ground against the polytheists, saying, "do not turn your backs on them" (*lā tuwallūhum al-adbār*). In the following verse (8:16), God warns them that any of them who "turns his back on them" (*yuwallihim... duburahu*) in flight will earn God's condemnation. The same sense of the word is used figuratively in *Sūrah Muḥammad*, 47:25, which describes those who have rejected God's message delivered through Muhammad as those who have turned their backs (*alladhīn irtaddū ʿalā adbārihim*) on the truth. (3) The end of something. *Sūrah Qāf*, 50:40 urges believers to extol God's glory "at every prayer's end" or "after the postures of adoration" (*adbār al-sujūd*). (4) Departing, receding into the past. *Sūrah al-Muddaththir*, 74:33 urges us to consider "the night when it departs (*al-layli idh adbara*)." (5) The last part of something. *Sūrah al-Anʿām*, 6:45 speaks of how "the last remnant of those folk who had been bent on evildoing was wiped out" (*quṭiʿa dābir al-qawmi alladhīna ẓalamū*). (6) Reflection or contemplation. *Sūrah al-Nisā'* 4:82 asks whether people "reflect on the Qur'an" (*afalā yatadabbarūn al-qu'rān*). (See also *Sūrah Muḥammad*, 47:24). (7) Management, disposal, governance. *Sūrah Yūnus*, 10:31 tells us that it is God Who "governs all that exists" (*yudabbiru al-amr*). (See *Sūrah al-Sajdah*, 32:5, *Sūrah al-Mu'minūn*, 23:68, and *Sūrah Ṣād*, 38:29).

15) *The concept of tadhakkur*

The triliteral root *dh-k-r* denotes several meanings: (1) male (*dhakar*) as opposed to female (*unthā*), (2) remembering (*dhikr*) as opposed to forgetting (*nisyān*), from which we derive the related meaning of mentioning or invocation (*dhikr*), which is a kind of remembrance with the tongue, and (3) honor, renown or good repute. Other derivatives of this root include the verbs *dhakkara*, to remind (verbal noun, *tadhkīr*), *dhākara* (*mudhākarah*) and *istadhkara* (*istidhkār*), meaning to study or recall, and the noun *tadhkirah* (a memento or keepsake, i.e., something that triggers or preserves a memory).

Derivatives of this root occur approximately 274 times in the Qur'an, and in the following senses: (1) A divine message or reminder. The Qur'an is spoken of in *Sūrah Ṣād*, 38:87 as "a reminder to all the worlds" (*dhikrun li al-ʿālamīn*). (See also *Sūrah al-Anbiyā'*, 21:24; and *Sūrah al-Qamar*, 54:25), (2) the Qur'anic revelation (*Sūrah al-Ḥijr*, 15:9). (3) Pre-Qur'anic revelation (the revelations given to Jews and Christians). The Prophet is told by God to tell those who deny the truth to "ask the followers of earlier revelation" (*is'alū ahl al-dhikr*) for greater understanding (*Sūrah al-Anbiyā'*, 21:7). (4) The revelation to Moses. This sense of the word *dhikr* is found in *Sūrah al-Anbiyā'*, 21:105, which speaks of the Psalms (*al-zabūr*) having come "after the Message (given to Moses)" (*baʿdi al-dhikri*). (5) Admonition, reminder, or warning. This sense of the word *dhikr* is found in *Sūrah Ṣād*, 38:1, which describes the Qur'an as being "full of admonition" (*dhī al-dhikr*, Abdullah Yusuf Ali; cf. the verbal form used in *Sūrah al-Anʿām*, 6:44). (6) Remembrance of God. Believers are told in *Sūrah al-Jumʿah*, 62:9 to "hasten to the remembrance of God (*fasʿaw ilā dhikr Allāh*)" when they hear the call to prayer (cf. *Sūrah Ṭāhā*, 20:124; *Sūrah Āl ʿImrān*, 3:135; *Sūrah al-Nisā'*, 4:103; *Sūrah al-Baqarah*, 2:152). (7) Honor or eminence. God tells the Prophet in *Sūrah al-Zukhruf*, 43:44 to hold fast the revelation he has been given, because it will be "[a source of] eminence for you and your people" (*dhikrun laka wa li qawmika*). (8) To mention. In *Sūrah Yūsuf*, 12:42, we are told that Joseph asked a fellow prisoner who would soon be freed to "mention me to your master" (*udhkurnī ʿinda rabbika*). (9) To observe, remember, or bear in mind. The Children of Israel were exhorted to "bear in mind" what was contained in the revelation they had received through Moses (*Sūrah al-Baqarah*, 2:63; *Sūrah Hūd*, 11:24; *Sūrah al-Nūr*, 24:1; *Sūrah al-Zumar*, 39:27). This sense of the word is also found in *Sūrah Ghāfir*, 40:44, where, after admonishing his people for their rejection of God's message, a certain believer in the time of Moses warned his hearers of the Day of Judgment. To this he added, "at that time you will remember (*sa tadhkurūna*) what I am telling you (*mā aqūlu lakum*)."

The verb *tadhakkar*, meaning "bear in mind" is often paired with the phrase "those endowed with insight" (*ūlū al-albāb*). For this pairing, see, for example, *Sūrah al-Baqarah*, 2:269; *Sūrah al-Raʿd*, 13:19; and *Sūrah Ṣād*, 38:29.

The word *dhikr* has been understood in different senses due to the way its meaning is specified by its various Qur'anic contexts. As we have seen, the word *dhikr* is used variously to refer to obedience, admonition, the Qur'an, elucidation, mentioning, reflection or contemplation. The act of remembering (*tadhakkur*) is an attempt to recover images stored in one's memory. Especially when one is remembering God, this process brings one into closer touch with his or her environment. As we saw in *Sūrah al-Aʿrāf*, 7:201, the act of bringing God to mind gives one a clearer perception of one's surroundings. In this context, the concept of *dhikr* is contrasted with unawareness, forgetfulness and oblivion. Remembering (*tadhakkur*) is similar to reflection (*tafakkur*), since reflection involves the contemplation of what one knows, while remembering involves the summoning of knowledge that one needs to be mindful of after a time of unawareness or forgetfulness. As we read in *Sūrah al-Aʿrāf*, 7:201, when those who are conscious of God are assailed by an evil thought, they "bring God to remembrance (*tadhakkarū*)" (Abdullah Yusuf Ali), and in so doing, are able to see the world around them more clearly (*fa idhā hum mubṣirūn*). The act of remembering (*tadhakkur*) confirms, preserves, and renders more effective the knowledge one already possesses, while the act of reflecting (*tafakkur*) may increase knowledge as well. The Qur'anic contexts in which the various forms of the word *tadhakkur* occur have to do with the clarification of matters of doctrine, comparisons between those with faith and those who deny the truth, reflection on final outcomes (judgment, resurrection), and self-examination. As mentioned, the verb *tadhakkar* is often associated with the phrase *ūlī al-albāb*, translated by Asad as "those endowed with insight," and by Abdullah Yusuf Ali as "men [sic] of understanding" (*Sūrah al-Baqarah*, 2:269 and *Sūrah al-Raʿd*, 13:19).

16) *The concept of ḥifẓ*

The triliteral root *ḥ-f-ẓ* denotes the act of preserving or observing. It is used in the sense of memorization, which serves to preserve knowledge, as well as in relation to the preservation of life, safety, food, and so on. One of the Divine Names is *al-Ḥafīẓ*, the Preserver, the One whose notice nothing escapes on earth or in the heavenly realms, while angels are sometimes referred to as *hafaẓah*, meaning guardians or caretakers who enumerate and record people's thoughts and actions.

Derivatives of the root *ḥ-f-ẓ* occur 44 times in the Qur'an, and in the following senses: (1) Entrusting to someone's care. *Sūrah al-Mā'idah*, 5:44 tells us that some of God's messages had been entrusted to people's care (*ustuḥfiẓū min kitābi Allāh*). (2) Guarding, preserving, protecting. *Sūrah al-Nisā'*, 4:34 speaks of righteous women who guard the privacy of their conjugal lives, while *Sūrah al-Ṣāffāt* 37:7 uses the noun *ḥifẓ* in relation to God's protection of the heavenly spheres. In *Sūrah Yūsuf*, 12:12, Joseph's brothers promise to protect him, saying,

"We shall guard him well" (*innā lahu la ḥāfiẓūn*; cf. 12:63). And in *Sūrah Yūsuf*, 12:55, Joseph promises to take good care of Egypt's resources, saying, "Behold, I shall be a good and knowing keeper" (*innī ḥafīẓun ʿalīm*). (3) Witnessing and recording. The phrase *ḥāfiẓīn kirāman kātibīn*, which translates literally as "noble preservers who record" refers to the angels God has appointed to watch over people and record their thoughts and actions (*Sūrah al-Infiṭār*, 82:10-11).

Preservation (*ḥifẓ*) is one of the primary functions of the human mind, which stores knowledge through memory, while memory is one measure of a person's intelligence. As such, the process of *ḥifẓ* refers to the establishment of what has been understood in one's mind lest it be forgotten and lost. This process is followed by emotive response (*shuʿūr*) and understanding, which is followed in turn by remembering and reflection. God condemns those who simply memorize without understanding, likening them to "an ass that carries a load of books" (*Sūrah al-Jumʿah*, 62:5). Similarly acquiring knowledge without memorization is like building an edifice on a steep precipice from which it is liable to slide at any moment into the abyss.

17) *The concept of waʿy*

The triliteral root w-ʿy denotes the act of holding or containing. Used figuratively, the verb *waʿā* refers to the act of retaining something in memory, hence, knowing it or being aware of it. The verbal noun *waʿy*, generally translated as "consciousness," refers to the heart's or mind's act of containing or preserving something, while the adjective *waʿiyyun* means knowledgeable, astute and understanding.

Derivatives of this root occur seven times in the Qur'an in the following senses: (1) A container. *Sūrah Yūsuf*, 12:76 refers to the travel bags of Joseph's brothers with the word *awʿiyatihim*, and to his brother Benjamin's bag with the singular *wiʿā'*. (2) Concealment. *Sūrah al-Inshiqāq*, 84:22-23 tells us that God is fully aware of what those who deny the truth "conceal" (*yūʿūn*). (3) Reflection and contemplation. *Sūrah al-Ḥāqqah*, 69:12 describes the great flood that occurred during the time of Noah as a message which "every wide-awake ear might consciously take in" (*taʿiyahā udhnun wāʿiyah*). (4) Withholding. *Sūrah al-Maʿārij*, 70:18 uses the verb *awʿā* to refer to the withholding of wealth that one has amassed.

18) *The concept of wijdān*

The triliteral root *w-j-d* denotes several different meanings. One of these is to find in the sense of reaching something one has sought. Another is to find in the sense of discovering or perceiving, as in, "I found Zayd [to be] generous and noble" (*wajadtu zaydan karīman*). Used in this sense, the verb *wajada* takes a double object.

Derivatives of the root *w-j-d* occur in 106 places in the Qur'an, and in two primary senses: (1) Discovery. We are told in *Sūrah Āl ʿImrān*, 3:37 that whenever Zachariah visited Mary in the sanctuary, he "found her provided with food" (*wajada ʿindahā rizqan*)." Similarly, we read in *Sūrah al-Baqarah*, 2:96 that although certain individuals claim to have a blissful afterlife awaiting them, "you will most certainly find that they cling to life more eagerly than any other people..." (*la tajidannahum aḥraṣ al-nāsi ʿalā ḥayāh*). A similar sense is found in *Sūrah al-Mā'idah*, 5:104 where we are told that when the polytheists of the Prophet's day were urged to respond to his message, they said, "Enough for us is that which we found our forefathers believing in and doing (*ḥasbunā mā wajadnā ʿalayhi ābā'anā*)."

19) *The concept of nisyān*

The root *n-s-y* denotes two basic meanings. The first is that of forgetting as opposed to remembering or memorizing something, while the second is that of omitting or leaving out. The triliteral verb is *nasiya/yansā*, while the verbal noun is *nisyān*.

Derivatives of the root *n-s-y* occur 45 times in the Qur'an in two basic senses: (1) being unaware of or oblivious to, and (2) omitting or neglecting. The first sense denotes the opposite of remembering, and from this we derive the adjective *nasī* (forgetful, oblivious), and *nisyān* (forgetting, oblivion). *Nisyān* has been described as the absence of a mental image from one's conscious mind, although it remains somewhere deep in the memory. The act of forgetting, or *nisyān* is condemned by God in the Qur'an in both of these senses, although it sometimes occurs unintentionally, in which case it may be excused. When the act of *nisyān* is attributed to God, it denotes conscious abandonment. In *Sūrah al-Aʿrāf*, 7:51, for example, God declares that just as deniers of the truth were heedless of Him during their earthly lives, "so We shall be oblivious of them today (*fa al-yawma nansāhum*) as they were oblivious of (*kamā nasū*) the coming of this their Day [of Judgment] (*liqā'a yawmihim hādhā*)." Another example of the use of this root is found in *Sūrah Ṭāhā*, 20:115, where God states, "Indeed, long ago did We impose Our commandment on Adam (*wa laqad ʿahidnā ilā ādama min qablu*); but he forgot [it] (*fa nasiya*)."

20) *The concept of sahw*

The triliteral root *s-h-w* refers primarily to inattentiveness and passivity. One might say, for example, *sahawtu ʿan al-ṣalāh*, "I was distracted from (or during) the ritual prayer." Whereas *sahw* denotes a minor and temporary lapse of memory or attentiveness, *nisyān* refers to something's complete absence from consciousness; nevertheless, the two words are sometimes used more or less synonymously. The heedlessness involved in *sahw* is of two types. One type takes place due to factors outside of a person's control, while the other, being born of neglect or rebellion, originates in a person's will. Hence, like *nisyān*, some instances of *sahw* are more blameworthy than others.

The plural active participle, *sāhūn* occurs twice in the Qur'an. *Sūrah al-Dhāriyāt*, 51:10-11 speaks in condemnation of those who guess blindly about things of which they know nothing and "who blunder along, in ignorance lost" (*hum fī ghamratin sāhūn*), while *Sūrah al-Māʿūn*, 107:4-5 chastises those who pray but "whose hearts from their prayer are remote" (*fawaylun lil-muṣallīn alladhīna hum ʿan ṣalātihim sāhūn*).

21) *The concept of ghaflah*

The root *gh-f-l* denotes the act of inadvertently neglecting or omitting something. The word *ghaflah* refers to a failure to perceive or comprehend something despite having the wherewithal to perceive or comprehend it. We would say, *ghafaltu ʿan al-shay'* to mean, "I accidentally omitted something," or "I failed to notice something." If, on the other hand, we said, *aghfaltuhu*, it would mean that I omitted or neglected something despite its having been mentioned to me. The derivative verbs *taghaffala* and *taghāfala* denote the act of pretending not to have noticed something (in others words, ignoring something deliberately), while the form *ghaffala* refers to the act of causing someone else to fail to notice something, that is, of concealing it.

Derivatives of this root occur 35 times in the Qur'an in the sense of distraction or lack of attentiveness due to a lack of wakefulness or diligence. In some situations this has occurred as a punishment from God, and sometimes due to a failure of memory. The Qur'an negates inattentiveness of God Himself, saying, "God is not unmindful of what you do!" (*Sūrah al-Baqarah*, 2:74; cf. *Sūrah Āl ʿImrān*, 3:99, and *Sūrah al-Mu'minūn*, 23:17).

22) *The concept of shakk*

One denotation of the root *sh-k-k* is that of interpenetration. One might say, *shakaktuhu bil-ramḥ*, "I pierced it with the spear." A second denotation is that of a lack of certainty (the verbal noun *shakkun* meaning doubt or suspicion). If we say, *shakka ʿalayhi al-amru*, we mean, "The matter was unclear or doubtful to him." A third denotation of the verb *shakka* is to cohere or be interconnected.

The root *sh-k-k* occurs fifteen times in the Qur'an in the sense of uncertainty. We read in *Sūrah al-Nisā'*, 4:157 that those who disagree about the matter of Jesus' death on the cross are in a state of confusion or doubt about this (*fī shakkin minhu*). In *Sūrah Yūnus*, 10:94, those who are in doubt concerning (*fī shakkin mimmā*) the Qur'anic message are exhorted to ask those who received earlier revelations to give them greater understanding. *Sūrah Hūd*, 11:62 relates that after receiving his message, the people to whom the Prophet Ṣāliḥ came told him that they were "in grave doubt" (*fī shakkin...murīb*) concerning what he was calling them to do. Similarly, *Sūrah Ibrāhīm*, 14:10 asks rhetorically whether there can be "any doubt about [the existence and oneness of] God, the Originator of the heavens and the earth?" (*afīllāhi shakkun, fāṭir al-samāwāti wa al-arḍ*).

23) *The concept of rayb*

The triliteral root *r-y-b* denotes suspicion, misgiving and/or alarm. The verbs *rāba/yarību* and *arāba/yurību* mean to disquiet, alarm, or fill with suspicion or misgivings.

Derivatives of this root occur 37 times in the Qur'an, and in the following senses: (1) Doubt or suspicion. Those involved in financial transactions are urged in *Sūrah al-Baqarah*, 2:282 to have a scribe record how much money is owed lest the parties to the transaction have reason to doubt one another (*allā tartābū*). Using the nominal derivative of the root, *Sūrah al-Baqarah*, 2:2 tells us that the divine writ found in the Qur'an is "without doubt" (*lā rayba fīhi*). The word *rayb* is similar to *shakk* in that they both describe mental states characterized by a lack of certainty. However, the verbal derivatives of these roots are used differently. Hence, while we might say, *rābanī al-amru* ("The matter made me uneasy, suspicious"), we cannot used the verb *shakka* in this construction (*shakkanī al-amru*) to convey the same meaning. (2) Distress, regret or disquiet. *Sūrah al-Tawbah*, 9:110 tells us that the transgressions people commit will be "a source of deep disquiet in their hearts" (*rībatan fī qulūbihim*). (3) The vicissitudes of fate. Every reference to the root *r-y-b* in the Qur'an has to do with doubt or uncertainty in the heart with the exception of *Sūrah al-Ṭūr*, 52:30, which refers to the uncertainties of life as *rayb al-manūn*, where the noun *manūn* is a reference to Death or Fate. Specifically, *Sūrah al-Ṭūr*, 52:30 relates the words of skeptics in the Prophet's day, who said, "[He is but] a poet – let us await what time will do unto Him (*rayb al-manūn*)."

SECOND: SENSATION-RELATED CONCEPTS

All means of perception, outward and inward, innate and acquired, previously acquired information, whether on one's own or from others, as well as certainties that God has revealed through His prophets, contribute to the process of knowledge acquisition. The physical senses are like windows through which the cognitive faculties look out at the world. Hence the first path to knowledge acquisition is through sensory perception. The input received through the senses is recorded, after which the cognitive processes begin as the perceiver forms an image or impression of the entity being perceived.

As has been noted, sensation is the first phase of knowledge acquisition. It represents the first interaction between the knowing subject and the entity to be known. You might smell something without knowing what it is that you are smelling, or without recognizing the fragrance. Hence, physical perception alone is not cognition. In order for cognition to occur, the conscious mind needs also to be involved in the process. This fact is affirmed by the Qur'an's statement that, "You will see them looking at you, but they see not" (*tarāhum yanẓurūna ilayka wa hum lā yubṣirūn*) (*Sūrah al-Aʿrāf*, 7:198). The act of looking (*naẓar*) consists in directing one's gaze toward something or someone whereby one's eye receives an image of the person or object being looked at. The physical reception of the image, however, falls short of actual recognition of the person or thing whose image has been recorded. One might look at one of God's prophets, for example, yet without recognizing him as a prophet of God.

The act of looking consists in turning one's eyes toward a visible object. The outcome of this action is that of sight (*ru'yah* or *baṣar*), which may lead to insight (*baṣīrah*), that is, a perception of the inward nature of the entity seen. However, when there is a disagreement about the nature or identity of a person or object seen, this is generally not due to a flaw in the process of sense perception but, rather, due to how sensory data is interpreted. In other words, the conflict exists in the realm of cognition. Otherwise, there would be no basis for either agreement or disagreement, since the basis of our communication is shared access to the same sensory data.

There can be no cognition without formation of a judgment about concrete entities. Without the physical senses, reason has nothing to go on; hence, sensory perception and reason must work together. If the senses are inoperative, reason too will be rendered inoperative.

We read in *Sūrah al-Naḥl*, 16:78 that "God has brought you forth from your mothers' wombs knowing nothing – but He has endowed you with hearing, and sight, and minds, so that you might have cause to be grateful." We are told clearly in this verse that human beings come into this world devoid of all knowledge. At the same time, it points to the sources of knowledge God has given us in the form of hearing, vision, and reason. All conceptualization begins with the senses, the most fundamental of which are hearing and sight. The senses of touch, taste, and smell are also God-given, of course; however, they are of less significance epistemologically speaking. One of the first senses that come into play after birth is that of touch, which enables the human infant to experience a wide range of physical entities. However, touch is incapable of distinguishing colors and sounds. Sight can distinguish colors, shapes, and numerous other features; hearing can distinguish sounds; and the sense of taste distinguishes flavors of various kinds, especially with the aid of the olfactory glands.

On the level of the intangible, a child gradually develops moral discernment, the ability to distinguish between the possible and the impossible, as well as the ability to generalize such that a judgment that applies to a given entity is seen to apply similarly to another, identical entity. Another insight gained as discernment matures is that opposites cannot coexist in a single entity in the same respect, and that if one of two opposing propositions is true, then the other must be false. These fundamental axioms or intuitive propositions gradually crystallize in a person's mind and, as they do so, he or she becomes able to deduce theoretical knowledge from both self-evident truths and concrete evidence.

THE ROLE OF SENSATION IN KNOWLEDGE ACQUISITION

Sensory data alone does not lead to knowledge; it needs the assistance of the mind, or reason, whose roles include those of weighing evidence, analogical reasoning, and generalization. The Qur'an itself presents sensation and sensory data as doors to knowledge. When we are commanded to look both to "the horizons" and to our inner selves for signs of God's existence and majesty we are being told to consider the sensory evidence that we derive from these realms. We experience the world around us via sight, hearing, smell, taste and touch, while we receive the words of the Revelation via sight and hearing. At the same time, a rigid division of external realities into the categories of tangible and intangible (the latter being perceptible only through reason) is inaccurate. It should be remembered that the messages brought by the prophets about the world of the unseen (*al-ghayb*), including paradise, hellfire, angels and jinn, are virtually always couched in concrete language which points, in fact, to concrete realities. The same is true of the blessings enjoyed by those in paradise and the torments suffered by those in hellfire, which are physical and tangible. As we read in *Sūrah Ṭāhā*, 20:96, "I saw what they saw not." Even the spirit, and the Divine Essence itself, are entities that can be perceived via sight. We are told in *Sūrah al-Anʿām*, 6:103 concerning God that, "No human vision can encompass Him (*lā tudrikuhu al-abṣāru*)." The fact that this verse negates the possibility that human vision can "encompass" (*tudriku*) God is, in itself, an affirmation that some vision, however incomplete, is possible. However, given the fact that such realities are absent from the world of sense perception as we now know it, the Qur'an refers to them as *al-ghayb*, which might be rendered, "the realm of the absent," as over against *al-shahādah*, or "the realm of the present."

The reality from which reason acquires its data thus includes not only intangible entities, but, in addition, physical, tangible entities that are perceived through the physical senses. Sensation concerns itself with the realm outside of human beings, as well as their own physical beings (our bodies). This realm encompasses everything that can be heard, seen, smelled, tasted or touched. There is also, as we have seen, an inward sense, which includes feelings of pleasure and pain, joy and sadness, love and hatred, all of which are associated in the Qur'an with the heart (*al-qalb*). It is the heart that reflects on the signs in the cosmos, thus acquiring insight and knowledge, and which then reminds others of the need to engage in the same kind of reflection.

THE REALM OF SENSATION

Our senses enable us to experience and examine the things around us and to distinguish them from each other in such a way that we can relate to them in the most appropriate and beneficial ways in meeting life's challenges. The Creator has endowed our senses with precisely the right degrees of sensitivity; hence, if they were to be altered in some way, our perceptions would cease to work to our benefit, and might actually bring us harm. If our hearing were one hundred times more acute than it is, we would be able to pick up sounds with higher and lower frequencies than those we are able to hear at present, and our world would become a disturbing cacophony. If our vision were sharper we would be able to see worlds that are presently invisible to us, and we might well feel overwhelmed by all the things that had suddenly entered our range of vision.

The world of *shahādah*, or "the realm of what is present," is by definition that which is accessible to the physical senses. If something is not accessible to the senses, it is by definition not part of *ʿālam al-shahādah*. In this case, it might be either in the realm of thought and emotion, or in the realm of the metaphysical, or *al-ghayb*, which is "absent." This is not to say that *al-ghayb* is not tangible or physical in any way; rather, as we have noted, it has a tangible, material aspect, but it is not accessible to our physical senses as they exist at present. This fact is repeated in various places in the Qur'an. In *Sūrah Qāf*, 50:22, for example God addresses the godless on the Day of Judgment, saying, "You have been unmindful of this [Day of Judgment]; but now We have lifted from you your veil, and sharp is your sight today." In other words, what is not visible to people's eyes now will be visible to them on the Day of Resurrection. *Sūrah al-Ḥāqqah*, 69:38-39 also testifies to this truth in the words, "I call to witness all that you can see, as well as all that you cannot see!"

What follows is an enumeration of Qur'anic concepts and terms that relate to sensation in one way or another:

1) *The concept of ḥass*

The root *ḥ-s-s* denotes the following meanings: (1) To kill, from which we derive the passive participle *ḥasīs* (from *maḥsūs*, on the pattern of *mafʿūl/faʿīl*), which is synonymous with *qatīl*, or slain (from *maqtūl*). (2) The sound made by someone who is suspicious, uncertain, or in pain (*ḥasīs*). (3) To sense, feel, see, know or be aware of. From this sense we derive the verb *aḥassa/yuḥissu* (verbal noun, *iḥsās*), the noun *ḥāssah* (sense, as in the sense of smell, hearing, etc., plural, *ḥawāss*), as well as *ḥāsūs*, which is synonymous with *jāsūs*, or spy. Thus, one might liken the five senses (*al-ḥawāss al-khams*) to the mind's "spies" (*ḥawāsīs/jawāsīs*), in that they provide the mental faculties with the tangible input they need in order to understand, form judgments, and formulate intellectual and emotional responses to the world.

The root *ḥ-s-s* occurs six times in the Qur'an, and in the following senses: (1) Killing. In *Sūrah Āl ʿImrān*, 3:152, God tells the Muslim fighters that He kept His promise to them when, with His permission, they were about to destroy their enemies (*idh taḥussūnahum bi idhni-hi*). (2) Perception via the senses. *Sūrah Āl ʿImrān*, 3:52 speaks of how "Jesus became aware of" (*aḥassa ʿĪsā*) his enemies' unwillingness to believe in the truth (cf. *Sūrah Maryam*, 19:98). (3) Investigation, search for information. In *Sūrah Yūsuf*, 12:87, Jacob tells his sons to search out information about Joseph and their brother Benjamin, saying, "try to obtain some tidings of Joseph and his brother (*tahassasū min yūsuf wa akhīhi*)."

2) *The concept of shuʿūr*

The root *sh-ʿ-r* denotes several meanings. The first of these is a plant. There is a type of tree referred to as a *shaʿrah* (plural, *shaʿār*, which also refers to a forest). A derivative phrase is *dāhiyah shaʿrā'*, meaning "a great calamity." A second denotation of this root is the act of feeling, sensing, or knowing. From this sense we derive the noun *shiʿār*, which refers to a byword or watchword by means of which fighters on one side in an armed conflict recognize each other. Related phrases and words include *shuʿūr*, meaning feeling or perception, *shiʿr*, poetry (plural, *ashʿār*), *layta shiʿri*, meaning, "If only I knew, perceived, or understood," *shāʿir* (plural, *shuʿarā'*), meaning a poet, that is, someone who is seen as perceiving and understanding things that other people do not; and *shaʿīrah* (plural, *shaʿā'ir*), which is a site or landmark associated with one of the rites of the pilgrimage to Makkah, or one of the rites themselves.

Derivatives of this root occur in 45 places in the Qur'an, and in the following senses: (1) Hair or fur (*ashʿār*). This sense of the word is used in *Sūrah al-Naḥl*, 16:80. (2) A poet. *Sūrah al-Shuʿarā'*, 26:224; and *Sūrah al-Anbiyā'*, 21:5. In both of these passages, poets are associated with lying, error and deceit. (3) Perception or realization. *Sūrah al-Baqarah*, 2:154 exhorts the Muslim community during a time of war, saying, "And say not of those who are slain in God's cause, 'They are dead': nay, they are alive, but you perceive it not" (*lā tashʿurūn*). Similarly, God warns people in *Sūrah al-Zumar*, 39:55 that chastisement might come upon them unexpectedly: "without your being aware [of its approach]" (*wa antum lā tashʿurūn*). (4) Site of a religious rite. *Sūrah al-Baqarah*, 2:158 refers to the sites of the pilgrimage rites as *shaʿā'ir Allāh*, "the symbols set up by God."

3) *The concept of ījās*

The root *w-j-s* denotes a fearful perception of something. The noun *wajs* refers to apprehension or dread, while the active participle, *wājis*, refers to a disquieting thought, premonition or foreboding. The phrase *tawajjasa al-ṭaʿām* means, "he nibbled on the food."

The past tense verbal form *awjasa* occurs three times in the Qur'an in the sense of an unstated feeling of dread or fear. We read in *Sūrah Hūd*, 11:70, for example, that when certain angelic visitors came to see the prophet Abraham and he noticed that they had not partaken of the food he had served them," he...became apprehensive of them" (*wa awjasa minhum khīfatan*). (See also *Sūrah Ṭāhā*, 20:67 and *Sūrah al-Dhāriyāt*, 51:28).

4) *The concept of īnās*

The root *a-n-s* denotes (1) the state of being familiar with, accustomed to, or at ease with; as such, it is contrasted with *waḥshah*, meaning forlornness, loneliness or alienation, and (2) the act of seeing, hearing or otherwise perceiving something. Derivatives include the adjective *anīs*, meaning affable, friendly, or cordial; as a noun, *anīs* refers to a pleasant companion.

The past tense verb form *ānasa* occurs seven times in the Qur'an, four of which are in the context of Moses' seeing the burning bush as he traveled with his family through the desert. We read in *Sūrah al-Qaṣaṣ*, 28:29 that Moses "perceived a fire" (*ānasa... nāran*) on the slope of Mount Sinai. He then told his family to wait, saying, "Behold, I perceive a fire (*innī ānastu nāran*)." (See also *Sūrah Ṭāhā*, 20:10 and *Sūrah al-Naml*, 27:7). It is from this root that we derive the word *insān*, meaning the pupil of the eye, which enables us to see things, and the collective noun *ins*, "human beings" who, unlike the jinn, are visible and tangible. The verbal noun *īnās* has thus been said to refer to clear, unambiguous sight, or the sight of something that brings reassurance or comfort. *Sūrah al-Nisā'*, 4:6 uses the verb *ānasa* in the sense of knowing, sensing or perceiving. After instructing believers to observe the orphans under their care, it instructs them with the words: "if you find them to be mature of mind (*fa'in ānastum minhum rushdan*), hand over to them their possessions (*fadfaᶜū ilayhim amwālahum*)" rather than squandering them for selfish ends.

5) *The concept of lams*

The root *l-m-s* denotes the act of touching or feeling with the hand, seeking, or perceiving. The verb *lamasa* or *lāmasa* is used metonymically to refer to sexual contact, while the sense of seeking or requesting is conveyed by the verbs *iltamasa* and *talammasa*.

Derivatives of the root *l-m-s* occur five times in the Qur'an, and in the following senses: (1) Seeking. The verb *lamasa* is used in this sense in the statement, "We reached out towards heaven" (*lamasnā al-samā'*) in *Sūrah al-Jinn*, 72:8. When, on the Day of Resurrection, the hypocrites seek light from the believers, they will be told, "Turn back, and seek a light [of your own] (*irjiᶜū... faltamisū nūran*)!" (*Sūrah al-Ḥadīd*, 57:13). (2) To touch with one's hands (*Sūrah al-Anᶜām*, 6:7). (3) Sexual intercourse. The verb *lāmasa* is used in this sense in the phrase, "have cohabited with a woman" (*lāmastum al-nisā'*) found in *Sūrah al-Nisā'*, 4:43 (cf. *Sūrah al-Mā'idah*, 5:6).

6) *The concept of yad*

Meaning "hand", the word *yad* (plural, *aydin* or *ayādin*) is used metaphorically in numerous senses.

The word *yad* and its derivatives occur 121 times in the Qur'an in the following senses: (1) The actual hand (*Sūrah al-Mā'idah*, 5:11). (2) Legal claim. *Sūrah al-Baqarah*, 2:237 uses the word *yad* in this sense in the context of discussing the rights of the various parties affected by a pre-consummation divorce agreement, saying that "he in whose hand is the marriage-tie" (*alladhī bi yadihi ᶜuqdat al-nikāḥ*), that is, the bride's guardian, can decide to forgo the half of the bridal dower to which he would be entitled in the case of a divorce. (3) Power. *Sūrah Ṣād*, 38:45 refers to Abraham, Isaac and Jacob as being "endowed with inner strength and vision" (*ūlī al-aydī wa al-abṣār*). (4) Regret. In *Sūrah al-Aᶜrāf*, 7:149 we read about how the people of Moses "would smite their hands in remorse" (*suqiṭa fī aydīhim*) when they realized their error. (5) Generosity. Describing God's graciousness, *Sūrah al-Mā'idah*, 5:64 states "but wide are His hands stretched out (*yadāhu mabsūṭatān*): He dispenses [bounty] as He wills (*yunfiqu kayfa yashā'*)."

Hence, the word *yad* is used primarily to refer to the actual hand, although it is sometimes used figuratively to speak of grace, generosity, or power. The word *yad* has also been used metaphorically to refer to the entire person and his or her actions. *Sūrah al-Ḥajj*, 22:10 tells us, for example, that when unrepentant sinners are being chastised in the afterlife, they will be told, "This is an outcome of what your own hands have wrought (*dhālika bi mā qaddamat yadāka*) – for, never does God do the least wrong to His creatures!" In *Sūrah al-Baqarah*, 2:79, those who have falsified scriptures are condemned "for what their hands have written" (*mimmā katabat aydīhim*). The reference to their hands having done the writing is a way of emphasizing that they, and not God, were the authors of this speech. Similarly, *Sūrah al-Tawbah*, 9:30 contains words of condemnation for those who teach misleading doctrines. Of them this verse states, "Such are the sayings which they utter with their mouths" (*dhālika qawluhum bi afwāhihim*) as a means of stressing the fact that what they are saying is their own invention. The image of the hand, or *yad*, is likewise used in numerous places to symbolize power, might, authority, high rank, protection, aid, and benevolent action.

7) *The concept of mass*

The root *m-s-s* originally denotes the action of touching something with one's hand, while denoting, figuratively, touching or affecting something or someone in a non-physical manner. The triliteral verb form is *massa/yamussu* (verbal noun, *misās* or *masīs*). The passive participle *mamsūs* is thus used to mean mentally deranged or insane, as though the person concerned had been 'touched' by jinn, while the active participle, *māss*, is used to describe a pressing need (*ḥājatun māssah*). (Cf. the statement, *massat ilayhi al-ḥājah*, "There is a great need for it.")

Derivatives of this root occur approximately 61 times in the Qur'an, and in the following senses: (1) Sexual intercourse. *Sūrah al-*

Aḥzāb, 33:49 instructs men in how to comport themselves if they marry believing women "and then divorce them before you have touched them" (*min qabli an tamussūhunna*), and in *Sūrah Āl ʿImrān*, 3:47, Mary the mother of Jesus asks, "How can I have a son when no man has ever touched me (*wa lam yamsasnī bashar*)?" (2) To afflict, affect. In *Sūrah al-Aʿrāf*, 7:95, we see people declaring, "Misfortune and hardship befell our forefathers as well" (*massa ābā'anā al-ḍarrā'u wa al-sarrā'*), while in *Sūrah Fāṭir*, 35:35, those blessed with Paradise describe it as a place "wherein no struggle can assail us (*lā yamussunā fīhā naṣabun*), and wherein no weariness can touch us (*wa lā yamussunā fīhā lughūb*)." (3) Confusion or mental disorder. *Sūrah al-Baqarah*, 2:275 compares those who indulge in usury to someone whose mind has been disordered by the 'touch' of Satan (*alladhī yatakhabbaṭuhu al-shayṭānu min al-mass*). (4) Contact of one person's skin with another's. This sense is found in *Sūrah Ṭāhā*, 20:97 in the phrase, *lā misāsa*, "Touch me not."

8) *The concept of samʿ*

The root *s-m-ʿ* denotes the perception of something via the ear. The noun *samʿ* thus refers to the ability to perceive sounds, and is used to refer figuratively to the ear, to the understanding, and to obedience to what one hears.

Derivatives of the root *s-m-ʿ* occur 185 times in the Qur'an, and in the following senses: (1) The capacity to perceive sounds. It is in this sense that it is used in *Sūrah al-Insān*, 76:2, where God describes Man as a being "endowed with hearing and sight" (*samīʿan baṣīran*). Similarly, God speaks in *Sūrah al-Aḥqāf*, 46:26 of endowing people "with hearing, and sight, and hearts" (*jaʿalnā lahum samʿan wa abṣāran wa afʾidah*). (2) Inward reception of the message one hears with the ear. *Sūrah al-Anfāl*, 8:21 warns people not to be "like those who say, 'We have heard' (*samiʿnā*), the while they do not hearken (*wa hum lā yasmaʿūn*)." This sense of the verb *samiʿa* is also found in *Sūrah al-Aḥqāf*, 46:26 quoted above, which goes on to speak of those who had been endowed with "hearing, and sight, and [knowledgeable] hearts," saying, "but neither their hearing, nor their sight, nor their hearts were of the least avail to them, seeing that they went on rejecting

God's messages." See *Sūrah al-Baqarah*, 2:7, which speaks of God having "sealed" certain people's hearts and hearing such that, even if they hear with their ears, they will not respond with belief.

Negations of the act of *samᶜ* in the Qur'an refer not to the physical capacity to pick up sounds, but, rather, to a failure to respond to the sounds heard and to the message they convey. Those who do not respond to God or His prophets are described in the Qur'an as "dead." As we read in *Sūrah al-Rūm*, 30:52, the Prophet is told, "you cannot make the dead hear (*innaka lā tusmiᶜu al-mawtā*): nor can you make the deaf [of heart] hear this call (*wa lā tusmiᶜu al-ṣumma al-duᶜā'*)."

9) *The concept of inṣāt*

The root *n-ṣ-t* denotes silence, or the act of becoming silent in order to listen to something. The triliteral verb is *naṣata/yanṣitu*, while the quadriliteral verb is *anṣata/yunṣitu* (verbal noun, *inṣāt*).

This latter verb occurs in the Qur'an twice in the imperative voice. Its first occurrence is in *Sūrah al-Aᶜrāf*, 7:204, where believers are commanded, when the Qur'an is recited, to "hearken unto it" (*istamiᶜū lahu*) "and listen in silence" (*wa anṣitū*). As for the second, it is found in *Sūrah al-Aḥqāf*, 46:29, which talks about certain unseen beings who, when they heard the Qur'an, said to each other, "Listen in silence (*anṣitū*)!" The verb *anṣata/yunṣitu* thus refers to the act of becoming quiet for the purpose of focusing intently on what one is hearing. When one quiets heart and mind in order to listen attentively and reflect on what one is hearing, the Qur'an brings mercy to its listeners in the form of understanding, knowledge and renewed faith.

10) *The concept of ṣamam*

The root *ṣ-m-m* denotes the process of coming together, thereby closing up an opening or gap. From this we derive the noun *ṣamam*, meaning deafness, the implication that something has stopped up the passageways through which sound reaches the ear, and *ṣimām*, meaning a plug or a valve.

The root *ṣ-m-m* occurs fifteen times in the Qur'an, and in the following senses: (1) Deafness. The noun *ṣamam* is used in this sense in *Sūrah Hūd*, 11:24. (Cf. *Sūrah al-Anᶜām*, 6:25; *Sūrah al-Isrā'*, 17:46).

(2) Neglecting or refusing to listen to the truth. We are told in *Sūrah al-Mā'idah*, 5:70-71 that because of their rebellion and rejection of God's messages, the children of Israel "became blind and deaf [of heart]" (*thumma ʿamū wa ṣammū*). Deafness, or *ṣamam*, is thus used figuratively to describe the condition of people who refuse to listen to the truth and who, if they do hear it, refuse to accept it. Such individuals are described as "deaf, dumb and blind" (*Sūrah al-Baqarah*, 2:18 and 171; and *Sūrah al-Isrā'*, 17:97).

11) *The concept of udhun*

The letters *a-dh-n* constitute two roots that are close in meaning, though distinct in pronunciation. The first of these denotes the ear (*al-udhun*), while the other denotes knowledge (*idhn*). Their meanings are related in that it is through the ear (*udhun*) that we gain knowledge (*idhn*) via audible sounds. One might say, *adhintu bi hādha al-amr* ("I learned of this matter"), or that so-and-so *ādhananī*, meaning that he informed me. In this latter case, the quadriliteral verb is *ādhana/yu'd-hinu* (verbal noun, *īdhān*). Also derived from this root is the quadriliteral form *adhdhana/yu'adhdhinu* (verbal noun, *ta'dhīn*), meaning to announce that the time for one of the five canonical prayers (salah) has begun, and the noun *adhān*, which refers to the call to prayer.

Derivatives of this root occur 101 times in the Qur'an, eighteen of which are references to the physical ear. For example, *Sūrah al-Mā'idah*, 5:45 makes reference to the Torah's law of retribution: "an eye for an eye, and a nose for a nose, and an ear for an ear..." (*wa al-udhun bil-udhun*). Using the word *udhun* in a figurative sense, *Sūrah al-Tawbah*, 9:61 refers to the way the Prophet's enemies would mock him, saying, "He is all ear (*huwa udhun*)," thereby insinuating that he would hear hallucinatory sounds and mistake them as revelations. To this the Qur'an replies, saying, "Say: '[Yes,] he is all ear, [listening] to what is good for you (*qul udhunu khayrin lakum*)!'" Similarly, *Sūrah al-Anʿām*, 6:25 uses the plural *ādhān* to refer not to people's physical ears, but to their willingness to listen to God's messages. Though they seem to listen to the Prophet, they are actually unresponsive, in their (spiritual) ears a kind of deafness (*fī ādhānihim waqran*). A third sense in which this root appears in the Qur'an is that of proclamation. In a description of a potential scene from the Day of Judgment, *Sūrah al-Aʿrāf*, 7:44 tells us that "a voice will loudly proclaim (*adhdhana mu'adhdhinun*)" that evildoers are only receiving their just due. A fourth sense borne by a derivative of this root is that of knowledge or command. *Sūrah Ghāfir*, 40:78 declares that no messenger could perform any miracle "other than by God's leave (or command) (*illā bi idhn-illāh*)." The noun *adhān* is used in *Sūrah al-Tawbah*, 9:3 in the sense of a proclamation, while *Sūrah Ibrāhīm*, 14:7 uses the derivative verb *ta'adhdhana* in the sense of announcing or proclaiming.

12) *The concept of baṣar*

The letters *b-ṣ-r* make up two roots, one of which denotes knowledge or perception of something. From this sense we derive the adjective *baṣīr*, meaning knowledgeable (of, *bi*) or discriminating with regard to (*bi*), and the noun *baṣīrah*, meaning insight, mental vision, or discernment. Given its relation to the concept of clarity and sight, the word *baṣīrah* can also be used in the sense of evidence or proof. The triliteral verb is *baṣura/yabṣaru* (verbal noun, *baṣar*), while the quadriliteral verb is *abṣara/yubṣiru* (verbal noun, *ibṣār*), both meaning to see or understand, although the former takes the preposition *bi* (cf. *Sūrah Ṭāhā*, 20:96), while the latter takes a direct object. The verbal noun *baṣar* (plural, *abṣār*; cf. *Sūrah al-Ḥashr*, 59:2) refers to eyesight, whereas *baṣīrah* is the vision of the mind or heart, or an integrated, complete knowledge of something. The verb *istabṣara* means to see, or to be endowed with reason, intelligence and insight, while the verb *tabaṣṣara/yatabaṣṣaru* (*tabaṣṣur*) means to reflect on or ponder.

As for the second root composed of the letters *b-ṣ-r*, it denotes the sewing together of two pieces of tanned leather or skin, while the noun *baṣrah* refers to loose stones.

Derivatives of the first root occur in 150 places in the Qur'an in the form of the verbal noun and all tenses of the verb, and in the following senses: (1) The vision of the heart. In *Sūrah Yūnus*, 10:43, God asks rhetorically, "Can you show the right way to the blind (*afa 'anta tahdī al-ʿumya*) even though they cannot see (*wa law kānū lā yubṣirūn*)?" (See also *Sūrah al-Dhāriyāt*, 51:21). (2) Eyesight. This sense is found in God's declaration that He has made Man "a being endowed with hearing and sight" (*Sūrah al-Insān*, 76:2; cf. *Sūrah Ṭāhā*, 20:125).

The adjective *baṣīr* is attributed to God in 42 verses of the Qur'an, in most of which it appears together with some other attribute or name. See, for example, *Sūrah al-Isrā'*, 17:1, which describes God as "All-Hearing, All-Seeing (*al-Samīʿ al-Baṣīr*)," *Sūrah Fāṭir*, 35:31, which describes Him as "Fully Aware, All-Seeing (*khabīr baṣīr*)." Note that in *Sūrah al-Isrā'*, 17:17, the quality of *baṣīrah* (insight) is linked to that of *khibrah* (awareness) in relation to people's inner states, while only that of *baṣīrah* is linked to their outward, visible actions. See *Sūrah al-Baqarah*, 2:265, which declares, "God sees all that you do" (*wa Allāhu bi mā taʿmalūna baṣīr*).

13) *The concept of ru'yah*
The letters *r-'-y* form a root that denotes looking and seeing with the physical eye or with the eye of the mind. The verbal noun *ra'yun* (plural, *ārā'*) refers to what a person sees with his or her mind; hence, an opinion, point of view, idea or belief. The reflexive verb form *tarā'ā* means to see each other, and the noun *ru'yah* refers to vision with either the eye or the heart. However, whereas the noun form *ru'yā* refers to the kind of vision one would have in one's sleep, the noun *ru'yah* refers to the seeing one does when awake. When the verb *ra'ā/yarā* is used in the sense of knowing, thinking or perceiving, it takes two direct objects. Tor example, the statement *ra'aytu zaydan khārijan* could mean either, "I thought Zayd had gone out," or, "I knew Zayd had gone out." When, by contrast, it is used in the sense of physical vision, it takes one direct object only.

Derivatives of this root occur 329 times in the Qur'an, and in the following senses: (1) Awareness. *Sūrah Saba'*, 34:6 states that those "who are endowed with [innate] knowledge are well aware that... (*yarā alladhīna ūtū al-ʿilma*)." Similarly, *Sūrah al-Anʿām*, 6:75 speaks of God's giving Abraham insight into His dominion over the heavens and the earth (*nurī ibrāhīma malakūta al-samāwāti wal-arḍ*). *Sūrah al-Tawbah*, 9:105 declares that "God will behold your deeds" (*sa yarā Allāhu aʿmalakum*), God's "seeing" clearly being a reference to His knowledge. And *Sūrah al-Nisā'*, 4:51 asks, "Are you not aware of those who... (*alam tara ilā alladhīna...*)?" (cf. *Sūrah al-Baqarah*, 2:258; *Sūrah Yāsīn*, 36:77) (2) Physical vision. *Sūrah al-Munāfiqūn*, 63:4 uses the word *ra'ā/yarā* in the sense of seeing with one's eyes, saying, "when you see them (*idhā ra'aytahum*), their outward appearance may please you" (*tuʿjibuka ajsāmuhum*) (cf. *Sūrah al-Najm*, 53:11; cf. *Sūrah Āl ʿImrān*, 3:13). (3) Reflection or consideration. This sense of the verb *ra'ā* is found in *Sūrah al-Naḥl*, 16:79, which asks, "Have, then, they [who deny the truth] never considered the birds, enabled [by God] to fly in mid-air (*alam yaraw ilā al-ṭayri musakhkharātin fī al-jaww*)?" (Cf. *Sūrah al-Anʿām*, 6:27). (4) Seeing and hearing. *Sūrah al-Anʿām*, 6:68 tells believers: "when you see (*idhā ra'ayta*)" those who disparage God's messages, turn away from them unless they begin speaking of something else.

14) *The concept of naẓar*

The basic denotation of the triliteral root *n-ẓ-r* is that of seeing, examining and reflecting on something. It can also refer to the act of waiting for or expecting something. The active participle *nāẓir* can refer to the eye, while the verbal noun *naẓar* refers to the process of thinking about, measuring and assessing something. The phrase *naẓara ilayhi* means "He looked at it," while the statement *naẓara fī al-amr* means, "He considered or studied the matter."

Derivatives of this root occur 139 times in the Qur'an and in the following senses: (1) Mercy. *Sūrah Āl ʿImrān*, 3:88 tells us that those who knowingly reject the truth will not be granted mercy or respite (*wa lā hum yunẓarūn*) in the life to come. (2) Expect or wait for. *Sūrah Yāsīn*, 36:49 tells us that for evildoers "nothing awaits them beyond (*mā yanẓurūna illā*) a single blast [of God's punishment] (*ṣayḥatan wāḥidatan*)." (See also *Sūrah al-Anʿām*, 6:158). (3) Consideration or reflection. Referring to those who deny the resurrection, *Sūrah al-Ghāshiyah*, 88:17 asks, "Do, then, they [who deny resurrection] never gaze at" (*afalā yanẓurūna ilā*) the clouds pregnant with water, [and observe] how they are created?" (For a similar sense, see also *Sūrah al-ʿAnkabūt*, 29:20; *Sūrah Āl ʿImrān*, 3:137; *Sūrah al-Anʿām*, 6:11; and *Sūrah Yūnus*, 10:101). (4) Beholding. *Sūrah al-Qiyāmah*, 75:23 describes the faces of those in Paradise as "Looking towards their Lord (*ilā rabbihā nāẓirah*)."

The verbal noun *naẓar* refers to the act of approaching something through vision, whether one's physical eye, or the eye of the mind ("look" – *Sūrah al-Muddathhir*, 74:21; "see" – *Sūrah al-Naml*, 27:27; "observe" – *Sūrah al-Ṭāriq*, 86:5 and *Sūrah Ghāfir*, 40:21; "consider" – *Sūrah ʿAbasa*, 80:24 and *Sūrah al-Aʿrāf*, 7:185). The quintiliteral form *intaẓara/yantaẓiru* (verbal noun, *intiẓār*) means to approach something with anticipation. You might look at (*tanẓuru ilā al-shay'*) something, but not see it (*wa lā tarāhu*). On the other hand, you might look at it and examine it closely, both with your physical eye and the eye of your mind.

15) *The concept of mushāhadah*

The letters *sh-h-d* form a root that denotes presence, knowledge, and the conveyance of knowledge to others. The triliteral verb is *shahida/yashhadu* (verbal noun, *shahādah*), while the noun *mashhad* refers to a scene, a sight, or a place of assembly. The active participle *shāhid* (plural, *shuhūd*) is a witness, as well as a tombstone (which "witnesses" to the presence of someone buried in a particular spot). The verb *shahida* can mean to bear witness or provide testimony as evidence of who is in the right and who is in the wrong (cf. *Sūrah al-Nisā'*, 4:41), while the noun *shahādah* can refer to someone's testimony, that is, a definitive eye-witness report. The noun *shahīd* (plural, *shuhadā'*) refers to a martyr who dies in witness to a cause, and to whose faithfulness the angels bear witness. The word *shahīd* can also refer to someone whose testimony is reliable, and someone who has knowledge and awareness of everything around him or her.

Derivatives of this root occur in 160 verses of the Qur'an, and in the following senses: (1) A witness. This sense is used in *Sūrah al-Nisā'*, 4:41 and 4:72; *Sūrah al-Burūj*, 85:7, and *Sūrah al-Nisā'*, 4:69. (2) Guardian angel. *Sūrah Qāf*, 50:21 tells us that on the Day of Resurrection, every soul will come forward with "an [angel] to drive (*sā'iq*) and an [angel] to bear witness (*wa shahīd*)." (3) The Muslim community. *Sūrah al-Baqarah*, 2:143 refers to the Muslim community as "witnesses" to other people (*shuhadā' ʿalā al-nās*). (4) Call upon someone as a witness. This sense is found in *Sūrah al-Ṭalāq*, 65:2 and *Sūrah al-Baqarah*, 2:23.

16) *The concept of ʿamā*

The letters *ʿ-m-y* form a root that denotes concealment and covering. The triliteral verb is *ʿamiya/yaʿmā*, meaning to be or become blind, and the verbal noun is *ʿamā*, meaning blindness. From this is derived the male singular adjective *aʿmā*, meaning blind or sightless (feminine singular, *ʿamyā'*, and plural masculine, *ʿamūn*, *ʿumy*, or *ʿumyān*. However, when people use the phrase *mā aʿmāhu*, meaning, "How blind he is!", they are not speaking of physical blindness.

Derivatives of the root *ʿ-m-y* occur 33 times in the Qur'an, and in the two following senses: (1) Blindness of the heart. As we read in *Sūrah al-Ḥajj*, 22:46, "verily, it is not their eyes that have become blind – but blind have become the hearts that are in their breasts (*wa lākin taʿmā al-qulūbu allatī fī al-ṣudūr*)!" Similarly, *Sūrah al-Isrā'*, 17:72 warns that whoever was spiritually blind in this life "(*man kāna fī hādhihi aʿmā*) will be blind in the life to come (*fa huwa fī al-ākhirati aʿmā*)." (Cf. *Sūrah Fāṭir*, 35:19). (2) Blindness of the eyes. Physical blindness is referred to in *Sūrah al-Aʿmā*, 80:2 and *Sūrah al-Nūr*, 24:61.

17) *The concept of ʿayn*

The root consisting of the letters *ʿ-y-n* has several denotations. One is the physical eye (*ʿayn*, plural, *aʿyun*, *ʿuyūn*, *aʿyān*), the member of the body that enables us to see. The word *ʿayn* can also refer to a spy, or to a spring of water. From this root we derive the quadriliteral verb *ʿāyana/yuʿāyinu* (verbal noun, *muʿāyanah* or *ʿiyān*), meaning to see or inspect. Hence, if one were to say, *laqītuhu ʿiyānan*, it would mean, "I met him in person, face to face." As for the noun *ʿīn*, it refers to a wild cow, the wild bull being referred to as *aʿyan*.

Derivatives of this root occur 65 times in the Qur'an, and in the following three senses: (1) The eye. *Sūrah Āl ʿImrān*, 3:13, *Sūrah Yūsuf*, 12:84, and *Sūrah al-Mā'idah*, 5:45 use the term *ʿayn* to refer to the physical eye. (2) A spring of water. This sense of the word *ʿayn* is found in *Sūrah al-Baqarah*, 2:60. (3) As a metaphor for care and protection. In *Sūrah Ṭāhā*, 20:39, God tells Moses of His intention that Moses be "formed under My eye," that is, under His divine protection and guidance.

4

Maʿrifah in the Qur'an

FIRST: THE DEFINITION OF *Maʿrifah*

AL-TAHNĀWĪ lists a set of definitions for *maʿrifah* which can be summarized as follows: *Maʿrifah* is knowledge in the sense of unqualified apprehension, be it a cognition that the individual forms himself or herself, or belief in a concept or affirmation presented from without. It includes the apprehension of a simple entity's essential nature, as well as a mental affirmation of the various states in which this entity might exist. It also includes the apprehension of a complex entity, whether as an original conceptualization or in affirmation of a conceptualization formed by someone else. Similarly, it includes apprehension of both the particular and the universal, whether in terms of basic understanding, or in terms of relevant legal rulings. The apprehension of the particular takes place on the basis of evidence, and after a previous lack of knowledge and understanding.

1) *The linguistic definition of maʿrifah*

According to Ibn Fāris, the letters *ʿ-r-f* form two roots, one of which denotes succession, continuity and cohesion, and the other of which denotes stillness and tranquility. The word *maʿrifah* (plural, *maʿārif*) is used in opposition to the word *nakirah*, where *maʿrifah* refers to a specific, known entity, while *nakirah* refers to an entity that is neither specified nor known. Moreover, the term *maʿrifah* is used in the context of commending someone's sound opinion, acute perception, or sharp intelligence.

2) *The definition of maʿrifah based on common usage*

The word *maʿrifah* is used to refer to a particular member of a species or group. In other words, it is a term that, by virtue of custom and unspoken agreement within a linguistic community, has come to refer to a specified, known entity. Pronouns, proper nouns, demonstrative pronouns, and regular nouns preceded by the definite article all serve to indicate that the entity referred to is *maʿrifah* (definite).

God declares in *Sūrah al-Dhāriyāt*, 51:56, "I have only created invisible beings and humankind in order for them to worship Me" (*mā khalaqtu al-jinna wa al-insa illā li yaʿbudūnī*). The phrase *li yaʿbudūnī* as "to worship me" implies the knowledge of faith, that is, the knowledge by faith of the Divine Being that we worship.

Scholastic theologians and logicians use the word *maʿrifah* to refer to a realization that is preceded by a lack of understanding. It is also used to refer to the formation of an image in the mind, a firm belief that corresponds to reality, and the apprehension of a universal or complex notion.

3) *The technical definition of maʿrifah*

The term *maʿrifah* occurs 24 times in the Qur'an, and 67 times in various other derivatives of the root *ʿ-r-f*. Most of these instances convey the sense of knowledge derived through the physical senses and pertaining to observable qualities or features. God declares in *Sūrah al-Baqarah*, 2:146, "They unto whom We have vouchsafed revelation aforetime know him (*yaʿrifūnahu*) as they know their own children (*kamā yaʿrifūna abnā'ahum*)." This sense of the verb *ʿarafa* is opposed to the Arabic verb *ankara*, meaning to deny or refuse to recognize. This sense of the word is used in *Sūrah al-Mu'minūn*, 23:69, where God asks, "Or is it, perchance, that they have not recognized their Apostle (*lam yaʿrifū rasūlahum*), and so they disavow him (*fa hum lahu munkirūn*)?" A somewhat different sense of the verb is found in *Sūrah Muḥammad*, 47:6, which speaks of how God will admit believers "to the paradise which He has made known to them (*ʿarrafahā lahum*)." The verb *ʿarrafa* might, in this context, also mean "made beautiful and pleasant."

Based on its use in the Qur'an, the verb *ʿarafa* refers to the act of acquiring knowledge or understanding via signals or signs that are perceptible in the earthly realm. *Sūrah al-Raḥman*, 55:41 tells that "those who were lost in sin shall be known (*yuʿrafu al-mujrimūn*) "by their marks (*bi simāhum*)." The verb *ʿarafa* is used in *Sūrah al-Muṭaffifīn*,

83:24 in the sense of seeing or perceiving. Hence, God tells the Prophet that when he sees believers in Paradise, he will perceive or see the radiance of bliss on their faces (*taʿrifu fī wujūhihim naḍrat al-naʿīm*). Whether the evidence on which knowledge is based is purely rational in nature or consists of wisdom and testimonies passed down through others, it will be received in either written or oral form. Knowledge based on rational evidence is referred to in *Sūrah al-Naml*, 27:93, which tells us that God "will make you see [the truth of] His messages, and then you shall know them [for what they are] (*fa taʿrifūnahā*)." (Cf. *Sūrah al-Aḥzāb*, 33:59.) A similar sense is conveyed in *Sūrah al-Naḥl*, 16:83, which tells us that those who deny the truth "are fully aware of God's blessings (*yaʿrifūna niʿmat Allāh*), but...they refuse to acknowledge them" (*thumma yunkirūnahā*)."

SECOND: THE NATURE OF *Maʿrifah*

1) *The concept of the nature of maʿrifah*

Knowledge is a quality that may be predicated of a living being. It is a relationship that comes into being between a knowing self and a known object. When we speak of "the nature of knowledge," we seek to define or specify the relationship between knower and known and the process by which it is formed.

The relationship embodied in knowledge is connected to the purpose for human existence on Earth and the matter of human survival. The relationship between the knowing self and the known object, which is formed within the consciousness of a discerning human being, may take the form of ideas or doctrines.

What concerns here in particular is the relationship between knowledge and existence. Which of the two is prior: essence, or existence? And if knowledge is acquired, then is what we come to know the essence of something? Or is it simply a form or an archetype? Further, is what we come to know on the level of universals, or of particulars? Where do universals exist? And what type of existence characterizes them? What are the tools or means of acquiring knowledge? And how do we acquire it?

2) *The nature of maʿrifah in the Qur'an*

Based on the foregoing we may say that knowledge as presented in the Qur'an consists of facts, precepts and rulings, as well as realizations and conceptualizations which we form about this or that entity as a result of what we receive via our sensory perceptions and/or our reason. The knowledge of which we speak here is a certain, indubitable apprehension that admits of no doubt and in relation to which there is no possibility of error or illusion.

(a) The source of *maʿrifah*

Everything finds its source in God Almighty. It is God who has brought all things into existence, including the cosmos and the laws that govern it. Knowledge is a divine creation and a grace with which He blesses human beings by virtue of the propensities and potentials that He has implanted within them. God has given us a natural desire to search for truth and means of acquiring knowledge. He "has brought you forth from your mothers' wombs knowing nothing – but He has endowed you with hearing, and sight, and minds, so that you might have cause to be grateful" (*Sūrah al-Naḥl*, 16:78). The gifts of hearing, sight and reason are thus among the conditions that make it possible for knowledge to be acquired.

Differences of opinion among Muslim schools of thought concerning how knowledge comes about have emerged from differences in their ways of understanding the Qur'anic verses that speak about the source of human knowledge. One such verse has to do with God's teaching of Adam: "And He imparted unto Adam the names of all things. Then He brought them within the ken of the angels and said: 'Declare unto Me the names of these [things]' (*Sūrah al-Baqarah*, 2:31)." By challenging the angels in this way, God was demonstrating Adam's superiority to them in knowledge, the special dignity that had been bestowed upon Adam, and God's majesty and power. This story indicates that the origin of knowledge lies in the initial receipt of information by our primal ancestor.

(b) Intuitive and acquired *maʿrifah*

Based on the aforementioned Qur'anic account concerning Adam, scholars have raised certain questions about what it was that Adam learned: Did God teach him all knowledge, or only its basic principles? Did God teach Adam by introducing the necessary knowledge into his mind while granting him the capacity for language, after which both language and knowledge would be acquired through a human instructional process? Further, what is the process by which language is taught and learned, and how is one's first knowledge gleaned?

(c) The first tier of *maʿrifah* obtained by the first human being

The Qur'anic statement quoted earlier that God "imparted to Adam the names of all things" suggests that God taught Adam language that signified the natures of things or that triggered the mental images associated with them. The understanding of a name requires us first to have comprehended its referent, that is, the entity it names. Without a referent, a name has no meaning. Hence, the entity named – the referent – has to be conceptualized first. A name's referent can be either a self-existent entity or a quality that inheres in something else such that when the name is mentioned, this quality comes automatically to mind.

Human *maʿrifah* subsequent to primordial cognitions

Not all acquired *maʿrifah* is based on logical evidence. This does not mean that the mind is inactive in some types of acquired knowledge. Rather, it means simply that the human capacity for knowledge acquisition is broader and more inclusive than the rational or logical faculties. A person might, for example, be provided with clear, sound, and comprehensible logical premises, yet remain unconvinced of the truths or facts to which these premises point.

Human beings have an inborn propensity to seek goodness, a propensity that helps them in turn to grasp and embrace truth. This innate capacity, which is marked by an inherent logic that goes beyond the codified logic of the mind, is reflected in the two basic kinds of evidence that God adduces for His oneness. The first of these is evidence from the physical universe, which is perceived by looking at the outside world, while the second is perceived by looking into ourselves. As God declares in *Sūrah Fuṣṣilat*, 41:53, "We shall make them fully understand Our messages [through what they perceive] in the utmost horizons [of the universe] and within themselves, so that it will become clear unto them that this [revelation] is indeed the truth." Similarly, we read in *Sūrah al-Dhāriyāt*, 51:20-21, "And on earth there are signs [of God's existence, visible] to all who are endowed with inner certainty, just as [there are signs thereof] within your own selves: can you not, then, see?" However, the mere availability of such evidence, outward and inward, is insufficient to bring about knowledge. We ourselves have to engage with the evidence in such a way that it leads to understanding and faith. There are individuals who dull their innate receptive and perceptive capacities through acts of disobedience. Such people render themselves incapable of benefiting even from the evidence they have at their disposal. Hence, rather than helping them, such evidence simply serves to condemn them for their refusal to receive it.

The Qur'an's frequent use of the Arabic term *laᶜalla*, meaning "perchance", or "in the hope that..." in relation to the topic of *maᶜrifah* is another indication that fulfillment of the external conditions for acquiring knowledge is no guarantee that the individual will necessarily learn and arrive at the truth. *Sūrah al-Baqarah*, 2:219, for example, reads: "God makes clear unto you His messages, so that you might reflect..." (*laᶜallakum tatafakkarūn*; cf. 2:266). Similarly we read in *Sūrah al-Baqarah*, 2:242, "God makes clear unto you His messages, so that you might [learn to] use your reason" (*laᶜallakum taᶜqilūn*; cf. *Sūrah al-Anᶜām*, 6:151). The *maᶜrifah* individuals can acquire thus depends on their readiness to receive it. The Qur'an depicts different tiers of knowledge or understanding. The first tier takes place on the level of physical perceptions made possible through the bodily senses and the conclusions reached through reason on the basis of these perceptions. The second tier might be termed special guidance which comes about through divine revelation. Those receptive to the divine light form such knowledge in gradually ascending levels, as opposed to the gradually descending levels experienced by those who are deluding themselves.

The acquisition of knowledge is thus related to human attitudes, or the will to benefit from the evidence one has. The initial tier, which consists in the realities around us and within us, is available to every able-bodied and able-minded adult. As God has declared, "We would never chastise [any community for the wrong they may do] ere We have sent an apostle [to them]" (*Sūrah al-Isrā'*, 17:15). Similarly, we are told in *Sūrah al-Nisā'*, 4:165 that God has sent messengers as bearers of both glad tidings and warning "so that people might have no excuse before God..." Hence, no one is excluded from this first tier of knowledge but those who, due to their young age or loss of mental faculties (through sleep or insanity), are not held morally accountable.

The second tier of knowledge, which leads to guidance, depends on the individual's attitude or readiness. As for the third tier of knowledge which entails an increase in guidance, faith and God-consciousness, it follows from the second, with the difference that this third tier is an added grace that comes from God alone and has nothing to do with human action or intervention.

The worldly sciences have two purposes. The first of these purposes pertains to this earthly realm, which is to impart knowledge that can be obtained by the believer and the nonbeliever alike by simply availing themselves of the resources God has placed at everyone's disposal. The believer, however, earns greater merit in that his or her reward will be not simply in this world, but in the next as well, in addition to the fact that he or she will be granted greater success in his or her efforts. As for the second purpose, it is to enable the believer to earn greater merit in the afterlife. The nonbeliever is deprived of this other-worldly reward. As we read in *Sūrah al-Anʿām*, 6:44, "When they had forgotten all that they had been told to take to heart, We threw open to them the gates of all [good] things until – even as they were rejoicing in what they had been granted – We suddenly took them to task: and lo! they were broken in spirit."

As for the believer, the more he or she learns about how to go about day-to-day affairs in this life, the stronger his or her faith becomes, and the higher the rank he or she is promised in the life to come.

Mastery of a task requires the fulfillment of two conditions: ability and wisdom. Ability consists in possessing both the basic material means and human resources needed, and the wherewithal to protect and preserve these resources. As for wisdom, it consists in knowledge and its good use and management. As God declares in *Sūrah al-Aʿrāf*, 7:96, "if the people of those communities had but attained to faith and been conscious of Us, We would indeed have opened up for them blessings out of heaven and earth..."

The Qur'an presents human beings' purpose on earth as that of stewardship (*istikhlāf*), which is a form of servanthood. Secular philosophy, by contrast, conceives of the human purpose in essentially materialistic terms. Consequently, the highest form of knowledge from the Qur'anic perspective is faith in God. Unbelief (*kufr*) is thus contrasted not only with faith (*īmān*), but with knowledge (*maʿrifah, ʿilm*). This is why the Qur'an treats the issue of knowledge in relation to the heart (*al-qalb, al-lubb, al-fū'ād*) more that it does in relation to any aspect of the human being. It is clear, then, that what the Qur'an intends by the term 'knowledge' is not simply a theoretical grasp of concepts and information but, rather, an awareness that is grounded in primordial human nature and the willingness to submit to God's rule.

The search for knowledge is a process that involves all human perceptions, both the physical and the nonphysical, as well as previously acquired knowledge, whether it was received from others, or divine revelation, as a result of which we might classify knowledge into three types: (1) innate, (2) intuitive and (3) theoretical. Innate knowledge is something with which a human being is born, such as an infant's instinctual knowledge of how to nurse from his or her mother. Intuitive knowledge includes perceptions and cognitions that take place as a matter of course, without the need for investigation or reasoning. One's sense of touch, for example, conveys a burning sensation if one touches fire. The individual thus gains experience with fire which, together with other interactions with his or her environment, builds up a reservoir of acquired knowledge that requires no conscious thought and reasoning. The physical senses might thus be likened to the windows of the mind onto the material, tangible world. As for theoretical knowledge, it requires study, investigation and intentional reasoning. The memory records the sensory data affirmed through concrete experiences. This data, together with information received from others, then becomes the material on the basis of which the mind goes to work forming and developing ideas and concepts.

The Qur'an affirms the importance of receiving knowledge from those who have gone before us, and calls upon us to integrate the knowledge gleaned through the Qur'an itself and the revelations received from earlier messengers of God and passed down through their followers. This integration takes places through a dual process of confirmation (*taṣdīq*) and sifting (*haymanah*). (See *Sūrah al-Mā'idah*, 5:48 and *Sūrah al-Shūrā*, 42:13.) The sifting process consists in approving every portion of earlier revelations that has not been corrupted or falsified.

(d) The object of *maʿrifah* as presented in the Qur'an is not essences, but attributes

Some scholars view philosophy as a process of generalization whereby individual manifestations of behavioral values, expressions of knowledge, and fields of learning in all their variety are traced back to a unifying source. The function of philosophy is to extract the implicit dimensions of the judgments we make, the ideas we form, and the beliefs we embrace, and give them direct, open expression. This conceptualization of philosophy supports the view that philosophical thought is intimately bound to religion or, rather, that the philosophical enterprise emerged as a kind of intellectual critique of religious and moral beliefs.

The Qur'an guides us to the evident realities from which we stand to benefit on the levels of both knowledge and action. However, it does not encourage us to delve into issues that cannot serve as a basis for what we do. This may be seen in *Sūrah al-Baqarah*, 2:189, which reads, "They will ask you about the new moons. Say: 'They indicate the periods for [various doings of] mankind, including the pilgrimage.'" Eminently practical, the answer provided here sidesteps the questioners' curiosity about other matters, such as why the moon appears like a mere thread at the beginning of the month, after which it fills out to form a full moon, after which it goes back to its former state. A similar point is conveyed in different terms by *Sūrah al-Mā'idah*, 5:101, "O you who have attained to faith! Do not ask about matters which, if they were to be made manifest to you..., might cause you hardship," and *Sūrah al-Isrā'*, 17:85, "They will ask you about [the nature of] divine inspiration. Say: 'This inspiration [comes] at my Sustainer's behest; and [you cannot understand its nature, since] you have been granted very little of [real] knowledge.'" The essential nature of things is known only to God.

What distinguishes the Islamic approach is that it acknowledges things' existence in the dual realms of 'the unseen' (*al-ghayb*) and 'the seen' (*al-shahādah*), that is, in one realm that is accessible to human reason and sensory perception, and in another that lies beyond these human capacities. The Islamic thought system recognizes human beings' ability to perceive various entities' existence and attributes; however, it denies our ability to know things' essential natures, holding that such knowledge is not required for us to fulfill our purpose in life.

The bond the Qur'an affirms between knowledge and the knowing human being is neglected by the so-called "scientific" research methods of this age, which destroy or deny the connection that God has drawn between us and the universe we live in. People are part and parcel of the cosmos, and their lives will be sound only when their hearts beat to its rhythm. The faith-based approach in no way diminishes the ability of the scientific method to bring us understanding of individual facts. On the contrary, it augments this understanding by connecting the facts to one another.

(e) *Maʿrifah* and existence

The Qur'an calls upon us to begin with existence as the basis for *maʿrifah*. There is no such thing as abstract research or abstract knowledge. Rather, faith is a phenomenon that emerges into consciousness from deep within the self. In any given society, doctrine is taught and life is lived in accordance with it even before the individual reaches the stage of conscious awareness. The individual believes in a doctrine before formulating a theory of knowledge, or *maʿrifah*. The role of *maʿrifah* is to enable people to examine their convictions and beliefs so that if they are convincing they can affirm them, and if they are unconvincing, they can reject them. This process is affected, of course, by environmental factors and upbringing as well as by innate disposition.

Maʿrifah entails awareness of what one believes. The origins of beliefs in the Qur'an are likewise the origins of human knowledge. Beliefs originate out of reflection on existent entities. As such, existence is the vessel that both contains and transcends the realm of *maʿrifah*, while *maʿrifah* is the awareness of what belief requires on the level of conduct and way of life.

The Qur'an awakens primordial human nature by inspiring faith in God as the sole Creator of the universe. It follows that the existence of God Almighty, and existence in general, are prior to human beings and human understanding. Existence is the cause and knowledge is one of its effects. The Qur'an thus affirms an externally existent entity which is independent of the knowing self and its perception or understanding. *Sūrah al-Baqarah*, 2:30 tells us that: "Thy Sustainer said to the angels: 'Behold, I am about to establish upon earth one who shall inherit it.'" In the following verse we are told that God "imparted to Adam the names of all things (2:31)." These two verses indicate that the heavens, the earth and the angels all exist independently of human beings, and that they were created before us. Hence, the existence of these entities was one source of human *maʿrifah*.

Moreover, external realities vis-à-vis human beings may be divided into two categories. The first consists of entities that belong to the realm of sensory perception, and which surround human beings in the world of nature, including plant life, animal life, inanimate beings, and other people. The second consists of entities that belong to the realm that transcends sensory perception, including the Eternal Tablet (*al-lawḥ al-maḥfūẓ*), which is the eternal prototype for the earthly Qur'an, Heaven and Hell, and the divine throne. The Qur'anic revelation was a wake-up call to human beings to "read" in the name of the Lord who created them, and who created the realm of existence of which they are a part, saying: "Read in the name of your Sustainer Who has created, created man out of a germ-cell! Read – for your Sustainer is the Most Bountiful One, Who has taught [man] the use of the pen, taught man what he did not know" (*Sūrah al-ʿAlaq*, 95:1-5).

As we have noted, existence is far broader than the realm of human knowledge. The Islamic teaching concerning the dual realms of what is inaccessible to human perception *(al-ghayb)* and what is humanly perceptible and knowable (*al-shahādah*) is central to the Qur'an. This teaching serves as one of the most powerful arguments for the relativity of knowledge and the finiteness, in both quantity and quality, of human understanding. God has made clear that the understanding and perceptive capacities God has granted us are for the purpose of enabling us to fulfill our role as stewards and vicegerents on Earth, a role which, in turn, is designed to help us achieve our ultimate purpose of being God's servants and worshippers. The human being with the greatest knowledge of all was the Prophet Muhammad, whom God commanded: "Say: 'O my Sustainer, cause me to grow in knowledge!'" (*Sūrah Ṭāhā*, 20:114). Similarly, we are reminded in *Sūrah Yūsuf*, 12:76 that "above everyone who is endowed with knowledge there is One who knows all."

THIRD: THE REALM OF *Maᶜrifah*

As we have seen, knowledge is divided by the Qur'an into two realms: that of *al-ghayb*, and that of *al-shahādah* (cf. *Sūrah al-Raᶜd*, 13:9). In relating to the world, we believe in the realm of *al-ghayb* by an act of faith without seeing it with our own eyes or sensing it in a tangible way; nor can our reason grasp its details or the manner in which it operates. Consequently, we might say that we have two different kinds of faith, one of which applies to the concrete world around us, and the other of which applies to the realm of *al-ghayb*. When relating to the former, we use both our physical senses and our minds, but in relating to the latter, our physical senses have no direct role to play. It bears noting here that God speaks of the universe in the Qur'an as consisting of numerous worlds. *Sūrah al-Fātiḥah*, 1:2 reads, "All praise is due to God alone, the Sustainer of all the worlds." From this we may conclude that there are numerous worlds, but that all of these worlds belong either to the realm of the humanly perceptible (*al-shahādah*), or the humanly imperceptible (*al-ghayb*).

1) *The relationship between al-ghayb and al-shahādah*
The realm of *al-shahādah* is often referred to in the Qur'an as *al-āfāq* ("the horizons"), which is manifested in the world of nature, while *al-ghayb* is often spoken of with reference to the inner, spiritual world of *al-anfus*, (literally, "the selves"), with these complementary realms often being mentioned in tandem. This is as it should be, since reflection on the outward signs manifested in the realm of *al-shahādah* can give us greater faith in what the Qur'an teaches about the realm of *al-ghayb*, while belief in *al-ghayb* can help us remain stronger and more hopeful in the face of life's challenges and difficulties, including situations in which we have to cope with the reality of death.

2) *The world of al-ghayb*

(a) The dictionary definition of *ghayb*

The root consisting of the letters *gh-y-b* denotes the act of concealing something. The verb *ghāba/yaghīb* (verbal nouns, *ghayb, ghaybah, ghuyūb*) thus means to be concealed from view. It is used to speak of the sun's setting, since when the sun sets it disappears from sight. Derivatives of this root are used figuratively to refer to realities that are known only to God. The related noun *ghayābah* refers to a depression in the ground, or to the bottom of something such as a well. It is used in *Sūrah Yūsuf*, 12:10, where one of Joseph's brothers tells the others to throw Joseph "into the dark depths of this well" (*fī ghayābat al-jubb*). As for the noun *ghībah*, it is used to refer to slander or backbiting, which is something one only dares engage in when the object of the person being spoken of is absent.

(b) The usage-related definition of *ghayb*

The word *ghayb* is used customarily to refer to something hidden, concealed or protected and, more specifically, to realities that are inaccessible ("absent") to the physical senses and/or are not self-evident to the mind. Al-Iṣfahānī defined *al-ghayb* as that for which is no evidence, of which there is no outward sign, and of which no created being has any knowledge. Since God is All-Knowing, nothing that exists belongs, from His perspective, to the realm of *ghayb*; rather, everything belongs, where God is concerned, to the realm of *shahādah*, or that which is perceptible and comprehensible.

Derivatives of the root *gh-y-b* occur 53 times in the Qur'an; these include four instances of the plural *al-ghuyūb*, and one instance of *ghaybah*. The masculine plural active participle *ghā'ibīn* (singular, *ghā'ib*) is used in *Sūrah al-Naml*, 27:20 in the sense of 'absent'. The feminine singular form of the same participle (*ghā'ibah*) refers in *Sūrah al-Naml*, 27:75 to something concealed or hidden: "...for there is nothing [so deeply] hidden (*ghā'ibah*) in the heavens or on earth but is recorded in (His] clear decree." The noun *ghayb* is used in *Sūrah al-Baqarah*, 2:3 to mean "that which is beyond the reach of human perception." In other words, *al-ghayb* can only be perceived via God's messengers and prophets, and denial of its existence is tantamount to atheism. *Sūrah al-Nisā'*, 4:34 speaks highly of wives who "guard in [the husband's] absence what God would have them guard" (*ḥāfiẓātun lil-ghaybi bi ma ḥafaza Allāhu*).

There are certain aspects of the realm of *al-ghayb* about which God has given us some knowledge. For example, the Qur'an includes the names of God (*asmā' Allāhi al-ḥusnā*), which tell us a great deal about God's nature; it also gives us information about the nature of life in the hereafter which we would otherwise have no way of knowing. Other aspects of the realm of *al-ghayb* are shrouded in complete mystery, and about these human beings can know nothing. *Sūrah al-Anʿām*, 6:59, for example, states that God has "the keys to the things that are beyond the reach of a created being's perception (*mafātiḥ al-ghayb*)," and "none knows them but He."

There are, in addition, two other types of *al-ghayb*, one of which is locational in nature, and the other temporal. The locational type of *al-ghayb* includes things we know nothing about because they are geographically remote from us, while the temporal type includes events that are either in the remote past, or in the unknown future. When future events become present to us, however, they remain in the realm of *al-ghayb* for people who are geographically remote from it.

(c) Features of *al-ghayb*

The world of *al-ghayb* represents the world of the intangible. However, even the tangible world might include certain aspects that are unknowable due to the types of geographical or temporal remoteness mentioned above. In addition, there are certain things God chooses not to disclose to anyone but a select few. *Sūrah al-Jinn*, 72:26-27 tells us that God alone "knows that which is beyond the reach of a created being's perception, and to none does He disclose aught of the mysteries of His Own unfathomable knowledge unless it be to an apostle whom He has been pleased to elect."

As for God's knowledge, it encompasses everything without exception in both the realm of the seen and the unseen. As we read in *Sūrah Saba'*, 34:3: "Not an atom's weight [of whatever there is] in the heavens or on earth escapes His knowledge; and neither is there anything smaller than that, or larger, but is recorded in [His] clear decree."

(d) Means for coming to know *al-ghayb*

Sensory perceptions can point beyond themselves to the world of the intangible, including the realities of lordship, divinity, divine attributes and prophecy. The mind is capable of grasping some universals, such as the existence of God and prophecy. However, neither sensory perception nor reason is capable of attaining a detailed knowledge of the world of *al-ghayb*, which can only be known fully through Divine Revelation. This fact is a consistent feature of the Islamic epistemological system. As God tells the Prophet in *Sūrah al-Shūrā*, 42:52,

> And thus, too, have We revealed to you a life-giving message, [coming] at Our behest. [Before this message came to you,] you did not know what revelation is, nor what faith [implies]: but [now] We have caused this [message] to be a light whereby We guide whom We will of Our servants.

In its call to believe in the world of the unseen, the Qur'an urges people to pursue scientific research. In other words, it encourages us to use the epistemological tools at our disposal to reflect on the evidence for God's creative power. It reminds us that this evidence is dispersed throughout the Earth and the heavenly realms, as well as inside of us.

As we read in *Sūrah Qāf*, 50:6-8, "Do they not look at the sky above them – how We have built it and made it beautiful and free of all faults? And the earth – We have spread it wide, and set upon it mountains firm, and caused it to bring forth plants of all beauteous kinds, thus offering an insight and a reminder unto every human being who willingly turns unto God."

(e) The principles of *al-ghayb*

The realm of *al-ghayb*, which constitutes a source of knowledge for human beings, has certain principles associated with it. These principles can be summed up as follows: (1) Existence has a beneficial purpose or end. (2) The laws of the cosmos are not subject to the human will. (3) The existence of God is the most important element of the world of *al-ghayb* with respect to human beings. (4) The afterlife constitutes the final outcome of the actions people have committed during their lives on Earth. (5) Life on Earth takes place in a realm of action and the pursuit of righteousness. (6) Though known to God, a person's individual fate (whether he or she is guided aright or falls into error) is a product of the choices he or she makes of his or her own free will. Consequently, there is no justification for passivity, defeatism or fatalism.

Divine Revelation is the source from which people derive the knowledge they need of the realm of *al-ghayb*. Revelation and human reason complement each other and work together to form human beings' attitudes toward the world and the extent to which they fulfill their purpose in life. For this reason, the Islamic epistemological method steers clear of dualistic oppositions between religion and the state, reason and written tradition, or traditionalism and modernity.

3) *The world of al-shahādah*

As we have seen, the terms *al-ghayb* and *al-shahādah* customarily appear in association with each other. Referring to the realm of sensory perception and those entities or concepts we can grasp with our minds, the realm of *shahādah* is perceived and understood by means of balanced cooperation between reason and the physical senses. By means of this kind of cooperation and balance, human beings can relate constructively to the world around them and achieve great things in fulfillment of their roles as God's stewards on Earth. In this process, human beings are expected to conduct themselves decisively and rationally, and to make proper use of the laws embedded within the universe based on a sound understanding of causality and the need for harmony among the various parts of the cosmic system.

(a) The lexical definition of the root *sh-h-d*

The letters *sh-h-d* form a root that denotes presence, knowledge, and the conveyance of knowledge to others. The verb *shahida/yashhadhu* denotes the act of witnessing or bearing witness, which implies the presence of the witness to the events or truths to which he or she is testifying. The noun *shahādah* denotes both the act of witnessing or bearing witness, and the testimony itself. The active participle *shāhid* refers to a witness, and the verbal noun *mushāhadah* refers to the act of seeing with one's own eyes. One of the names of God is *al-Shahīd*, which means, "the One Whose knowledge nothing escapes," because He is present to all and everything at all times. When speaking of God's absolute knowledge (*ʿilm*), we refer to Him as *al-ʿAlīm*. When such knowledge is construed as encompassing matters that are hidden, concealed or mysterious, we refer to Him as *al-Khabīr*, and when it is construed as encompassing matters that are visible and evident, we refer to Him as *al-Shahīd*.

(b) The usage-based definition of *sh-h-d*

Derivates of the root *sh-h-d* occur 124 times in the Qur'an, and in the following senses. In *Sūrah al-Burūj*, 85:7 the word *shuhūd* (plural of *shāhid*) is used to refer to those who are 'witnesses' to what they themselves are doing to others. The word *shahādah* can refer to an act of witnessing that takes place via physical sight, or via insight or understanding. In either case, the word denotes a definitive report that constitutes evidence in favor of what the witness is saying. The verb *shahida* is used in *Sūrah al-Zukhruf*, 43:19 in the sense of knowing about something by virtue of having seen it with one's own eyes. Of those who claim that the angels are females, God asks rhetorically, "did they witness their creation (*ashahidū khalqahum*)?" (Cf. *Sūrah al-Kahf*, 18:51.) The same verb, *shahida*, is used in *Sūrah al-Baqarah*, 2:84 in the sense of bearing witness or testifying to the truth of something. And the word *shahādah* is used in *Sūrah al-Raʿd*, 13:9 to refer to "all that can be witnessed by a creature's senses or mind."

(c) Categories of *shahādah*

The realm of existence that can be understood through human reason is referred to in the Qur'an by the terms *al-āfāq* ('horizons') and *al-anfus* ('souls' or 'selves'). These terms are found in *Sūrah Fuṣṣilat*, 41:53 quoted earlier, where God states, "We shall make them fully understand Our messages [through what they perceive] in the utmost horizons [of the universe] (*fī al-āfāq*) and within themselves (*wa fī anfusihim*), so that it will become clear unto them that this [revelation] is indeed the truth." In a discussion of the meaning of the term *al-āfāq*, al-Shawkānī quotes Ibn Yazīd, a leading early scholar of Islam, as stating, "*Al-āfāq* are the signs observed in the sky." Commentators Qatādah and al-Ḍaḥḥāk defined the term as referring to "God's deeds among the people of the world." ʿAṭā understood it to refer to "astronomical, meteorological and terrestrial entities and phenomena, including the sun, the moon, the stars, night and day, winds, and the like." Ibn Kathīr for his part interpreted the phrase *al-āfāq* as referring to "the Muslim conquests and Islam's triumph over other regions and religions." As for al-Rāzī, he opined that the term denoted "astronomical and planetary signs, the signs of day and night, in light, shadow and darkness, the four elements [fire, water, earth and air], and the three compounds known as mineral, animal and vegetable."

(d) The relationship between the realms of *al-āfāq* and *al-anfus*

It is clear that these two realms are closely linked based on the fact that whenever one of them is mentioned in the Qur'an, the other is mentioned as well. One example of this pairing is found in *Sūrah al-Kahf*, 18:51. Referring to the angels, God declares, "I did not make them witnesses of the creation of the heavens and the earth, nor of the creation of their own selves." Another such pairing is found in *Sūrah al-*

Dhāriyāt, 51:20-21 quoted earlier: "And on earth there are signs [of God's existence, visible] to all who are endowed with inner certainty, just as [there are signs thereof] within your own selves: can you not, then, see?"

The Qur'an thus emphasizes the interconnection and complementariness of these two spheres: the fact that the universe has been placed at human beings' disposal negates the notion that there is an inherent struggle or conflict between human beings and the rest of the cosmos. On the contrary, in order for human beings to be good stewards of the Earth and to "colonize" Earth in pursuit of happiness and prosperity, they must strive for a sound understanding of both "the horizons" (*al-āfāq*) and of the human psyche and its legitimate needs (*al-anfus*). The better we understand the universe, the better able we are to make good use of it. Hence, human progress and development depend on the ability to know and relate to both the outer world (*al-āfāq*) and our inner worlds (*al-anfus*). In this way only can we strive for the common good of humanity.

FOURTH: QUR'ANIC CRITERIA FOR *Maʿrifah*

The Qur'an demonstrates a concern for disciplined thought on the levels of both ethics and knowledge. Ethical integrity as it relates to knowledge, important though it is, is insufficient. It is not enough for a scholar to have pure motives for his work without also conveying information accurately and completely. Nor is it enough to be academically disciplined in terms of accuracy and thoroughness without putting one's knowledge to the proper ethical uses. Rather, we need to hold ourselves to strict standards both ethically and academically in our pursuit of knowledge. The Qur'an seeks to guide us toward beneficial knowledge within the proper boundaries. In order to achieve true epistemological progress, which requires integration of our various sources of knowledge, we must demonstrate proper respect for both the Divine Law and human reason. We need to formulate rules that will both facilitate and regulate scholarship by ensuring that our research methods are sound and free of debilitating errors.

1) *Qur'anic ethical standards of maʿrifah*
The importance of ethical standards in relation to knowledge lies in the fact that such standards guide the choices we make as to how we will put such knowledge to use. The Qur'an speaks of ethical values either in terms of legal rulings, or in terms of human beings' innate moral consciousness. People do not, of course, always obey their consciences. Nevertheless, conscience remains deeply embedded in the human psyche. Consequently, one tends to be intuitively aware of having violated a moral principle. The purpose of knowledge is to empower human beings to be God's vicegerents by bringing prosperity both to themselves and to the Earth in keeping with God's commands, and it is the Qur'an that informs us of what these commands are. The precepts set down in the Qur'an provide us with guidelines for relating to others and to the wider Cosmos in such a way that we use our God-given knowledge constructively rather than destructively.

(a) Prohibiting strife and contention

Competition in the sense of aspiration is one thing, and conflict and strife are another. Aspiration has a noble, laudable purpose (cf. *Sūrah al-Muṭaffifīn*, 83:26), whereas strife and contention lead to nothing but division. As God has said, "do not be at variance with one another, lest you lose heart and your moral strength desert you." There are two types of disagreement. The first type is permissible. In fact, it is one of the hallmarks of the Islamic academic and intellectual heritage, having served to fuel an intellectual revolution and the accumulation of vast epistemological wealth. Differences of opinion among Muslim scholars over questions of scriptural and theological interpretation have helped to deepen our understanding of the truth and to achieve significant benefits in the theoretical and practical realms alike. However, numerous verses of the Qur'an criticize the behavior of Jews and Christians whose rulings and judgments violated principles of which they had clear knowledge. God warns in *Sūrah Āl ʿImrān*, 3:105, "Be not like those who have drawn apart from one another and have taken to conflicting views after all evidence of the truth has come unto them; for them tremendous suffering is in store." One of the most devastating things that can happen to the general populace and the intellectual elite alike is for them to succumb to the spiritual weaknesses that led to the demise of bygone civilizations. One such weakness consists in knowledge losing its moral foundations and high-minded aims, with the result that it goes from being knowledge of God and a source of virtue to being a destructive force that tears at the fabric of the society and destroys its religious unity.

We know from the study of intellectual and doctrinal history that there are numerous potential causes of difference and disagreement. Whenever societies take steps in the direction of progress and higher civilization, the rifts among their members tend to widen. The result is the emergence of competing schools of thought, religions, sects and denominations. None of this is evil in and of itself. However, such developments turn destructive when people surrender to selfish whims. God warned the Prophet in *Sūrah al-Baqarah*, 2:145 that if he followed the "(vain) desires" (*ahwā'*, plural of *hawā*) of those who opposed his way, he would be a wrongdoer. To submit to Divine Revelation is to stand opposed to mere human caprice and vain desire. God asks rhetorically in *Sūrah Muḥammad*, 47:14, "Is then one who is on a clear [path] from his Lord no better than one to whom the evil of his conduct seems pleasing, and such as follow their own lusts (*ittabaʿū ahwā'ahum*)?"

The Qur'an and the Sunnah are the two primary sources of knowledge for the Muslim community. Hence, disputes that arise from opposition to what is taught by Divine Revelation are caused by people going the way of their own caprices, whether out of love for worldly gain, hatred for people of faith, or intellectual hubris. In *Sūrah al-Qaṣaṣ*, 28:78 we read about how a certain wealthy man of Moses' day defiantly declared, "[My wealth] has been given to me only by virtue of the knowledge that is in me!" Knowledge is, first and foremost, a gift from God, and should be recognized as such. Apart from this recognition, knowledge becomes a veil that blinds us to our need for our lives and relationships to be ordered by the Divine Law.

(b) Objectivity

By "objectivity", I am referring to the act of stepping back from one's emotions and prejudices in relation to an issue or question concerning which a decision or judgment needs to be made. Thus defined, objectivity requires honesty and humility. Another concomitant of objectivity is academic integrity, which includes a commitment to practices such as attributing statements to their proper sources and not reading one's own thoughts or intentions into what another person has said. Consequently, objectivity can be quite difficult to achieve and maintain.

The term 'objectivity' as such does not appear anywhere in the Qur'an. However the concept of objectivity as defined above is alluded to in numerous places in the Qur'an as a necessity for making sound judgments and relating fairly to others. An example of objectivity presents itself in the balanced way in which, when God speaks about various communities, including the Jews and the Christians, He points to both their strengths and their weaknesses, their virtues and their vices. We read in *Sūrah Āl ʿImrān*, 3:75: "And among the followers of earlier revelation there is many a one who, if you entrust him with a treasure, will [faithfully] restore it to you; and there is among them many a one who, if you entrust him with a tiny gold coin, will not restore it to you unless you keep standing over him." (Cf. *Sūrah Āl ʿImrān*, 3:110-113.) Hence, although it has become popular to equate 'objectivity' with non-adherence to any value system or doctrinal consideration, one could not describe someone who adheres to the standards of Islamic law as lacking in objectivity. Rather, the Qur'an calls upon believers to strive for impartiality and fairness while cautioning against the dangers of neglecting these noble virtues. The Muslim is expected to relate to whatever subject or issue he or she studies without overreacting and without prejudice for or against one group or another depending on worldly fortunes or status, venal desires and ambitions, or baseless caprices and passions.

(c) A warning against suppression of the truth

God warns, "...do not overlay the truth with falsehood, and do not knowingly suppress the truth" (*Sūrah al-Baqarah*, 2:42). Elsewhere, God warns those who do engage in such concealment of the great spiritual torment that lies in store for them: "Verily, as for those who suppress aught of the revelation which God has bestowed from on high, and barter it away for a trifling gain – they but fill their bellies with fire. And God will not speak unto them on the Day of Resurrection, nor will He cleanse them [of their sins]; and grievous suffering awaits them" (*Sūrah al-Baqarah*, 2:174).

Those who are obliged to answer a question are forbidden to conceal or suppress what they know. However, in particular situations and when dealing with certain individuals, one may be duty-bound to suppress certain information because those to whom one is speaking would be unable to comprehend this information, and would thereby be liable to misconstrue it and, worse still, disbelieve God and His Messenger.

(d) The dangers of being selective in the search for knowledge

Addressing the children of Israel, God asks, "Do you, then, believe in some parts of the divine writ and deny the truth of other parts? What, then, could be the reward of those among you who do such things but ignominy in the life of this world and, on the Day of Resurrection, commitment to most grievous suffering?" (*Sūrah al-Baqarah*, 2:85). This admonition reminds us of the need to develop an inclusive view of whatever subject we are studying. Rather than falling into narrow, atomistic, compartmentalized views of reality, we need to adhere to a method that provides us with a balanced mix of experience and information. At the same time, we should be diligent about purging our thought systems of foreign, extraneous, or spurious elements and ideas.

(e) Speculation and surmise

The Qur'an places no store by beliefs based on mere conjecture no matter how many people happen to subscribe to them. Truth is not measured by the number of people who embrace it any more than falsehood is identified by the scarcity of its followers. As we read in *Sūrah al-Anʿām*, 6:116, "if you pay heed to the majority of those [who live] on earth, they will but lead you astray from the path of God: they follow but [other people's] conjectures, and they themselves do nothing but guess." Similarly, *Sūrah al-Baqarah*, 2:78 urges us not to depend on "unlettered people who have no real knowledge of the divine writ, [following] only wishful beliefs and depending on nothing but conjecture." It is clear, then, that true knowledge requires that we demand the kind of accuracy and precision that will lead to certainty.

(f) The prohibition of falsification and lying

In *Sūrah Āl ʿImrān*, 3:71 God says, "O followers of earlier revelation! Why do you cloak the truth with falsehood and conceal the truth of which you are [so well] aware?" A similar admonition comes in *Sūrah al-Baqarah*, 2:79: "Woe, then, unto those who write down, with their own hands, [something which they claim to be] divine writ, and then say, 'This is from God,' in order to acquire a trifling gain thereby; woe, then, unto them for what their hands have written, and woe unto them for all that they may have gained!" Deliberate corruption of holy writ is a moral transgression. This sort of transgression is spoken of in *Sūrah Āl ʿImrān*, 3:78, which reads, "Behold, there are indeed some among them who distort the Bible with their tongues, so as to make you think that [what they say] is from the Bible, the while it is not from the Bible." When sound knowledge is set aside, it is bound to be replaced by untruths. If, however, the epistemological method being followed is based on sources that yield solid facts, the results we obtain will be accurate and sound, uncontaminated by the vices of cheating, deception, hypocrisy, and pedantry. We are admonished in *Sūrah al-Naḥl*, 16:116, "Do not utter falsehoods by letting your tongues determine [at your own discretion], 'This is lawful and that is forbidden,' thus attributing your own lying inventions to God."

2) *Scientific standards of truth in the Qur'an*

(a) Refuse to accept claims not backed up by evidence

The Qur'an affirms the importance of verifying the accuracy of any information on which we are going to base an attitude or position. This verification takes place based on two types of evidence that we will term revelational and rational. Revelational evidence is evidence derived from the Qur'an or the Sunnah of the Prophet, while rational evidence consists of indisputable rational premises. In numerous verses of the Qur'an we encounter demands for evidence for claims people make on controversial matters. In response to those who worship beings other than God and appeal to tradition in support of their practice, God commands the Prophet, "Say: 'Have you any [certain] knowledge which you could proffer to us? You follow but [other people's] conjectures, and you yourselves do nothing but guess'" (*Sūrah al-Anʿām*, 6:148). Similarly we read in *Sūrah al-Aḥqāf*, 46:4, "Say: 'Have you [really] given thought to what it is that you invoke instead of God? Show me what these [beings or forces) have created anywhere on earth! Or had they, perchance, a share in [creating] the heavens? [If so,] bring me any divine writ preceding this one, or any [other] vestige of knowledge – if what you claim is true!'" Claims devoid of proof avail nothing. As we read in *Sūrah al-Naml*, 27:64: "Could there be any divine power besides God? Say: '[If you think so,] produce your evidence – if you truly believe in your claim!'" A similar message is conveyed by *Sūrah al-Kahf*, 18:15: "These people of ours have taken to worshipping [other] deities instead of Him, without being able to adduce any reasonable evidence in support of their beliefs; and who could be more wicked than he who invents a lie about God?" For other references to evidence that God provides for the truth of His message, see *Sūrah al-Anʿām*, 6:83, *Sūrah al-Baqarah*, 2:211, *Sūrah al-Mā'idah*, 5:110, and *Sūrah al-Anʿām*, 6:104.

(b) Do not delve into matters of which you have no knowledge

This is a cardinal Qur'anic rule for those who aspire to sound thinking and sound research, which requires that we know both our strengths and our limitations. *Sūrah al-Anʿām*, 6:68 admonishes the Prophet to turn his back on those who speak ignorantly about God's messages, while *Sūrah al-Isrā'*, 17:36 instructs all and sundry as follows: "And never concern yourself with anything of which you have no knowledge: verily, [your] hearing and sight and heart – all of them – will be called to account for it [on Judgment Day]."

(c) Make careful use of words

Sound academic research requires the precise use of terms. This point is made in another context in *Sūrah al-Ḥujurāt*, 49:14, which reads, "The Bedouin say, 'We have attained to faith.' Say [unto them, O Muhammad]: 'You have not [yet] attained to faith; you should [rather] say, "We have [outwardly] surrendered" – for [true] faith has not yet entered your hearts.'" In *Sūrah al-Baqarah*, 2:104, the Muslim community is addressed with the words: "O you who have attained to faith! Do not say [to the Prophet], 'Listen to us,' but rather say, 'Have patience with us,' and hearken [unto him], since grievous suffering awaits those who deny the truth." (Or, as Yusuf Ali translates the same passage, "O ye of Faith! Say not [to the Messenger] words of ambiguous import, but words of respect; and hearken [to him]: To those without Faith is a grievous punishment.")

Believers are expected to speak respectfully and not to use words that could lead either to misunderstanding or to wrongdoing. It should always be remembered that the circumstances, the timing, the environment, the situation, and the person to whom one is speaking all play a role in how one's words will be perceived and, hence, the effect they will have. Conversely, when words or statements are taken out of their original context, serious misunderstandings, errors and confusion can result. It is a given, then, that the Muslim academic or researcher must take special care in the way in which he or she uses language, recognizing that words are defined by their contexts as much as they are by lexicons, and that other people's language should be interpreted based on the way in which they themselves understand it.

Just as specialists in this or that field of knowledge develop an in-house jargon that would be incomprehensible to an outsider, the people of this or that community or society come, over time, to attribute new meanings to the words and expressions they use in day-to-day interactions. In order to be recognized as competent in a given field, one has to have mastered that field's special terminology or jargon. Similarly, the academic or scientific methodology which we glean from the Qur'an teaches us not to form judgments about people until we have made certain that we understand the meanings of the words with which they communicate.

Terminology plays a pivotal role in virtually all forms of intellectual creativity and in the discussions and debates to which they give rise. The more a field broadens and the more issues ramify, the more critical terminology becomes for conveying facts clearly and succinctly and for streamlining the exchange of ideas. On the other hand, one danger of newly evolving terminology, particularly in this age of doctrinal, intellectual and cultural clashes, is that it has the potential to crowd out the traditional terms used in academic and cultural spheres to the point where, little by little, it replaces the Islamic beliefs, notions, and moral values to which these traditional terms originally gave expression.

(d) Strive for a proper fit between your field of study and your scientific method

The importance of such a "good fit" is alluded to in *Sūrah al-Zukhruf*, 43:19, which reads, "And [yet] they claim that the angels – who in themselves are but beings created by the Most Gracious – are females: [but] did they witness their creation? This false claim of theirs will be recorded, and they will be called to account [for it on Judgment Day]!" The idolaters of the Prophet's day were espousing an epistemological view according to which the angels are females. Elsewhere we are told that these same people attributed "daughters" to God: "Or, [if you believe in God, how can you believe that] He has daughters, whereas you yourselves would have sons?" God challenges their claim by asking whether they had been present at the angels' creation. What this means is that the claim that the angels are females and that they are God's daughters can only be shown to be valid or invalid, true or untrue, by appeal to empirical evidence. The only empirical evidence that would fill the bill in such a situation would have been for the people making the claim either to have witnessed the angels' creation, or to have seen these angels at some later time, neither of which was a requirement they could fulfill. It could only be concluded, therefore, that those making this claim were engaged in unfounded speculation. In this connection, *Sūrah al-Anʿām*, 6:100-101 reads, "And yet, some have come to attribute to all manner of invisible beings a place side by side with God – although it is He who has created them [all]; and in their ignorance they have invented for Him sons and daughters!

Limitless is He in His glory, and sublimely exalted above anything that men may devise by way of definition: the Originator of the heavens and the earth! How could it be that He should have a child without there ever having been a mate for Him – since it is He who has created everything, and He alone knows everything?" Such people's claims lacked any basis in fact, nor were they founded on any scientific method appropriate to their epistemological field, since the realm about which they were making their claim was that of *al-ghayb*, which lies beyond the ken of human perception. Worse still, they attributed perfection to themselves and imperfection to God!

The importance of a proper fit between the field of knowledge one is dealing with and the scientific method one employs cannot be stressed too highly. No scientific progress occurs without research, and scientific research depends on method. Sound method yields sound research; faulty method yields faulty research.

(e) Strive for a proper fit between the epistemological field in question and your intellectual capacities

It goes without saying that intellectual capacities have their limitations. This is true on both the level of intelligence or reason in general, and on the level of individual abilities, which vary from one person to another. The Qur'an makes clear that there are certain matters that are beyond the reach of human understanding or knowledge. These include the Divine Essence, the nature of Spirit, when the Day of Resurrection will come, the world of the angels, the inner workings of the Universe, how successful we will be in our livelihoods, what our lifespans will be, and the ultimate fates of both individuals and nations. We have not been equipped to know these things, nor are we held responsible for doing so. As we read in *Sūrah al-Aʿrāf*, 7:187:

> They will ask you [O Prophet] about the Last Hour: "When will it come to pass?" Say: "Verily, knowledge thereof rests with my Sustainer alone. None but He will reveal it in its time. Heavily will it weigh on the heavens and the earth; [and] it will not fall upon you otherwise than of a sudden." They will ask you – as if you could gain insight into this [mystery] by dint of persistent inquiry! Say: "Knowledge thereof rests with my Sustainer alone; but [of this] most people are unaware."

A similar message is found in *Sūrah Luqmān*, 31:34:

> Verily, with God alone rests the knowledge of when the Last Hour will come; and He [it is Who] sends down rain; and He [alone] knows what is in the wombs: whereas no one knows what he will reap tomorrow, and no one knows in what land he will die. Verily, God [alone] is All-Knowing, All-Aware.

Muslims must bind their reason to their religion; in other words, they must use their minds, but with awareness of the limits of the mind in the face of mysteries to which God has not granted us access. Otherwise, we may squander our mental energy on pursuits that yield no benefit. Muslims should inquire into those things God has urged them to gain knowledge of, and they should do so in keeping with the limits set down in the Divine Law as given in the Qur'an and the Sunnah of the Prophet. Only then will the Muslim community be able to protect itself from error and achieve the good both in this life and the next.

(f) Achieve a thorough grasp of the issue at hand

Formulation of an appropriate ruling on an issue requires an accurate understanding of that issue. This understanding is built in turn on a thorough acquaintance with all its aspects, since otherwise, the ruling might be invalidated by factors that were not taken into consideration in the beginning. This is why inclusive thinking is so vital. Judging an idea, person, group or school of thought based on a partial examination will lead to a decision, attitude or ruling that is unfair in one way or another, which is in violation of what God has commanded us in *Sūrah al-Mā'idah*, 5:8: "O you who have attained to faith! Be ever steadfast in your devotion to God, bearing witness to the truth in all equity; and never let hatred of anyone lead you into the sin of deviating from justice. Be just: this is closest to being God-conscious. And remain conscious of God: verily God is aware of all that you do."

The Qur'an speaks harshly of those who form judgments based on incomplete knowledge: "Nay, but they are bent on giving the lie to everything the wisdom whereof they do not comprehend, and ere its inner meaning has become clear to them. Even thus did those who lived before their time give the lie to the truth: and behold what happened in the end to those evildoers" (*Sūrah Yūnus*, 10:39). As for a fair and sound judgment, it is based on both complete understanding and a charitable motive. Hence, rulings set forth in the Qur'an may be followed by a statement such as: "God wants to make [all this] clear unto you, and to guide you onto the [righteous] ways of life of those who preceded you, and to turn unto you in His mercy: for God is All-Knowing, Wise" (*Sūrah al-Nisā'*, 4:26).

When a ruling is based on a thorough comprehension of the issue at hand and when it is applicable to all the forms such an issue might take, this helps to prevent unfair generalization of such a ruling to situations or people to which, or whom, it does not apply. If the cause that gave rise to some past ruling recurs in another situation, the same ruling will apply; otherwise, it will not. Therefore it is of great importance to distinguish between one situation and another lest our rulings be misapplied. A principle related to this is that only the person guilty of a crime should be punished for it. As we read in *Sūrah Fāṭir*, 35:18:

> No bearer of burdens shall be made to bear another's burden; and if one weighed down by his load calls upon [another] to help him carry it, nothing thereof may be carried [by that other], even if it be one's near of kin. Hence, you can [truly] warn only those who stand in awe of their Sustainer although He is beyond the reach of their perception, and are constant in prayer, and [know that] whoever grows in purity, attains to purity but for the good of his own self, and [that] with God is all journeys' end.

It follows, then, that if a scholar makes an error, we have no right to hold other scholars accountable for it. Similarly, if one member of a group, sect or religion commits an error or even a crime, this does not give us the right to issue a blanket judgment against all other members of this group or religion. Rather, the ruling or verdict applies only to the guilty party and to the relevant situation. *Sūrah Āl ʿImrān*, 3:110-115 makes clear that although some "followers of earlier revelation" are iniquitous,

> they are not all alike: among the followers of earlier revelation there are

upright people, who recite God's messages throughout the night and prostrate themselves [before Him]. They believe in God and the Last Day, and enjoin the doing of what is right and forbid the doing of what is wrong, and vie with one another in doing good works: and these are among the righteous. And whatever good they do, they shall never be denied the reward thereof: for, God has full knowledge of those who are conscious of Him. (cf. *Sūrah Yūnus*, 10:40)

The Muslim should derive knowledge from the proper sources while at the same time being open to the knowledge and experience of others. Different types of knowledge are derived from different sources. Revelational knowledge, for example, is derived from Divine Revelation, while human knowledge is derived from a variety of other sources. When a question arises about this or that, the Qur'an directs the inquirers to the appropriate source of knowledge. In *Sūrah al-Anbiyā'*, 21:7, God says to the Prophet, "For [even] before your time, We never sent [as Our apostles] any but [mortal] men, whom We inspired – hence, [tell the deniers of the truth,] 'If you do not know this, ask the followers of earlier revelation.'" If the type of knowledge we are seeking has to do with the material world, then it makes most sense to seek this from those who possess this type of knowledge rather than from someone else. Similarly, the tools and methods we employ in gathering information should be suitable to the type of knowledge we are after. So long as the knowledge people possess is of benefit and its uses are in keeping with the Divine Law, we are called upon to pursue greater understanding of their cultures, their academic disciplines, and the learning they have accumulated over the centuries so that we, too, can spread blessing through the creative use of information and its applications.

In *Sūrah al-Kahf*, 18:65-66, we read about how Moses, encountering a servant of God who had been given special wisdom (identified in commentaries as Khidr), asked if he could follow this servant and learn from him even though he (Khidr) was less well-known, and possibly of lower rank, than was Moses. Similarly, we find Adam's son Cain expressing the need to learn from the example of a crow, even though a bird might be considered a lower form of life than a human being. After killing his brother Abel, Cain saw a raven which showed him how to bury his brother, and he learned from the raven's concrete example. We read in *Sūrah al-Mā'idah*, 5:31:

> Thereupon God sent forth a raven which scratched the earth, to show him how he might conceal the nakedness of his brother's body. [And Cain] cried out: "Oh, woe is me! Am I then too weak to do what this raven did, and to conceal the nakedness of my brother's body?" – and was thereupon smitten with remorse.

We also find that the Queen of Sheba, before surrendering herself to the one God worshipped by Solomon, was possessed of a profound wisdom which God Himself affirms in the Qur'an. The Qur'an quotes her as saying, "Verily, whenever kings enter a country they corrupt it, and turn the noblest of its people into the most abject. And this is the way they [always] behave" (*Sūrah al-Naml*, 27:34).

When gleaning information from others, we need to distinguish between what constitutes 'cultural invasion' and cultural exchange. The fear of subjecting themselves to cultural hegemony by others has prevented many Muslims from benefitting from sound knowledge and exploring the horizons that would have enabled them to overcome backwardness of various sorts and contribute to positive, constructive change in their societies. However, a truly progressive scientific approach is prepared to glean knowledge from whatever source necessary so long as the knowledge it contains is accurate and lends itself to the service of the good, and this regardless of the character of the person or group that serves as this source. As we have seen, the Qur'an calls upon Muslims to derive benefit from earlier revelations by affirming whatever knowledge they supply provided that it is in congruence with the Islamic message. Some of the contents of earlier revelations, according to Islamic teaching, have suffered corruption, as a result of which discernment is in order so as to make it possible to adopt what is still sound in these messages and to reject what has been corrupted or falsified. Muslims are to study, analyze and critique the contents of earlier revelations in such a way that they draw from them what is good, true and beneficial.

The Qur'an was revealed both to complete and to abrogate previous revelations. God tells the Prophet in *Sūrah al-Mā'idah*, 5:48, "And unto you [O Prophet] have We vouchsafed this divine writ, setting forth the truth, confirming the truth of whatever there still remains of earlier revelations and determining what is true therein." *Sūrah al-Aḥqāf*, 46:12 reads, "And yet, before this there was the revelation of Moses, a guide and a [sign of God's] grace; and this [Qur'an] is a divine writ confirming the truth [of the Torah] in the Arabic tongue, to warn those who are bent on evildoing, and [to bring] a glad tiding to the doers of good." In the same vein, *Sūrah al-Ṣaff*, 61:6 reads, "And [this happened, too,] when Jesus, the son of Mary, said: 'O children of Israel! Behold, I am an apostle of God unto you, [sent] to confirm the truth of whatever there still remains of the Torah, and to give [you] the glad tiding of an apostle who shall come after me, whose name shall be Ahmad.'" This passage is a confirmation that successive revelations represent an accumulation of knowledge, with the later building upon what was left by the earlier. Similarly, it illustrates the phenomenon whereby the Qur'an confirms all of the knowledge that was brought in earlier times through divine revelation because such knowledge is intended for everyone. Islam's revealed precepts and doctrines, being marked by the highest levels of certainty, stand in judgment over other teachings and serve as a criterion by which we are to judge the truth of other revelations and sources of knowledge.

This is the approach that should be taken to the heritage passed down to us by bygone nations and civilizations, as well as to our own Islamic scientific heritage. Our Islamic academic heritage undoubtedly contains both truth and error, since it consists of human interpretations. Such interpretations, the aim of which was to arrive at truth, left a massive body of writings that have both benefited and burdened later generations. Our job is to sift through what we have; whatever we find to be in agreement with the revealed message, we should accept, and whatever conflicts with it, we should set aside.

5
ʿIlm in the Qur'an

ʿILM IS ONE of the most frequently occurring terms in the Qur'an, as are derivatives of other roots denoting similar or related concepts. *ʿIlm*, generally translated as 'knowledge', is the only thing God commanded the Prophet to pray to receive more of. Arriving at a definition of *ʿilm* requires a discussion of numerous themes, including both the lexical meaning of the term *ʿilm* and its customary uses. We first come to a discussion of the word's lexical definition and the features that set it apart from other terms within the same semantic field, as well as the ways in which it is linked to such terms in various contexts.

FIRST: THE DEFINITION AND TYPES OF *ʿIlm*

1) *The lexical definition of ʿilm*

ʿIlm is the opposite of *jahl*, or ignorance. It refers to perception or knowledge in general terms. *ʿIlm* might also be defined as the confident belief that something is as it truly is. Philologists have proposed that the word *ʿilm* derives its meaning from the word *ʿalāmah*, meaning sign, symbol or signal. The term *maʿlam* (plural, *maʿālim*) refers to a signpost, guidepost, landmark or distinguishing feature of a place or an object. Unlike most other verbal nouns, the word *ʿilm* can be pluralized (*ʿulūm*), in which connection it denotes a field of study or academic discipline. The active participle *ʿālim* (plural, *ʿulamā'*) refers to a scientist (literally, a 'knower' or 'one who knows'), while the related word *ʿalīm* means knowledgeable and, when referring to God, All-Knowing (cf. *Sūrah al-Anʿām*, 6:101: "He alone knows everything" – *wa huwa bi kulli shay'in ʿalīm*). The verb *ʿalima/yaʿlamu* (which can take a direct object or be followed by the preposition *bi*) means to be aware of, to sense, to know, to master, to comprehend, or to be certain of. Speaking of the person who turns his back on truth, *Sūrah al-ʿAlaq*, 96:14 asks,

"Does he, then, not know (*alam yaʿlam*) that God sees [all] (*anna Allāh yarā*)?" Used in the sense of 'distinguish', the verb appears in *Sūrah al-Baqarah*, 2:220, which reminds us that God "knows the person who means mischief from the person who means good" (*yaʿlamu al-mufsid min al-muṣliḥ*).

2) *The usage-based definition*

Most definitions of *ʿilm* identify it as a certain belief that corresponds to reality, a definitive judgment that is not subject to doubt. All such definitions distinguish between *ʿilm* and *takhayyul*, that is, fantasy or imagination. *ʿIlm* is accurate to the extent that it corresponds to actual reality. The definition of *ʿilm* as a perception of something as it actually is includes two possibilities. In one of these, it refers to a perception of the nature or essence of something, and in the other, it refers to a judgment regarding the presence or absence of an attribute in someone or something. The first usage is illustrated in the statement, "you may not know them, [but] God knows them (*lā taʿlamūnahum, Allāhu yaʿlamuhum*)" (*Sūrah al-Anfāl*, 8:60). As for the second type of usage, it takes two direct objects, as in the phrase, "and if you have thus ascertained that they are believers... (*in ʿalimtumūhunna mu'mināt*)" (*Sūrah al-Mumtaḥanah*, 60:10). Al-Jurjānī defined *ʿilm* as "a certain belief that corresponds to reality." God refers to Himself in the Qur'an as *al-ʿĀlim* (the One who knows) and *al-ʿAlīm* (the All-Knowing). The Qur'an attributes the verb *ʿalima/yaʿlamu* to God, and describes God as possessing *ʿilm*. God is also described as *ʿallām al-ghuyūb* (*Sūrah al-Mā'idah*, 5:109), which means that nothing is hidden from His knowledge or perception: He knows what was, what is, what will be, what is not, and how things that are not would be if they were. God is aware of the faith of believers, the unbelief of unbelievers, and the sins of the disobedient. However, God's knowledge of what people will do in the future does not rob of their freedom; hence, each individuals remains responsible for his or her actions, words and beliefs. God's *ʿilm* is the cause behind the existence of the world (*al-ʿālam*), which is, in turn, the cause behind the *ʿilm* of human beings. God's *ʿilm* encompasses all aspects of existence, both outward (*ẓāhir*) and inward (*bāṭin*). Being eternal, God's knowledge is not dependent on events in time.

Nor is it acquired through the senses or reasoning as is the knowledge of human beings.

3) *Divisions of ʿilm*

Scholars have divided *ʿilm* into two categories. The first is that of *ʿilm qadīm*, that is, timeless or eternal knowledge, which can be predicated of God alone. The second is *ʿilm ḥadīth*, or temporal knowledge, which is predicated of creatures. Temporal knowledge is further divided into the dual categories of intuitive, which refers to the kind of elementary knowledge that one gains through one or more of the five senses and which requires no conscious thought or reflection; and acquired knowledge, which is obtained via conscious mental effort and a deliberate learning process. This is the import behind the saying of the Prophet: *innamā al-ʿilmu bi al-taʿallum*, "Knowledge comes through learning." The differences among individuals with respect to acquired knowledge are alluded to in *Sūrah al-Raʿd*, 13:17, which states that God "sends down water from the skies, and the channels flow, each according to its measure." In other words, people vary in their God-given ability to take in and 'channel' information and knowledge. The type of knowledge classed above as *ʿilm ḍarūrī*, or intuitive knowledge, is available to all able-bodied and able-minded individuals. The laws God has revealed to human beings over the ages have been revealed on the level of intuitive knowledge, that is, in language that is accessible to people of all levels of intelligence. For this reason, all people of mature mind are equally accountable for their response to the basic requirements of their religion. As for the minute details concerning the components and conditions for acts of worship, grammatical questions, analysis of linguistic structures and the like, these belong to the category of acquired knowledge, or *ʿilm muktasab*.

Lastly, *ʿilm* is divided into the dual categories of theoretical (*naẓarī*) and practical (*ʿamalī*). Theoretical knowledge is knowledge that, once it has been acquired on the level of understanding, is complete. This category includes knowledge of physical realities such as scientific facts. As for practical knowledge, it is knowledge which, in order to be complete, must be applied in practice; this category includes, for example, knowledge of rites of worship.

SECOND: LEVELS AND CRITERIA OF *ʿIlm*

1) *Levels of ʿilm*

The outside world (*al-ʿālam al-khārijī*) is what makes *ʿilm* possible. Since the senses are the only means we have of communicating with the tangible realm, the first stage of accessing knowledge is that of sensation (*iḥsās*), which is the interaction of the senses with tangible entities through the reception of data from sensory stimuli. This sensory data is transferred to the psyche in an ascending progression from simple, primary receptive processes to something more complex. This is followed by *idrāk*, or cognition, which involves a representation of the external reality to the perceiver. This representation is stored in the mind; this is then followed by *tadhakkur*, or recollection, in which the individual attempts to recover on the conscious level what remains of the data stored in the previous stage. When the desired images are restored to the conscious mind there occurs a process of *fahm*, or understanding, which is generally associated with a word or expression you have heard someone utter.

A further level of understanding might be referred to as *fiqh*, which involves a comprehension of what the person addressing you intends through what he or she is saying to you. Beyond this we have a level referred to as *dirāyah*, or cognizance, which is the knowledge that results from repeated introductions to the subject at hand. *Yaqīn*, or complete certainty, applies to the state in which you have learned something so thoroughly that no other possibility is imaginable to you. The term *dhihn*, usually rendered simply as mind or intellect, refers to the willingness to acquire knowledge one does not yet have, while *fikr* refers to the mental process of shifting back and forth between concepts and ideas on one hand, and the phenomena, principles or facts that demonstrate the validity of such concepts and ideas on the other. As for *ḥads*, sometimes translated as 'intuition', it refers to what distinguishes the act of thinking. The term *dhakā'*, usually rendered as 'intelligence', refers to the power of intuition, while *fiṭnah*, or perceptiveness, refers to the ability to attend to the content one needs to know; and *kays*, or 'subtlety', is the ability to deduce what is most useful or beneficial. The term *ra'y* refers to the process of conjuring and reflecting on the premises one has been presented with, while *tabayyun* refers to the process of arriving at clarity concerning something that was ambiguous or obscure. The term *istibṣār*, similarly, refers to knowledge gained through reflection, while the term *iḥāṭah* refers to a thorough grasp of something from all angles. The term *ẓann* refers to the process of adopting a position not as a certainty but, rather, with an awareness that there are two sides to the issue at hand, neither of which is clearly superior to the other. And lastly, the term *ʿaql* refers to an essence by means of which you perceive intangible realities through the mediation of sensory perception.

Ibn al-Qayyim proposed another division of the levels of *ʿilm* which begins with the higher levels and descends to the lower. The order in which he lists these levels is as follows: (1) The level at which God speaks directly to His servant, unmediated, when the servant is in a state of wakefulness. This highest level of knowledge is spoken of in *Sūrah al-Nisā'* 4:164, which tells us that "God spoke His word unto Moses." (2) The level of revelation reserved for God's prophets. God told the Prophet Muhammad, "Behold, We have inspired you just as We inspired Noah and all the prophets after him" (*Sūrah al-Nisā'*, 4:163). (3) The level that involves the sending of an angelic messenger to a human being to convey what God has commanded him to convey. These first three levels of *ʿilm* are reserved for God's prophets alone. (4) The level of inspiration at which it is as though God were addressing someone in actual words. This level is lower than that bestowed on prophets and apostles, which involves the giving of a new law of divine origin. The Prophet attributed this level of knowledge to ʿUmar ibn al-Khaṭṭāb, saying, "Among the nations that came before you there were inspired individuals. If anyone in our community fits this description, it is ʿUmar ibn al-Khaṭṭāb." (5) The level that involves conveying understanding to others. *Sūrah al-Anbiyā'*, 21:78-79 speaks of this level of knowledge, telling how God gave special understanding to Solomon in relation to a case that was brought before him. (6) The level of general explication. This level involves explicating the truth and distinguishing it from falsehood based on proofs, evidence and signs so that truth becomes visible to the heart just as physical entities are visible to the eye. This level constitutes the evidence on the basis of which

God will call us to account on the Day of Resurrection. Until or unless this evidence reaches people, God will not chastise them or cause them to go astray. *Sūrah al-Tawbah*, 9:115 assures us that "God would never – after having invited them to His guidance – condemn people for going astray before He has made [entirely] clear to them of what they should beware." (7) The level of knowledge that involves special guidance of some sort. This guidance is generally marked by providential leading, God-given success, chosenness, and protection from disappointment and betrayal. This phenomenon is alluded to in *Sūrah al-Qaṣaṣ*, 28:56, where God tells the Prophet, "You cannot guide aright everyone you love: but it is God who guides..." (cf. *Sūrah al-Naḥl*, 16:37). (8) The level at which one is caused to hear what God wants one to hear. *Sūrah al-Anfāl*, 8:23 affirms that "if God had seen any good in them, He would certainly have made them hear..." (cf. *Sūrah Fāṭir*, 35:22). (9) The level of enlightenment (*ilhām*). *Sūrah al-Shams*, 91:7-8 tells us that God has "enlightened" the soul concerning its iniquitous tendencies as well as its capacity for God-consciousness (*alhamahā fujūrahā wa taqwāhā*). (10) The level that involves receiving a truthful vision from God. The beginning of the divine revelations which the Prophet received are said to have begun with a "truthful vision" (*ru'yā ṣādiqah*).

2) *The criteria of sound ʿilm*

As was noted earlier in this discussion, ethical rectitude in relation to *ʿilm*, however necessary it is, is not sufficient; by the same token, academic discipline and rigor are not sufficient by themselves, since no amount of rigor or accuracy will render research acceptable if it conflicts with recognized standards of virtue and morality. The most important criteria by which one must abide in relation to *ʿilm* include the following:

Objectivity. Scientific theories and hypotheses must be based on thorough research derived from definitive, demonstrable evidence. Researchers must distance themselves from personal emotions and sensitivities, especially when studying the humanities and social sciences, which are affected significantly by individual interpretations. Objectivity is a fundamental measure of one's ability to arrive at truth and to be fair in one's judgments.

Academic integrity. This criterion concerns itself with the protection of human rights on all levels. It is expressed in *Sūrah al-Shuʿarā'*, 26:183, which commands us: "Do not deprive people of what is rightfully theirs; and do not act wickedly on earth by spreading corruption." One aspect of academic integrity is the practice of giving credit to those from whom one has received information and/or whose research has paved the way for one's own. Another aspect of academic integrity is complete truthfulness, which is a fundamental expression of one's respect for self and others. The Qur'an is replete with verses that address the matter of truthfulness. We read, for example, in *Sūrah al-Tawbah*, 9:119, "O you who have attained to faith! Remain conscious of God, and be among those who are true to their word!" Similarly, *Sūrah al-Zumar*, 39:33 identifies those who bring the truth and accept the truth wholeheartedly with the truly God-conscious. Hence, truthfulness is intimately linked with consciousness of God and faith.

The ethics of polite disagreement. God commands us in *Sūrah al-Naḥl*, 16:125 to invite others to the path of God "with wisdom and goodly exhortation, and argue with them in the most kindly manner." The practice of arguing "in the most kindly manner" requires that one not be rude or harsh in dealing with others. The Prophet himself was reminded that if he had treated his followers harshly, they would have scattered from around him when God addressed him, saying: "it was by God's grace that you dealt gently with your followers: for if you had been harsh and hard of heart, they would indeed have broken away from you" (*Sūrah Āl ʿImrān*, 3:159). When discussion and debate are undertaken for the purpose of bringing benefit and communicating truth, there is no place for belittlement and provocation of one's opponent, or attempts to impugn his or her motives. On the contrary, we should commend our opponent on his or her learning and accomplishments, and express ourselves politely and gently. The Qur'an forbids us to goad others. *Sūrah al-Isrā'*, 17:53 reads, "Tell My servants that they should speak in the most kindly manner [unto those who do not share their beliefs]: verily, Satan is always ready to stir up discord between people..." The prophets are known to have been considerate and tactful in their dealings with others, including even their mortal foes, as they set forth the truth. God commanded Moses and Aaron, "go forth, both of you, unto Pharaoh: for, verily, he has transgressed all bounds of equity! But speak unto him in a mild manner, so that he might bethink himself or [at least] be filled with apprehension" (*Sūrah Ṭāhā*, 20:43).

Putting Evidence before Theorization and Rule Formation

Verifying one's sources and quoting from them correctly will not be sufficient if those sources are themselves unreliable. Consequently, the Qur'anic approach to research is to demand evidence for the accuracy of whatever claim is being presented. One of the marks of those committed to the pursuit of truth is that they do not formulate a belief until after examining the evidence. As for those in the grip of falsehood, they base their belief on either their own whims and fancies, or on what they have been taught to believe by others. They then go in search of evidence that will lend their beliefs an appearance of validity and legitimacy. In this way they attempt to evade having to confront the truth and receive true guidance.

Evidence may be derived from the Qur'an and the Sunnah, from rational argumentation, or from sensory data. Each issue and question being examined calls for specific methods, approaches, and types of evidence; hence, the evidence or procedure appropriate to one question or field of study might not be appropriate for another. In *Sūrah al-Anʿām*, 6:148 God commanded the Prophet: "Say: 'Have you any [certain] knowledge which you could proffer to us? You follow but [other people's] conjectures, and you yourselves do nothing but guess.'"

It should be remembered that evidence goes by many names in the Qur'an. In the verse just cited, for example, it is referred to as 'knowledge' (*ʿilm*). Elsewhere it is referred to as 'proof' (*burhān*; cf. *Sūrah al-Mu'minūn*, 23:117), for example, 'authority' (*sulṭān*; cf. *Sūrah Yūnus*, 10:68), and 'argument' (*ḥujjah*; cf. *Sūrah al-Anʿām*, 6:83), 'sign' (*āyah*; cf. *Sūrah al-Baqarah*, 2:211), evidence of the truth (*bayyinah*; cf. *Sūrah al-Aḥqāf*, 46:7), and 'means of insight' (*baṣā'ir*; cf. *Sūrah al-Anʿām*, 6:104).

Careful Use of Scientific language

A researcher must have a good grasp of the terminology relating to his or her field of specialization given the impact it has on people's attitudes and feelings. Technical terms come into being in order to meet a need; then, given their ability to influence people's understanding of things, they evolve the potential to bring either benefit or harm. Technical terms are keys to knowledge; as such, they can exert either a positive or a negative impact on people's thinking and behavior. A single term can convey several different ideas combined, some of them explicit, others implicit, some conscious, others subliminal. A given word may direct the mind toward meanings with which it has been previously associated while, at the same, giving these meanings new associations. When a term is used, it comes embedded in a whole host of related circumstances and expectations, thoughts and feelings, hopes and fears, times and places, specializations and civilizations, all of which help determine its import. Hence, anyone who attempts to understand it outside of its context is bound to fall into error and confusion.

The Right Fit Between Intellectual Capacities and One's Field of Study

The tools of knowledge available to human beings have limited capacities and a finite scope. There is, for example, a range of frequencies that the human ear is unable to detect. Human beings also have a limited range of vision; there are colors that the human eye cannot distinguish, and images too tiny or far away to be seen with the naked eye. The mind, too, is limited in what it can absorb and comprehend. Hence, another rule of academic pursuit is not to delve into matters that are beyond one's capacity to understand thoroughly, since to do so would be waste of time and energy. On this point we read in *Sūrah al-Aʿrāf*, 7:187:

> They will ask you [O Prophet] about the Last Hour: When will it come to pass? Say: "Verily, knowledge thereof rests with my Sustainer alone. None but He will reveal it in its time. Heavily will it weigh on the heavens and the earth; [and] it will not fall upon you otherwise than of a sudden." They will ask you – as if you could gain insight into this [mystery] by dint of persistent

> inquiry! Say: "Knowledge thereof rests with my Sustainer alone; but [of this] most people are unaware."

THIRD: THE QUR'AN'S COMPREHENSIVE VIEW OF *ʿIlm*

As presented in the pages of the Qur'an, *ʿilm* encompasses both this world and the next. It concerns itself with the questions that occupy us as human beings, most particularly how the creation came into existence, how it has developed, and the end it can anticipate; the oneness of God; and the universe in all its fullness – Earth, the heavenly realm, the stars, the planets. The Qur'an calls upon its readers to reflect on these cosmic phenomena, saying, "He it is who has set up for you the stars so that you might be guided by them in the midst of the deep darkness of land and sea: clearly, indeed, have We spelled out these messages unto people of [innate] knowledge!" (*Sūrah al-Anʿām*, 6:97).

The comprehensive nature of the Qur'anic concept of *ʿilm* manifests itself with special clarity in *Sūrah al-ʿAlaq*, 96:1, where God commands, "Read in the name of your Sustainer, who has created..." When read in its broadest sense, this verse may be understood to be addressed to all human beings – believer and unbeliever, righteous and unrighteous. As al-Shawkānī notes in his commentary on this verse, the verb "read" requires that there be something which "is read." However, the object of the command to "read" is not mentioned, which signals that it might include any number of things.

The act of reading being spoken of here begins with God's command; the means by which it takes place is provided by God, and the end, or purpose, for which it is done is centered in God. This being the case, it excludes racist, bigoted purposes, blind adherence to tradition, and unthinking prejudice in favor of a particular race, ethnic group, school or philosophy. The act of reading as presented here takes on a universal dimension, since the message we are being instructed to read and deliver to others is addressed to the entire world and deals with all of people's needs both in this life and the next.

The One who commands us to read is Our Creator, our Sustainer, and our Lord. Being intimately familiar both with what He has created and what is best for that creation, God is supremely qualified to determine what approach we will take to this reading of ours. A thoughtful reading of the Qur'an reveals that the *ʿilm* it speaks of revolves around three principle themes. The first of these is the oneness of God in His lordship and sovereignty, His names and His attributes, and the worship-related questions that follow from these. The second theme is the Cosmos, and the divine wisdom and mysteries it manifests. And the third theme is the peoples of the world and the ways in which they relate to the Creator and the creation.

Each of these themes is associated with specialized fields of study. The first has given rise to the fields of Islamic theology and jurisprudence in their respective specializations and branches; the second, to the natural sciences; and the third, to the humanities. The interrelated dimensions of existence as presented and treated in the Qur'an yield an inclusive picture of *ʿilm*. This conceptualization of *ʿilm* leads neither to an atheistic materialism, nor to a utopian, earth-denying asceticism. Rather, it affirms a moderate stance that strikes a balance between these two extremes. As we are told in *Sūrah al-Mulk*, 67:15, God "has made the earth easy to live upon: go about, then, in all its regions, and partake of the sustenance which He provides: but [always bear in mind that] unto Him you shall be resurrected."

FOURTH: CATEGORIES OF *Maʿrifah*

The Qur'an calls upon Muslims to think scientifically about all aspects of life, both in this world and in the next. Given this inclusive understanding of *ʿilm*, some scholars have divided it into three categories: (1) theology and jurisprudence, (2) the natural sciences, and (3) the humanities.

Theology and jurisprudence. Theology and jurisprudence treat the principles and rites of the religion, that is, doctrine and forms of worship. The purpose of these areas of study is to enable Muslims to understand their purpose and end in life, and how to relate to their Lord and to the rest of creation. God declares in *Sūrah al-Dhāriyāt*, 51:56, "I have not created the invisible beings and men to any end other than that they may [know and] worship Me." In order to achieve this purpose, we need to understand the tasks before us, including the commands and prohibitions we have received from God. These commands and prohibitions then need to be applied in a studied, scientific manner; as a consequence, there are numerous branches of Islamic legal, theological and doctrinal studies. These include the field of jurisprudence, which is the study of Islamic Law and the ways in which rulings are derived from its foundations and principles in relation to forms of worship, financial transactions, personal transactions, penalties for violations of the law, and so on.

The natural sciences. A pursuit common to all nations and civilizations, the natural sciences are related to the way in which we manage our earthly affairs. The knowledge gleaned through the natural sciences is cumulative; hence, those who come later build on what was discovered by those who came before them. New discoveries and accomplishments in the realm of the natural sciences provide us with additional evidence of God's greatness and bounty toward us; they also provide a foundation on which to build an advancing civilization. Every Qur'anic command to investigate or reflect on plant life, animal life, the heavenly realms, the earth, or ourselves is implicitly related to the natural sciences. Indeed, human beings' ability to exercise their God-given powers on earth, be they economic, financial, industrial, cultural or scientific, is dependent on the knowledge they acquire through such disciplines and their practical applications.

Muslims' efforts to spread the message of Islam and establish God's religion on earth do not take place in some fantasy realm but, rather, in the context of our earthly existence and our relations with other communities. When Muslims are backward and decadent, this does nothing to promote the Islamic message. The importance of seeking not simply the world to come, but the good of the present world, is affirmed in *Sūrah al-Qaṣaṣ*, 28:77, where God commands us to "seek...[the good of] the life to come, without forgetting your [rightful] share in this world." We seek our "rightful share in this world" by, among other things, studying the various facets of the material world so as to put them to the most beneficial uses for all.

The humanities. The field known as "the humanities" encompasses a number of disciplines, including Sociology, Psychology, Political Science, History, Economics, and others. The Qur'an has provided us with definitive answers concerning the origin and nature of human beings, the purpose for our existence, freedom and responsibility, social relations, human interaction with the natural environment and its effects, and the extent and limitations of human power and authority over the rest of the world. Hence, fields of study such as those listed above were not classified separately in the early days of Islam. In the modern West, by contrast, these topics have become the subjects of distinct academic disciplines.

When looking at studies done in the fields of Sociology, Psychology, Political Science, History, Economics, and related areas, we should bear in mind that what is beneficial for human beings in one place or society is not necessarily beneficial for them in some other location or community. Studies done in a Western setting may not be applicable in an Eastern setting, and vice-versa. No sociological, psychological, or economic study should be taken out of context; rather, its results and conclusions should be examined with a view to the cultural, historical, political, religious, and socioeconomic milieu in which the study took place, and any extrapolations made from it should be made with care.

FIFTH: A COMPARISON BETWEEN *Maᶜrifah* AND *ᶜIlm*

In order to determine the precise distinctions between *maᶜrifah* and *ᶜilm*, we must delve into scholars' discussions of these terms, which touch on matters both linguistic and doctrinal. Given the fact that scholars tend to use terms arbitrarily and in the service of their own ideas, we will need to trace these terms back to their linguistic roots so as to define them accurately and assign them to the correct semantic fields. *ᶜIlm* is characterized by differing degrees of certainty and uncertainty; moreover, it involves a thought process that requires both intelligence and presence of mind. *ᶜIlm* might be superficial and abstract; conversely, it might be thorough, detailed and concrete. For this reason, there are numerous words that are used more or less synonymously with both *ᶜilm* and *maᶜrifah*. Each of these synonyms is related in one way to knowledge as a whole, and in another, to a specialized niche of some sort. In what follows we will attempt to trace the most important Qur'anic synonyms for these two terms and identify the features that distinguish each one from the rest.

Lexical and Usage-Related Differences

In order to get a clearer picture of the relationship between the terms *maʿrifah* and *ʿilm*, we will need to examine each one's lexical definition and usages, and then compare them on this basis.

(1) *Lexical differences*

The term *ʿilm* came to be applied to certain kinds of knowledge based on the meaning of the word *ʿalāmah*, which refers to a sign or signal that points to or identifies something or someone. As for the term *maʿrifah*, it is used primarily in contrast to the word *nakirah*, which refers to something or someone unknown or unidentified. Similarly, the word *ʿirfān*, meaning recognition or acknowledgment, is used in contrast to *jahl*, meaning ignorance or lack of awareness, while the verb *taʿarrafa*, when used with a direct object, means to explore or discover. *Maʿrifah* refers to knowledge that follows upon an absence of knowledge, either because one had never known about the entity in question, or because one had once known about it but had then forgotten what one knew. In the second situation, it would be as though the information one once had had disappeared from one's mind, but was then brought up from the subconscious. As for the verb *ʿarafa/yaʿrifu*, it takes a single direct object. One might say, for example, *ʿaraftu al-dār*, "I recognized the house." The verb is used in a similar sense in *Sūrah Yūsuf*, 12:58, where we are told that while Joseph recognized his brothers "he knew them" (*ʿarafahum*) after their long separation, they did not recognize him (*wa hum lahu munkirūn*). The verb *ʿalima/yaʿlamu*, by contrast, requires two direct objects when used in the sense of recognition. As we saw earlier, it is used in this manner in *Sūrah al-Mumtaḥanah*, 60:10, "if you recognize them as believers... (*in ʿalimtumūhunna mu'mināt*)."

The point of similarity between the verbs *maʿrifah* and *ʿilm* is that both refer to a kind of knowledge and awareness. *Maʿrifah*, however, has an active and personal dimension that is not present in the concept of *ʿilm*, which is more purely theoretical. So, for example, it might be said *maʿrifat Allāh* (the knowledge of God) refers to a confirmed *ʿilm* of God coupled with action that is a reflection of this *ʿilm*.

(2) *Usage-related differences*
Some view *maʿrifah* as more specialized or specific than *ʿilm*, in that *maʿrifah* refers to an awareness of the distinctive nature of something as contrasted with other entities. The term *maʿrifah* denotes the act of distinguishing someone or something known from someone or something unknown, while the term *ʿilm* does not. *Maʿrifah* also refers to a knowledge or awareness at which one arrives via a process of thinking and reflection, and is used to refer to the recognition or knowledge of something or someone whose outer effects can be perceived, but whose inner essence cannot be known. Thus one might say, *ʿaraftu Allāh*, "I know/came to know God." One might also say, *ʿaraftu zaydan*, "I recognized Zayd," without meaning that one knows Zayd's inner essence.

Maʿrifah is further distinguished from *ʿilm* by the fact that whereas *maʿrifah* is used in contradistinction to a lack of recognition (*inkār*) or ingratitude (*juḥūd*), *ʿilm* is used in contrast to ignorance (*jahl*) and caprice or lust (*hawā*). *Sūrah al-Māʾidah*, 5:83 speaks of people's eyes overflowing with tears when they hear God's word "for they recognise the truth (*mimmā ʿarafū min al-ḥaqq*)," while we read in *Sūrah al-Baqarah*, 2:146 that the Jews and Christians of the Prophet's day "know it [the truth] as they know their own children" (*yaʿrifūnahu kamā yaʿrifūna abnāʾahum*)." As for the verb *ʿalima/yaʿlamu*, it is used more frequently to refer to knowledge of facts, as in the Qur'an's exhortation in *Sūrah Muḥammad*, 47:19: "Know, then, [O man,] that there is no deity save God (*faʿlam annahu lā ilāha illā Allāh*)."

6

Tools for Acquiring Knowledge in the Qur'an

AMONG THE physical senses through which we receive sensory data as a means of obtaining knowledge, the two that receive the most attention in the Qur'an are hearing and sight, as well as their associated organs: the ear and the eye. As for the sense of touch mediated through the hands, its role in knowledge acquisition is presented as a support or aid to visual perception via writing or holding something for the sake of examining it.

FIRST: THE FUNCTION OF THE SENSES IN KNOWLEDGE ACQUISITION

As we have seen, scholars generally classify *ʿilm* as either intuitive or acquired. The physical senses serve to convey data to the brain and, as such, they represent the first stage of cognition. According to many researchers in philosophy and other fields, the senses are subject to error and, as a consequence, cannot provide us with certainty. On this point they are in agreement with a number of ancient philosophers, some of them Muslim thinkers the likes of Abū Ḥāmid al-Ghazālī, Ibn Ḥazm, and others. In support of the claim that the senses are unreliable, some thinkers have appealed to *Sūrah al-Nūr*, 24:39, which reads, "But as for those who are bent on denying the truth, their [good] deeds are like a mirage in the desert, which the thirsty supposes to be water – until, when he approaches it, he finds that it was nothing." Numerous other references support this line of thinking as well. The physical senses are, in fact, relative rather than absolute. However, they are still capable of providing certainty when they are in agreement with logic and common sense. At the same time, the five senses cannot take in all possible data. Hence, if someone were given some additional sense over and above the five we already enjoy, he/she might discover many things of which he had never been aware before. As has been noted, our surroundings are replete with images that we are unable to perceive with the naked eye and frequencies that are either too high or too low for us to hear. As we read in *Sūrah al-Ḥāqqah*, 69:38-39, "I call to witness all that you can see, as well as all that you cannot see!"

There are those who even go so far as to claim what we perceive with our physical senses is nothing but fantasy and illusion. As for the Qur'an, it does not cast doubt on either sight or hearing, although it acknowledges that certain factors might impair these senses. In *Sūrah al-Ḥijr*, 15:15, we are told that if skeptics of the Qur'an had been given a veritable staircase to heaven on which to ascend, "they would surely have said, 'It is only our eyes that are spellbound! Nay, we have been bewitched!'" In other words, a person's sight might be rendered ineffective because his or her mind has been clouded, or because his or her eyes are under a magic spell. Elsewhere God speaks of sealing people's hearts in such a way that they are no longer able to hear. Speaking of those who are not heedful of His message, God declares in *Sūrah al-Aʿrāf*, 7:100: "if We so willed, We could smite them [too] by means of their sins, sealing their hearts so that they cannot hear [the truth]." The hearing spoken of in this verse is not physical; rather, it refers to the ability to receive the truth in one's heart and respond to it. Indeed, whenever the Qur'an refers to the senses in a negative manner or speaks of them being incapacitated, it is referring to a level of perception higher than that of the physical. More specifically, it is referring to God's dulling of human beings' receptivity to truth as punishment for having willfully ignored His guidance despite having heard, seen, and understood the evidence in its favor. In a situation such as this, individuals who choose to disregard the guidance that has come to them via their inward sense of right and wrong will not be given any further, more profound guidance such as that received by prophets and apostles.

God has given us the physical senses so that each of us, within his or her own limitations and circumstances, may benefit from them. The gift of the physical senses has been given to all people without exception, although individuals differ in the extent to which they put them to good use, and although one sense might be sharper than another in a given individual. At the same time, however, the senses are not the only path to knowledge that we have been given, and sole dependence on the physical senses is fraught with peril. God has given people three means by which to attain to knowledge, and holds us responsible for their use. As we read in *Sūrah al-Naḥl*, 16:78, "God has brought you forth from your mothers' wombs knowing nothing – but He has endowed you with hearing, and sight, and minds, so that you might have cause to be grateful." It is clear, then, that unlike certain philosophical schools of thought, the Qur'an casts no doubt on the reliability of the senses, nor does it deny their importance. It is equally clear, on the other hand, that the Qur'an gives the senses no greater importance than it does the faculty of reason; in this respect, Islam parts ways with radical empiricists who place the physical senses above all else. The Islamic position on the senses is one of moderation whereby the senses are viewed as the source of the 'raw material' which is then put to use by other means of perception and cognition.

SECOND: HEARING AND SIGHT IN THE QUR'AN

1) *The ear and hearing in the Qur'an*

The Arabic feminine noun *udhun* (plural, *ādhān*) refers to the ear in both human beings and animals. Speaking of those who care nothing for the truth, God says in *Sūrah al-Aʿrāf*, 7:179,

> And most certainly have We destined for hell many of the invisible beings and men who have hearts with which they fail to grasp the truth, and eyes with which they fail to see, and ears with which they fail to hear. They are like cattle – nay, they are even less conscious of the right way: it is they, they who are the [truly] heedless!

The sense of hearing is mentioned 139 times in the Qur'an, more frequently than any of the other physical senses. As noted in an earlier section, the sounds one hears may or may not lead to understanding. Speaking of certain nations of bygone times, God states in *Sūrah al-Aḥqāf*, 46:26: "We had endowed them with hearing, and sight, and [knowledgeable] hearts: but neither their hearing, nor their sight, nor their hearts were of the least avail to them, seeing that they went on rejecting God's messages."

The word *sam*ᶜ or hearing is associated in the Qur'an with numerous related concepts and processes, including: perception, understanding, reason, responsiveness, acceptance, and obedience. The verb *sami*ᶜ*a/yasma*ᶜ*u* takes a single direct object. As for the active participle *sāmi*ᶜ, or hearer, it is more inclusive than the word *mukhāṭab*, which refers to the person being spoken to, since you may hear a message that is not addressed to you in particular. The noun *sam*ᶜ may be used to refer not only to the act of hearing but to the ear as well. We read in *Sūrah al-Baqarah*, 2:6-7, "Behold, as for those who are bent on denying the truth – it is all one to them whether you warn them or do not warn them: they will not believe. God has sealed their hearts and their hearing (*sam*ᶜ*ihim*)...." Similarly, the word *sam*ᶜ is used to refer not only to the act of hearing, but to the process of understanding what has been heard and responding to it in obedience. As we read in *Sūrah al-Anfāl*, 8:31, "And whenever Our messages were conveyed to them, they would say, 'We have heard [all this] before (*qālū qad sami*ᶜ*nā*).'" In other words, they had heard the message with their ears, but they had not responded with acceptance and obedience. *Sam*ᶜ associated with understanding and positive response is also illustrated in *Sūrah al-Jinn*, 72:1-2, where we are told that after hearing the Qur'an recited, certain 'invisible beings' said to others of their kind, "Verily, we have heard a wondrous discourse, guiding towards consciousness of what is right; and so We have come to believe in it..." (Cf. *Sūrah al-Rūm*, 30:52 and *Sūrah al-Nūr*, 24:51.)

It will have been seen, then, that the kind of *sam*ᶜ that is commended in the Qur'an is accompanied by understanding, obedience to God's commands, refraining from acts that have been forbidden, and so on. Without understanding, obedience and faithful response, the *sam*ᶜ may as well not have taken place. This applies equally to believers and unbelievers. Turning away from the truth is equated with turning away from what one has heard such that someone who rejects the truth is, in essence, deaf. We read in *Sūrah Luqmān*, 31:7: "For, whenever Our messages are conveyed to such a one, he turns away in his arrogance as though he had not heard them – as though there were deafness in his ears..." Such a person has heard the message with his or her physical ears; however, he or she might as well not have heard the message, since it was not met with belief or obedience; hence, the purpose for which the message was addressed to him or her was not achieved.

2) *The eye and seeing in the Qur'an*

The Arabic noun *ʿayn* refers first and foremost to the physical eye. Used metaphorically, it may refer also to the essence of the object perceived via the eye or other sensory organs. What concerns us in this context is the role played by the eye in cognitive processes. God asks rhetorically of the person who does not seek the truth through the senses he has been given, "Have We not given him two eyes...and shown him the two highways [of good and evil]?" (*Sūrah al-Balad*, 90:8,10). The function of the eye as presented in the Qur'an is that of seeing (*Sūrah Āl ʿImrān*, 3:13; *Sūrah al-Aʿrāf*, 7:179; *Sūrah al-Anbiyā'*, 21:61).

References to eyes abound in the Qur'an in a variety of contexts: God's causing people's eyes to be dulled (*Sūrah Yāsīn*, 36:66); the eye being gladdened (*Sūrah al-Aḥzāb*, 33:51); turning one's eyes on the things of this world (*Sūrah Ṭāhā*, 20:131); one's eyes holding someone in contempt (*Sūrah Hūd*, 11:31); eyes overflowing with tears (*Sūrah al-Tawbah*, 9:92); eyes being veiled from the remembrance of God (*Sūrah al-Kahf*, 18:101); eyes rolling in terror (*Sūrah al-Aḥzāb*, 33:19); and eyes delighting in a sight (*Sūrah al-Zukhruf*, 43:71).

An action mentioned frequently in the Qur'an with relevance to the eye is that of *naẓar* (the verb being *naẓara/yanẓuru*), meaning 'to look'. The action of looking involves focusing one's eyes steadily on something in such a way that one can form a thorough and accurate image of the entity being looked at. Consequently, the word *naẓar* is often used to refer to a process of reflection and examination. It is possible to look at something in the sense of directing one's eyes toward it without actually perceiving it or seeing it. When used with the preposition *fī* (*naẓara fī*), the verb conveys the sense of investigating or carefully studying something; used with the preposition *li* or with a direct object, the verb *naẓara* is used to refer to the act of having mercy or compassion on. These, however, are only a few of the numerous ways and senses in which the verb *naẓara/yanẓuru* is used in the Qur'an.

3) *A comparison between samᶜ and baṣar in the Qur'an*

(a) The differences between *samᶜ* (hearing) and *baṣar* (sight) in the view of scholars

Scholars have differed over which of the two, *samᶜ* or *baṣar*, is superior. Some scholars argue for the superiority of *samᶜ* (hearing) over *baṣar* (sight). In favor of this view they cite *Sūrah Yūnus*, 10:42-43: "And there are among them such as (pretend to) listen to you: but can you cause the deaf to hearken even though they will not use their reason? And there are among them such as [pretend to) look towards you: but can you show the right way to the blind even though they cannot see?" According to these scholars, the passage just quoted associates 'deafness' with a refusal to use one's reason; however, it associates a failure to look not with a loss of the use of reason, but only with a loss of sight. Other scholars, by contrast, view *baṣar* as superior to *samᶜ*. These scholars argue that the best of all blessings bestowed by God on human beings is the beatific vision (*al-naẓar ilā Allāh*), which takes place via the sense of sight. They also argue that the reality perceived via sight is more complete and perfect than that perceived via hearing, just the locus of sight is more honorable than the locus of hearing.

(b) The pairing of *samᶜ* and *baṣar* in the Qur'an

The Qur'an mentions *samᶜ* and *baṣar* either separately or jointly in 36 places (see, for example, *Sūrah Yūnus*, 10:31, and *Sūrah al-Naḥl*, 16:78). There are several reasons the Qur'an tends most frequently to mention hearing and sight together when discussing the various paths of knowledge available to human beings. These reasons are as follows: (1) Hearing and sight are among the most important means of attaining to knowledge about God. (2) Hearing and sight are the two most important pathways between knowledge and reason. (3) The loss of these two senses deprives the individual to a significant extent of the ability to obtain knowledge through the spoken and written word. (4) Hearing enables one to perceive sounds in both light and darkness, and despite the presence of certain barriers between speaker and listener. As for sight, it requires the presence of light and the absence of physical barriers. Furthermore, a person is more likely to wake up from a sound than from the presence of light. The sense of hearing is the first to be activated when one wakes from sleep, and the last to be deactivated when one goes to sleep (since the sense of hearing continues to operate even when one has one's eyes closed).

(c) The reasons for the Qur'an's mention of hearing before seeing

It will be noted that hearing tends to be mentioned prior to sight when the two are paired in the Qur'an. The reason for this order appears to lie in the tendency to list the superior of two entities prior to the inferior and this phenomenon has been viewed as evidence of the Qur'an's literary and rhetorical miraculousness. The consistency of this order in the Qur'an has been cited as evidence of hearing's superiority over sight in relation to knowledge acquisition. The arguments for such superiority are taken, moreover, not only from the Qur'an, but from other realities as well. One notes that numerous verses of the Qur'an pair *samᶜ* (hearing) with *ᶜaql* (reason) without a similar pairing between *baṣar* (sight) and *ᶜaql*. This first pairing is found in *Sūrah al-Mulk*, 67:10, where inhabitants of hell fire are quoted as saying, "Had we but listened [to those warnings], or [at least] used our own reason, we would not [now] be among those who are destined for the blazing flame!" Similarly, the divine names *al-Samīᶜ* (the All-Hearing) and *al-ᶜAlīm* (the All-Knowing) are paired in the Qur'an (see *Sūrah al-Baqarah*, 2:127,137,181, etc.), whereas the divine name *al-Baṣīr* (the All-Seeing) is not paired with *al-ᶜAlīm*.

On the purely epistemological level, hearing may be viewed as superior to sight for a number of reasons: (1) Hearing plays a more important role in holding people accountable before God. (2) Hearing is capable of conveying events both present and future, whereas sight can only convey what is present and visible to the eye. (3) You can hear sounds that are not immediately present to you; in order to see something, however, the object must be directly before you, or at least within the range of your peripheral vision. (4) One's sense of hearing operates night and day, in the darkness and in the light. The first sense that becomes active when a person wakes up is the sense of hearing, even if the person has his or her eyes closed. (5) Someone who has lost his or her hearing also loses the ability to speak due to the inability to hear himself or herself (not to mention others) and, hence, to carry on meaningful dialogue.

(d) Reasons for mentioning *baṣar* before *samᶜ* in the Qur'an

The places in which sight (*baṣar*) is mentioned before hearing (*samᶜ*) in Qur'anic pairings of these terms are generally associated with censure, impairment, and punishment, whereas the places in which hearing is mentioned before sight are associated with commendation. This reversed order does not negate the superiority of the sense of hearing; on the contrary, it confirms it. Passages in which sight is mentioned before hearing include 7:179, which condemns people who "eyes with which they fail to see, and ears with which they fail to hear"; *Sūrah Hūd*, 11:24 speaks of "the blind and deaf and the seeing and hearing," asking, "Can these two be deemed alike in [their] nature?" *Sūrah al-Isrā'*, 17:97 warns of the fate of those who have rejected God's messages saying: "We shall gather them together on the Day of Resurrection, [they will lie] prone upon their faces, blind and dumb and deaf, with hell as their goal." In a similar vein, *Sūrah al-Sajdah*, 32:12 describes the condition of those who had turned away from God on earth and who, on the Day of Resurrection, hang their heads before God and cry, "O our Sustainer! [Now] we have seen, and we have heard! Return us, then, [to our earthly life) that we may do good deeds..."

THIRD: THE *Qalb* IN THE QUR'AN

The physical senses are completed in the knowledge-acquisition process by the *qalb*, generally rendered as the heart. Closely related terms used in the Qur'an are *fū'ād*, *lubb*, and *ᶜaql*. The function of the *qalb* is that of comprehension, just as the function of the *udhun* is hearing and the function of the *ᶜayn* is sight. The *qalb*, or *fū'ād*, is paired with the senses of hearing and sight in approximately 20 verses of the Qur'an, all of which portray the *qalb* as being an internal apparatus whose role complements that of the outer senses, particularly hearing and sight. This complementary relationship is suggested by the fact that these entities are mentioned in association with each other in

Sūrah al-Naḥl, 16:78, which speaks of God endowing us with "hearing [ears], and sight [eyes], and hearts [minds]" (*al-samʿa wa al-abṣāra wa al-afʾidah*).

1) *The concept of the qalb in the Qur'an*

Scholars have equated the *qalb* with the *fūʾād*, with reason (*ʿaql*), and with the inward essence ('heart') of a thing. From the root *q-l-b* we derive the verb *taqallaba/yataqallabu* (verbal noun, *taqallub*), meaning to fluctuate or vary. The adjective *qullab* refers to someone who is adaptable, versatile, and of varied skills and talents.

The word *qalb* is used in the Qur'an to denote three things: (1) Reason (*ʿaql*). This meaning is illustrated in *Sūrah Qāf*, 50:37, which reads: "In this, behold, there is indeed a reminder for everyone whose heart is wide-awake – that is, [everyone who] lends ear with a conscious mind." (2) Opinion or point of view (*ra'y*). This meaning is illustrated in *Sūrah al-Ḥashr*, 59:14 which, in talking about those who oppose truth, states that "their hearts are at odds [with one another]: this, because they are people who will not use their reason." (3) The physical organ itself. *Sūrah al-Ḥajj*, 22:46 thus refers to "the hearts that are in their breasts."

The word *qalb* can thus be used to refer to one's powers of reason, just as the word *udhun* (ear) can be used to refer to the sense of hearing, and the word *ʿayn* (eye) can be used to refer to the sense of sight.

2) *Qur'anic terms synonymous with qalb*

The epistemological concepts in the Qur'an may be divided into two types. The first has to do with sensory organs (eyes, ears, and the like), while the second has to do with their functions (sight, hearing, and so on). A function might be mentioned alone without the organ that performs it, since the purpose for its mention is not to convey information about the body as such, but to convey knowledge and encourage action. In other situations, the sensory organ might be mentioned alone by way of allusion to its function. Thus, for example, the heart (*qalb*) might be mentioned in an allusion to reason, the allusion becoming clear from the surrounding context.

In what follows I discuss entities to which the Qur'an attributes some of the cognitive functions of the *qalb*, thereby indicating that these entities are viewed as synonymous with the word *qalb*.

(a) *Fū'ād*

As was noted in an earlier discussion, the root *f-'-d* denotes fever, heat and intensity, and the heart (*qalb*) is sometimes referred with the noun *fū'ād* due to its warmth. Unlike the term *qalb*, however, the word *fū'ād* is used consistently in reference to the non-material dimension of the heart. It is in this non-material sense that the word *fū'ād* is used in *Sūrah al-Isrā'*, 17:36, where God declares that "never concern thyself with anything of which thou hast no knowledge" for our "hearing (*al-sam*ᶜ) and sight (*wa al-baṣar*) and heart (*wa al-fū'ād*) – all of them – will be called to account for it [on Judgment Day]."

Ibn Ashur observed that the term *af'idah* (plural of *fū'ād*) is frequently used in the Qur'an to refer to reason or the mind. At the same time, however, the word *fū'ād* is sometimes used in reference to a specific cognitive or perceptive capacity. This can be deduced from the way it is paired, as in *Sūrah al-Isrā'*, 17:36 above, with the faculties of hearing and sight. In other words, the term *fū'ād* may be seen here not to be referring to the physical sensory organ itself (the heart that pumps blood throughout the body), but rather to the 'heart's' spiritual or intellectual function. When the term *sam*ᶜ and *baṣar* are paired with the word *qalb*, the pairing is most always in a negative context, that is, one that refers to ingratitude, hardness of heart, etc., whereas the term *fū'ād* is paired with these same functions in contexts of gratitude, faith and the like.

A comparison between the Qur'anic verses containing the words *fū'ād* and *qalb* indicates that the *fū'ād* is associated with spiritual vision and the ability to distinguish a true vision from a false one; we read in *Sūrah al-Najm*, 53:11 that "The [servant's] heart did not give the lie to what he saw" (*mā kadhdhaba al-fū'ādu mā ra'ā*)," whereas the term *qalb*, by contrast, is associated with waywardness, denial, conjecture, blindness, and hypocrisy. The word *fū'ād* is also associated in places with emptiness. We read in *Sūrah al-Qaṣaṣ*, 28:10 that after casting the infant Moses into the river at God's command, "the heart of

Moses' mother became empty" (*aṣbaḥa fū'ādu ummi mūsā fārighan*). Asad renders this phrase with the words, "an aching void grew up in the heart of the mother of Moses." Virtually all commentators agree that the "void" or "emptiness" described here is an allusion to the fear Moses' mother was experiencing. In *Sūrah Ibrāhīm*, 14:43 we read that on the Day of Judgment, evildoers will be "running confusedly to and fro, with their heads upraised [in supplication]...and their hearts an abysmal void" (*wa af'idatuhum hawā'*). The phrase *af'idatuhum hawā'* means literally, "their hearts [will be] air." In a positive context, God tells the Prophet that the reason He has related to him the stories of earlier prophets was to make his heart (*fū'ād*) firm (*Sūrah Hūd*, 11:120).

Both the *fū'ād* and the *qalb* are described in the Qur'an as subject to tumultuous change. In relation to those who have refused to believe in His messages, God declares in *Sūrah al-Anʿām*, 6:110, "We [too] shall turn to [confusion] their hearts and their eyes (*nuqallibu af'idatahum wa abṣārahum*)." And in *Sūrah al-Nūr*, 24:37, the Day of Judgment is referred as "the Day on which all hearts and eyes will be convulsed" (*tataqallabu fīhi al-qulūbu wa al-abṣār*).

(b) *Lubb*

As mentioned in the earlier discussion of the triliteral root *l-b-b* and its derivatives, the word *lubb* is often used in the plural (*albāb*) to speak of people who have been granted special understanding of God's ways and messages. Referred to as *ūlī al-albāb* ("those endowed with insight"), these are individuals who exercise conscientious obedience to God and whose reflection on revealed texts enables them to discern the divine wisdom that is manifested in God's laws but which is not visible to others. Moreover, because of the deeper understanding they have been given, such individuals are held more strictly accountable for their attitudes and actions than others would be.

(c) *Abṣār*

The noun *abṣār* (plural of the noun *baṣar*, meaning sight) occurs in *Sūrah Āl ʿImrān*, 3:13 in the phrase *ūlī al-abṣār*, those "who have eyes to see." According to al-Rāghib, the related term *baṣīrah* refers to the perceptive faculty of the heart. It is rarely used to refer to the organ of sight, that is, to the physical eye. Similarly, the verb *baṣura* is rarely used to refer to the physical act of seeing unless it is associated somehow with the vision of the heart. The noun *baṣīrah* denotes inward powers of perception, and is rarely understood in any other sense. Al-Ṭabarī interpreted the phrase, *ūlī al-abṣār* to mean "those possessed of keen understanding." The function of *baṣīrah* ("insight"), that is, the light by means of which the heart "sees", is to engage in reflection. As such, *baṣīrah* enables one to see the truth of what he or she has received through God's messengers. Consequently, it is *baṣīrah* that delivers one from uncertainty, either through faith or through direct vision. And while the *baṣīrah* is associated with the moral lessons derived from God's messages, the *lubb* is associated with the act of bringing these lessons to mind. Speaking of those who do not heed God's messages, *Sūrah al-Ḥajj*, 22:46 asks, "Have they, then, never journeyed about the earth, letting their hearts gain wisdom, and causing their ears to hear? Yet, verily, it is not their eyes that have become blind (*lā taʿmā al-abṣār*) – but blind have become the hearts that are in their breasts (*wa lākin taʿmā al-qulūb allatī fī al-ṣudūr*)!"

(d) *Ṣadr*

As seen earlier, the word *ṣadr* refers to the uppermost or foremost part of something. It can also refer to the beginning of something, as in the phrase, *ṣadr al-islām*, which refers to the early years of Islam. Similar phrases are *ṣadr al-nahār* (the early part of the day), *ṣadr al-layl* (the early part of the night), *ṣadr al-shitā'* (early winter) and *ṣadr al-ṣayf* (early summer). In keeping with its definition as the uppermost or anterior portion of something, the noun *ṣadr* is used to refer to the chest in both human beings and animals and, more specifically, to the rib cage.

The triliteral root *ṣ-d-r* and its derivatives occur 44 times in the Qur'an. The ways in which these words are used in the Qur'an indicates that the *ṣadr* plays a role in the process of knowledge acquisition in relation to the heart as the seat of perception. The *ṣadr* contains the *qalb*, which contains the *fū'ād*, which contains the *lubb*. The *ṣadr* is to the heart what the white of the eye is to the pupil, what a courtyard is to a house, or what the environs of Makkah are to Makkah. For just as it is the white of the eye on which follicles form when someone suffers from trachoma, it is the *ṣadr* into which doubts, misgivings, temptations and other disturbing thoughts enter. The *ṣadr* is also the seat of lusts, cravings, and other promptings of the lower self, while at the same time being the locus of faith, surrender to God, learning and knowledge.

The following passages illustrate some of the ways in which the word *ṣadr* is used in the Qur'an. *Sūrah al-Naḥl*, 16:106 warns of the fate that will meet someone "who willingly opens up his heart to a denial of the truth" (*man sharaḥa bil-kufri ṣadran*). Conversely, *Sūrah al-Anʿām*, 6:125 tells us that when God wills to guide someone, "his bosom He opens wide with willingness towards self-surrender [to Him]" (*yashraḥ ṣadrahu lil-islām*). When announcing to the Prophet that He has a revelation to bestow upon him, God said in *Sūrah al-Aʿrāf*, 7:2, "So let your heart be oppressed no more (*lā yakun fī ṣadrika ḥarajun*). *Sūrah Hūd*, 11:5 assures us that no matter how we may try to hide from God, He "He has full knowledge of what is in the hearts [of men]" (*innahu ʿalīmun bi dhāt al-ṣudūr*; cf. *Sūrah al-Mulk*, 67:13). *Sūrah al-Ḥajj*, 22:46 tells us that when people are astray, it is not their physical eyes that are blinded but, rather, "the hearts that are in their breasts" (*al-qulūb allatī fī al-ṣudūr*).

As has been mentioned, the *ṣadr* is identified as the seat of troubling, anxious thoughts. We read in *Sūrah al-Nās*, 114:5 that Satan "whispers in people's hearts" (*yuwaswisu fī ṣudūri al-nās*). Speaking of those who question God's messages without evidence to support their doubts, *Sūrah Ghāfir*, 40:56 states that "in their hearts is nothing but overweening self-conceit" (*in fī ṣudūrihim illā kibrun*). Speaking of a time of war and tribulation, *Sūrah Āl ʿImrān*, 3:154 declares that God allowed this hardship in order to test what was in their hearts (*li yabtalī Allāhu mā fī ṣudūrikum*). *Sūrah al-ʿĀdiyāt*, 100:10 speaks of how, on the Day of Judgment, "all that is [hidden] in people's hearts" (*mā fī al-sudūr*) will be revealed. *Sūrah al-Ḥashr*, 59:13 speaks of the fear in the hearts of the unbelievers (*fī ṣudūrihim*), while *Sūrah Yūnus*, 10:57 declares that God's messages contain a cure for the ailments in people's hearts (*shifā'un li mā fī al-ṣudūr*).

3) *The motions and states of the heart in the Qur'an*
The functions of the heart can be divided into two main categories: cognitive and emotive. The cognitive category includes processes relating to knowledge and conceptualization: thinking, reflecting, idea formation, recollection of information one has learned in the past, and the acquisition of new information. As for the emotive category, it has to do with the will: desires and intentions, inclinations and disinclinations. In this realm there exists a gradation from a mere inclination, to attachment, to enslavement. The will gives rise to intention or determination, which is a decision of the heart to use one's bodily members in the commission of a given act, be it praiseworthy or blameworthy. If no action results, the intention remains in the realm of wishing or craving. Only when a decision takes firm root does it become determination and develop into action.

The Qur'an speaks of the heart (the *qalb*) in numerous ways. It describes actions undertaken by the heart as well as attributes that make it a multifaceted world unto itself. The heart is the seat of mental images and knowledge, of feelings and sentiments; in some situations the heart combines the cognitive and the emotive, while adding a deeper dimension to both.

Cognition and Perception

This realm includes conceptualizations, images, and ideas, the aptitude for knowledge and learning, the internal thought processes that arise out of experience, and the ability to discriminate, memorize, recall, and produce information.

The Will

The will encompasses temperament and mood, which include cravings, sentiments, desires, and inclinations. The realm of the will includes the dualities of seeking out and abandoning, love and hate, intimacy and alienation, as well as awareness of right and wrong, possibility and impossibility. Will and determination are what emerges after a thought process that yields certainty, faith, belief, and inner peace.

As discussed in an earlier section, some Qur'anic statements relating to the *qalb* describe processes that arise from the heart itself or actions undertaken by the heart (fearing, trembling, and the like), while others describe processes which the heart undergoes (such as being sealed, strengthened, examined, and so on).

To live sound lives, human beings need four things: (1) knowledge of what is beneficial and desirable and, therefore, to be sought after, (2) knowledge of what is harmful and undesirable and, therefore, to be avoided, (3) a means of achieving what is beneficial and desirable, and (4) a means of avoiding what is harmful and undesirable. Our wills tend to be subject to our desires and whims, and the impressions and notions formed based on our sense perceptions. However, conceptualizations formed based on sensory experience are subject to refinement and alteration as our awareness increases and we develop greater powers of discernment. Given these powers, we are able to decide whether to suppress a desire or to satisfy it, and to act accordingly. Human action is thus based on three foundations: cognition ("What actions are called for and/or possible?"), will ("What do I choose to do?"), and ability ("What action am I capable of?").

4) *The importance of the qalb in knowledge acquisition*

God has created the *qalb* as the seat of both knowledge and will. It is the site of both our perception of reality as it is, and our conception of how it should be (our ideals). Knowledge and action both grow out of thought processes. Thought processes give rises to conceptions, which give rise in turn to decisions, which lead to action. When an action is repeated, this results in the formation of habits. Along with knowledge and will, each of us has worldly attachments, inborn character traits, and life experiences that have contributed to our psychological makeup. Given the complexity of our makeup as human beings, it is impossible for us to fully control the thoughts that come to us, of course, and we are sometimes beleaguered by thoughts that seem to assault us against our wills. However, we have been given the gifts of reason and faith, which enable us to distinguish which thoughts to welcome and act upon, and which ones to resist and suppress. When put to use, these gifts make it possible for us to live our lives fully, and to give everyone his/her due, and everything its due.

7

Waḥy (Revelation) and *Nubuwwah* (Prophethood)

IF WE HOLD that there is a need for revelation – *waḥy* – what we are saying is that there is a need for a point of contact between the realms of *al-shahādah* and *al-ghayb*. If we assume the reality of what is referred to as *waḥy*, or divine revelation – the speech of the Creator which has taken the form of the messages sent to us through the prophets – then on this basis we may categorize people on the basis of their relationship to this revelation. These categories include: (1) those who have received God's messages and believed in them and obeyed them, (2) those who have received these messages and rejected them for whatever reason, and (3) those who have not received these messages. People's relationship to the messages of divine revelation holds implications for the ways in which they relate not only to their Maker, but to one another.

There has been disagreement down the ages over who the Creator is, what the Creator's attributes are, and, assuming there to be a divine revelation, whether to take the Creator's revelation as a source of knowledge and a basis for people's ways of life such that they are willing to appeal to the divine revelation as their authority in relation to all aspects of their existence. In other words, their difference has been over whether to treat the divine revelation as the sole source of truth, or whether to draw on other sources as well. The Qur'an's response to this dispute is to ask: "Say: 'Can any of those beings to whom you ascribe a share in God's divinity create [life] in the first instance, and then bring it forth anew?' Say: 'It is God [alone] who creates [all life] in the first instance, and then brings it forth anew. How perverted, then, are your minds!'" (*Sūrah Yūnus*, 10:34).

Throughout human history people have tended to seek knowledge through two sources. The first of these is the material world (the cosmos), and the second is the spiritual realm. This spiritual realm has included the spiritual experiences and expertise of those recognized as righteous, trustworthy, learned individuals. Some civilizations looked to the heavenly spheres and the movements of the stars and planets as a source of guidance. Some treated idols as symbols of spiritual realities given their inborn desire to worship and seek the unknown. Idol worship has also taken the form of giving free reign to one's instinctual urges rather than looking outward for guidance. Of such people the Qur'an speaks when it asks: "Have you ever considered [the kind of man] who makes his own desires his deity?" (*Sūrah al-Furqān*, 25:43).

As has been mentioned, there is an age-old dispute over whether human beings stand in need of a divine revelation which constitutes the sole source of trustworthy knowledge and guidance – in other words, the sole path to knowledge of *al-ghayb*: the realm that lies beyond the reach of human perception. Given agreement on the need for such a divine revelation, there has arisen the issue of who could be viewed as a trustworthy conduit or transmitter of revelation. In other words, what prophet or divine messenger could be affirmed to be sinless and infallible, and which message could be vouched for as the one genuine divine revelation? In this connection we read in *Sūrah Yūnus*, 10:37, "Now this Qur'an could not possibly have been devised by anyone save God: nay indeed, it confirms the truth of whatever there still remains [of earlier revelations] and clearly spells out the revelation [which comes] – let there be no doubt about it – from the Sustainer of all the worlds."

The Qur'an, as divine revelation, and the Prophet as its conduit, might be viewed as bridges between *al-ghayb* and *al-shahādah*. Both the Qur'an and the Prophet are material entities to which people can gain access through their senses, but which point beyond themselves to a realm out of reach of human sensory perception. A prophet and the message he brings are thus intermediaries between the human and the divine.

Based on the foregoing, we can identify four purposes of divine revelation and prophethood: (1) The conveyance of good news and warning. As God says to the Prophet in *Sūrah Saba'*, 34:28, "Now [as for thee, O Muhammad,] We have not sent thee otherwise than to mankind at large, to be a herald of glad tidings and a warner." (Cf.

Sūrah al-Aḥqāf, 46:9.) (2) To bring people out of the darkness of ignorance and error and into the light of right guidance. As God announces in *Sūrah Ibrāhīm*, 14:1, He has sent down the Qur'an in order to "bring forth all mankind, by their Sustainer's leave, out of the depths of darkness into the light." (3) To resolve disputes among people. Thus God tells the Prophet, "And upon you [too] have We bestowed from on high this divine writ for no other reason than that you might make clear unto them all [questions of faith] on which they have come to hold divergent views, and [thus offer] guidance and grace unto people who will believe" (*Sūrah al-Naḥl*, 16:64). (4) To define people's relationship to God in terms of the ways they are to worship and obey Him, and how they are to relate to each other.

Divine revelation is only bestowed on a prophet. Consequently, there is a need for prophets to serve as conduits through which divine revelation is conveyed to people at large. It is God alone who determines who will be chosen as a prophet. As we read in *Sūrah Ghāfir*, 40:78, "And it was not given to any apostle to bring forth a miracle other than by God's leave." This verse might also be understood to mean that no apostle can bring a divine message to others but by God's leave. Similarly, as we are told in *Sūrah al-Jinn*, 72:26-27, "He [alone] knows that which is beyond the reach of a created being's perception, and to none does He disclose aught of the mysteries of His Own unfathomable knowledge, unless it be to an apostle whom He has been pleased to elect." Ever since the days of Adam confirmation of an individual's status as a prophet has been demonstrated via well-attested proofs. As we read in *Sūrah Āl ʿImrān*, 3:33, "Behold, God raised Adam, and Noah, and the House of Abraham, and the House of ʿImran above all mankind." God graces prophets with miracles that are initially for the benefit of the prophet themselves, as a means of reassuring them that they are, in fact, God's messengers, and that revelation is being bestowed on them. Once they are certain of their role and identity, prophets will have the boldness to deliver the message they have been entrusted with. At this point, then, the miracles a prophet has been given to perform serve as a reassurance not only to the prophet, but to the people to whom his message is being communicated. In the story of Moses, for example, we are told that before sending him to

Pharaoh, God enabled Moses to perform the miracle of throwing his staff down and seeing it turn into a serpent. It was only after this that God commanded Moses to go to Pharaoh (*Sūrah Ṭāhā*, 20:17-24) with "the divine writ – and [thus] a standard by which to discern the true from the false" (*Sūrah al-Baqarah*, 2:53; cf. 2:176; *Sūrah al-Isrā'*, 17:9).

A true prophet of God, though human, is a person of exceptional character: prudent, virtuous, obedient, and chosen by God to deliver His revealed message. A prophet must of course speak the language of the people to whom he has been sent, and demonstrate his claim to be a prophet by performing miracles that would be impossible without divine intervention. The prophet's miracles thus become a source of certainty for those who witness them, as they can be sure that his message is a revelation from God.

Once a prophet has delivered the divinely revealed message to the people to whom he has been sent, his audience will be divided into groups depending on what their response to him and his message has been. Those who have heard his message and witnessed his miracles will be divided among those who affirm his identity as a prophet and his message as a divine revelation, and those who reject his message and his miracles. Others might not even have heard of a given prophet or believe in the phenomenon of prophethood. In order to demonstrate the truthfulness of his message and the genuineness of his identity, a prophet needs two types of evidential proof. One consists of proof of the possibility and necessity of prophethood and divine revelation. The second is proof that he himself is a prophet who is delivering a divine revelation from its very Source. To this end a prophet is sent with two types of signs: verbal and nonverbal. The verbal signs consist of a spoken and/or written revelation, while the nonverbal signs consist of supernatural feats, usually termed miracles, that could only be performed by someone who has been given special power and authority from God.

A divinely revealed message will be comprehensive in nature in the sense that it encompasses all parts of the perceptible realm in which people live. It also connects the perceptible realm with the realm that lies beyond the grasp of human perception. Of this latter realm, there are parts that God has revealed only to His angelic messengers. Other parts, God has revealed to the angels and the prophets. Still others, He has made known to people through His apostles. And lastly, there is a part that God reveals to no one, and of which He alone is knowledgeable. This part is referred to in the Qur'an as "the keys of the unseen (*mafātīḥ al-ghayb*), the treasures that none knows but He ...." (*Sūrah al-Anʿām*, 6:59; cf. *Sūrah Āl ʿImrān*, 3:40). As a divinely given source of knowledge, the divine revelation granted to human beings encompasses only a fraction of *al-ghayb*, while the created universe, likewise a source of knowledge, consists of elements that are perceptible to human beings, and others that are not.

In sum, the sources of knowledge available to us might be classed as either uncreated, or created. As a source of knowledge, *waḥy* speaks of both entities that lie beyond the grasp of human perception, and of realities that human beings can grasp with their senses and their minds. As such, *waḥy* is something that can be perceived, studied, understood and reflected on. It is also, and equally importantly, something to be acted upon as a means of drawing nearer to God, and establishing justice on Earth. As God declares in *Sūrah al-Ḥadīd*, 57:25, "Indeed, [even aforetime] did We send forth Our apostles with all evidence of [this] truth; and through them We bestowed revelation from on high, and [thus gave you] a balance [wherewith to weigh right and wrong], so that people might behave with equity."

NOTES

[1] The Arabic term *taʿjīz*, translated here as impossibility, refers to the use of the imperative not to give an actual command, but to demonstrate the impossibility of what is being "commanded." Thus, for example, when the Qur'an exhorts skeptics to produce a surah like what is found in the Qur'an (see, for example, *Sūrah al-Baqarah*, 2:23), the intent is not actually to command them to do this, since they would be unable to do so even if they tried. Rather, the intent is to make the point that such a feat would be unachievable.

[2] As in the case of *taʿjīz*, the term *irshād* refers here to the use of the imperative voice for a purpose other than that of giving an actual command. For example, when the Qur'an exhorts people who have lent money to write down the transaction, it is simply advising them to do so as a matter of good practice, but not commanding them to do so (see *Sūrah al-Baqarah*, 2:282).